40⁰⁰

Imagining Medea

Imagining
Medea

Rhodessa Jones & Theater for Incarcerated Women

RENA FRADEN

Foreword by Angela Y. Davis

The University of North Carolina Press

Chapel Hill and London

© 2001 The University of North Carolina Press
All rights reserved
Manufactured in the United States of America
This book was set in Carter Cone Galliard
by Tseng Information Systems, Inc.
The paper in this book meets the guidelines for permanence and
durability of the Committee on Production Guidelines for Book
Longevity of the Council on Library Resources.

Frontispiece: "The Storyteller." Ceramic sculpture by Lorraine Capparell, 1994.
27″×19″×11″. Model: Rhodessa Jones. Photograph by the artist, 1994

This volume was published with the generous assistance of the
Greensboro Women's Fund of the University of North Carolina Press.
Founding Contributors: Linda Arnold Carlisle, Sally Schindel Cone,
Anne Faircloth, Bonnie McElveen Hunter, Linda Bullard Jennings,
Janice J. Kerley (in honor of Margaret Supplee Smith), Nancy Rouzer May,
and Betty Hughes Nichols.

Quotations from all five Medea Project productions are taken from unpublished
manuscripts that are the property of Cultural Odyssey, 762 Fulton Street, Suite 306,
San Francisco, CA 94102. Reproduced here by permission of Cultural Odyssey.

Library of Congress Cataloging-in-Publication Data
Fraden, Rena.
Imagining Medea : Rhodessa Jones and theater for incarcerated women /
by Rena Fraden.
p. cm. — (Gender and American culture)
Includes bibliographical references and index.
ISBN 0-8078-2659-6 (alk. paper) — ISBN 0-8078-4984-7 (pbk. : alk. paper)
1. Jones, Rhodessa.   2. Medea Project: Theater for Incarcerated Women.
3. Prison theater—California.   4. Women prisoners—Services for—California.
I. Title.   II. Gender & American culture
HV8861 .F73   2001
365'.66'082—dc21   2001033301

05 04 03 02 01   5 4 3 2 1

For my daughters

RUTHIE & EVA

CONTENTS

ILLUSTRATIONS

Rhodessa Jones's Medea Project has accomplished something that is still extremely rare in this era of gigantic prison populations and increasingly complex relations linking state-inflicted punishment and corporate striving for profit: through its dramatization of the "real," the project has demonstrated that prison walls are not entirely unscalable. The Medea Project offers us the insight that cultural performance can carve out routes along which imprisoned women's stories—the stories of the most marginalized women in our society—can be trafficked in the free world.

In *Imagining Medea: Rhodessa Jones and Theater for Incarcerated Women*, Rena Fraden has written a powerful account of the nine-year collaboration between women in the San Francisco County Jail system and women performers who, when they are not working in a rehearsal space in jail, inhabit the free world. This collaboration is choreographed by Rhodessa Jones—both in its specific performances and as a protracted effort to keep open the routes that allow audiences outside to celebrate stories from inside and that create access for those inside to fleeting moments on public stages in the free world.

I first encountered the Medea Project when it was still in its formative period. In 1991, while Jones was working with the first group of women prisoners in the San Francisco County Jail, I was teaching a course at the jail entitled "Women's Cultural Awareness." Rhodessa and I would occasionally meet in the well-monitored corridors of the jail in San Bruno and would share ideas and insights. When she told me about her desire to have her students perform not only for their sister prisoners but also for public audiences in San Francisco, I remember my own skepticism. Now, of course, I feel ashamed that I doubted her ability to create these momentary escape routes from jail, especially since I can remember how powerful metaphors evoking the yearning for freedom informed the rehearsal session I attended at the jail.

Less than a year after these conversations, the Medea Project was already preparing for its debut performance at Theater Artaud in San Francisco, *Reality Is Just Outside the Window*. Of course I attended that performance and have attended numerous others since then. Nine years later, I am even more impressed by Jones's ability to expand and complicate the performance space known as the Medea Project: Theater for Incarcerated Women. To trace the development of this project is no easy task. Just as Rhodessa Jones is always aware of the fragility of the representations her actors produce—where is the distinction, for example, between representing the life of the sex worker and reproducing the exploitative ideologies that inform our ideas about prostitutes—so Rena Fraden is also aware of the deeply contradictory role she plays as the interpreter of this work.

To pursue this analogy, one might say that just as these theater performances are inconceivable except as precarious products of well-earned trust, mutually practiced by all involved, so Fraden had to discover a writing strategy that would trouble the inevitable hierarchies that usually define relations between prisoners and free persons, between lay people and professionals, informants and scholars. To develop an effective writing strategy, she also had to discover a democratic form within which to stage encounters between the theorists she invokes and the actors who offer her the primary material about the Medea Project. How, for example, can she allow Michel Foucault to converse with Paulette Jones, whose participation in many Medea Project performances can be measured by the number of times she has returned to jail despite her sincere desire to interrupt this cycle? According to Paulette Jones, "Art does not save me. I really wish that it did, but it does not. And that's been the hardest thing to accept." Her words, and those of other members of the company, reflect an attempt to theorize the conditions of women prisoners as well as the role of this art in altering—or not altering—individual trajectories. This theorizing on the ground is as important to Fraden's book as the analyses she borrows from the realm of "high theory."

Rena Fraden's account is also remarkable for its honesty—a trait Rhodessa Jones always demands from the women with whom she works. Fraden refuses to allow her readers to romanticize the space—inside and outside the jail—created by the Medea Project. While the rehearsals and performances may indeed create momentary transcendences, imprisonment continues to define the women's everyday realities, where their social and psychic problems continue to play themselves out. Moreover, as Fraden writes, "Jones cannot help but direct the audience's attention to what constitutes the boundaries of a prison and a theater. The theater too may operate as an institution of coercion, containing the women, disciplining them."

One of the important contributions of the Medea Project has been to demystify the relationship between crime and punishment. As prison populations have soared in the United States, the conventional assumption that increased levels of crime are the cause of expanding prison populations has been widely contested. Activists and scholars, who have tried to develop a more nuanced understanding of the punishment process—and especially the role of racism in it—have deployed the concept of the "prison industrial complex" to point out that the proliferation of prisons and prisoners is linked to larger economic and political structures and ideologies and not primarily to individual criminal conduct nor to efforts to curb "crime." Vast numbers of corporations with global markets rely on prisons as an important market and thus have acquired clandestine stakes in the continued expansion of the prison system. Because the overwhelming majority of prisoners in United States prisons and jails are people of color, corporate stakes in a flourishing apparatus of punishment necessarily relies on and promotes old and new structures of racism.

Women have been especially hurt by these developments. Although women comprise a relatively small percentage of the entire prison population, they constitute, nevertheless, the fastest growing segment of prisoners. There are now more women in prison in the state of California alone than there were in the country as a whole in 1970. Because race is a major factor determining who goes to prison and who doesn't, women of color are the fastest growing group among women prisoners.

Both this book and the theater project it explores make an important contribution to contemporary activist efforts to rescue imprisoned women of color from the invisibility to which they historically have been relegated. Women not only constitute the fastest growing population of prisoners, they are also more directly affected by the proliferation of jails and prisons than their male counterparts. Women constitute the primary support for other prisoners, both male and female. Women write letters to prisoners, send books, make and accept expensive telephone calls, coordinate long journeys to out-of-the-way prisons. In other words, as women's presence behind the walls continues to grow, so does their performance of the invisible labor summoned by the expanding prison population as a whole.

The Medea Project refuses to let the women prisoners and their collaborators remain unseen and unheard. Instead, it insists on a hypervisibility of women's bodies, histories, and psyches. And Rena Fraden's engagement with this project not only acquaints broader audiences with Rhodessa Jones's important work, it also encourages us all to think deeply and critically about our own responsibility to redesign a social landscape on which coercion and confinement—and especially punishment for profit—will eventually wither away.

Angela Y. Davis

I first saw Rhodessa Jones in 1994 in Berkeley, California, performing her autobiographical work *The Blue Stories: Black Erotica about Letting Go*. After the performance, she came on stage with two other women, and they began to talk about their collaboration on the Medea Project: Theater for Incarcerated Women. I had never heard, at that point, of Rhodessa Jones or the Medea Project, but, unlike some performers, she seemed accessible and open, inviting the audience not only to ask questions but to find a way to work with her. So I invited her to Pomona College to perform and to speak to students about her work.

When I saw the fourth Medea production, *Buried Fire*, in 1996, I was stunned and exhilarated by the power of the performers and the response the audience gave them. From workshops in the jails with incarcerated women, and in collaboration with artists from the community, Jones had produced an evening of stirring theater—mixing music, myth, dance, and autobiography. With short runs, no published text, and mostly local press coverage, the Medea Project's performances are historically fragile. Inspired by Jones and the performance, I believed that by describing their efforts, I might honor and celebrate the individuals, organizations, and the spirit of San Francisco (my hometown) that created and sustained this social art work. I began this book as a celebratory "recording" of the Medea Project. The "real" performance of the Medea Project, I soon came to understand, started long before opening night—in the negotiations to make the private public, in the workshops that took place inside and outside the jail. Encapsulated in book form, I thought the Medea Project might enjoy a shelf life longer than a night in the theater, reach a bigger audience than the one lucky enough to have seen a performance, and be presented as a rich, complicated, and powerful process, involving many more people than one hears and sees on stage.

As I began to focus on chronicling the process, I came to feel more and more acutely the contrast between descriptions that isolate a performance or an interview and descriptions that acknowledge their provisionality and fluidity. It is notoriously difficult to capture the sense of a "live" performance: it is never exactly the same, and it will affect different members of the audience differently. I do not claim to have created an all-inclusive accounting or definitive history of the Medea Project. Instead, I have conceived of this book as an example of what cultural critic Kobena Mercer calls a *practice of interruption:* "an ongoing conversation or dialogue that seeks to deepen our knowledge of the way texts 'work' as they circulate in the contingent and contradictory circumstances of the public sphere." "In this approach," writes Mercer, "it is not even necessary to construct a general or definitive framework for interpretation, as what arises instead is a practice of interruption, which does not aim to have the last word on the aesthetic value of a given text, but which recognizes the contextual character of the relations between authors, text and audiences as they encounter each other in the worldly spaces of the public sphere."[1] In creating this book, I interviewed some people, they told me something about themselves, I saw some of the performances and workshops. Even though I missed a lot, I saw how the Medea Project began and grew to conceive of itself. I was drawn to it because of the extraordinary relations I sensed among the very different authors, texts, and audiences who participated in it. This book celebrates everyone who is on the record and, just as importantly, everyone who is off—those still very much a part of history, just not *this* version of history. To present any history honestly, one must acknowledge its limitations. The history this book presents is incomplete not only because of all I have not observed and surveyed, but also because the Medea Project itself is not yet history. It is in medias res, unstable, uncertain as to who is in or out or back in again, its techniques and goals developing, the people involved changing over time. Therefore, it would be premature to construct a definitive framework of interpretation or to believe that this book could contain the last word on the project's value, aesthetic or otherwise. Relationships, partnerships, productions are still being planned. The project still has a future. There are possibilities for changes, both those that we might imagine and those that have not been imagined yet.

I think of this book, with its emphasis on chronicling process rather than evaluating production, as being more in line with the ethos of community artists than with the practice of historians. In describing the way community artists in Edinburgh talked about their projects, feminist geographer Gillian Rose observes that most of the time she found people refused to interpret what a project meant. It is not that community artists don't understand the power of language to define, but they are suspicious of the ways language can be used to qualify, reduce, and restrain efforts to perform differently. They resist the impulse to assign meaning and instead prefer to talk about the importance of the process and participation. "'Process,'" writes Rose, "refers to how participants learn skills and create art when they become involved in a project. . . . [W]hat many shared was a sense in which the point of process is to produce more process, more participation. . . . Participation entails more of itself. It regenerates itself, and this is its purpose. The process of participation is therefore never quite complete. It is a performance constantly reconstituting itself."[2] This notion of the never-ending process of participation is, I have come to believe, fundamental to how the Medea Project operates. The particular qualities of this artwork or that artwork are not as significant as the act of creating itself. Everything starts from participation, and whatever the other outcomes, that participation is in and of itself enough. What the participation comes to mean in the life of a person may not be known now or ever be knowable, but one should not therefore infer that participation has not made a difference. Participation opens up more possibilities for exchange, different combinatory ways to make community; it may enable change, though it cannot ensure it.

If the final goal of participation in the Medea Project is absolutely utopian (and revolutionary)—to create a community that nurtures the best of human instincts, liberates creativity, raises critical consciousness, and redistributes power—it is not surprising that any account will show the project falling short of that goal. What is surprising is that it can do so much, and my goal, in this account, is to show how. This is a case study that describes how the Medea Project creates an alternative, sometimes oppositional space, and how it reshapes theoretical and practical boundaries that mark off the aesthetic, commercial, political, moral, personal, and religious realms we inhabit at present, evaluating which methods work best at creating more permeable boundaries. It is my hope that it provides an example of how other projects might constitute and imagine themselves in relation to their community. The Medea Project means to intervene in the way we imagine the boundaries of community. It makes room for specific political programs, pedagogical enlightenment, sedition, artistic creativity, social critique, and human fellowship. It invites and depends upon participation. In that spirit, I think of this book as another form of taking part; it is not the last word, but a kind of interruption that might provoke responses to what has been left over and left out, inspiring others who will have more to say and more to do.

I want to add one note about the personal epiphanies I came to in working on this project. While I do not mean this book to be autobiographical, I am enough part of the Zeitgeist to acknowledge the necessity of explaining my own "subject position," at least so far as I am able. Jones always tells the participants in the Medea Project that no one can sit on the sidelines. At one point early on in interviewing Jones, I exclaimed, "So, you *do* direct!" We went on talking for another few hours, and then, a few days later, I received an angry card from her, even a despairing one, in which she said she'd been thinking about my exclamation and she couldn't believe that I hadn't *gotten* it. Of *course* she was a director. This was *her* project; *she* walked the floor, as she put it. When I went back to the tape of the interview, it became clear to me that I was responding to a more mundane and particular point, not knowing—because I hadn't yet watched her as a director—how she shaped the material the women wrote for her, or when she began to shape it, or how much she intervened in the writing and producing. But when she called me up short and asked me to declare my intentions, I found myself having to answer, to talk back, which was at once both exhilarating and rather daunting. Many times over the years I followed the project, I wished for the anonymity of the historical archives, the blessed silence of dead people, and the refuge of a subject that would be of little interest to few people. On the other hand, being *in* the process, insofar as I was—listening to the amazing sounds of absolutely alive, cantankerous, loud, defiant people, subjects who had definite interests, sometimes in conflict with each other; finding myself sometimes an obstacle, someone who had to explain herself because she was not trusted, someone who had to be taught and who sometimes had to respond—all this conspired to make my own thinking about difference and voice sharper and more intellectually necessary.

In negotiating the terms of our relationship through this book, Rhodessa Jones and I have both had to cede some of the control that, as artist and as author, we usually depend upon. Through my conversations with everyone else concerning rights over material, songs, and interviews, I had to determine what mattered and what belonged to whom. I was forced to think about who owns the stories, the songs, the ideas in the performances, and I had to make choices about how these voices could be transcribed on paper. When black dialect spoken aloud sounded street smart but on the page looked dumb or clumsy, how to convey what seemed to me worth hearing—the rhythms, the sound, and the meaning that was in the attitude? I don't believe I have completely caught the

unique sounds on these pages, the swagger and cadences of each participant, which made their talk so rich, but I believe some of their poetic
power rings through in the prose translation.

I also puzzled over what sound my own voice should have. As I imagined who might come to read this book and who this book was *for*, and
as I metamorphosed from editor to author, I experimented with various
voices and versions of authority, from academic theoretician to popular
journalist. In *Fighting Words: Black Women and the Search for Justice*, Patricia Hill Collins wonders, "How could I possibly write for so many possible audiences in language that they would understand and find credible?
In responding to this dilemma, I decided to write in the multiple languages used by the different audiences that I encounter on a daily basis.
. . . I decided to speak as many languages as I could, rather than feeling
that I had to pick one in order to establish a 'tone' for the volume."[3] I
suppose, in some way, I've opted for the same hybrid tone. At the Medea
Project, I listened to many different languages spoken by different people,
to people switching midstream from street to classical, and to the vocabu-
lary of the academy. It was the mixture of languages and disciplines that
was challenging to capture and which may be a more realistic portrayal of
how we use what we know as we head into the new millennium. Within
the subset of academic disciplines, I found myself sometimes employing
biography and history, statistics and postmodern theories of identity, ref-
erencing urban politics and performance art. Early on, Sean Reynolds
read my prospectus and objected to my use of the word "methodology."
Over that word she wrote emphatically, "JARGON!"—as in "bad word
choice." Coming as I did from the academic minefields of late-twentieth-
century cultural theory, "methodology" seemed pretty mild to me as
far as jargon goes. From the beginning I was struggling to figure out
which methodologies I could use to describe this hybrid project. I worried whether the foregrounding of *any* methodology would imprison me
irretrievably in a "high theory" voice. What method would *not* imprison
me? Which voice *should* I use? How much could I—or should I—mask
my past history of reading and writing? And who was to tell me? And
how was I to decide?

The Medea Project is "Theater *for* Incarcerated Women"—that's what
Rhodessa Jones has called it—but it seemed to me I could either be
a metaphorical part of that incarcerated womanhood and thus find a
place within it (we're all potential Medeas, we're all incarcerated women,

imprisoned in various psychological bondages—to love, to children, to human experience) or be written out altogether, if incarceration is taken literally to refer only to women behind the bars of the jail at 850 Bryant Street in San Francisco. But the Medea Project spoke to me, and it spoke to others in the audience, and if I had to think about what methodologies (or methods) I might use to describe the force of the prepositions ("of," "by," "for") and who was being positioned where, I figured those questions would have to be part of the book. Still, the marginalial "JARGON!" did give me pause. And in that long pause, I read some more, and thought some more, and took more time to figure out how to write in my own voice about the voices of others. There is a delicate balance between critical distance and passionate advocacy, as there is between writing *of* and *about* without wanting to write *for* or *instead of* someone else. Not everyone will be satisfied that I have positioned myself properly or caught the proper inflection. But I remember one evening when some of the core group of the Medea Project sat down and looked at me and said, "Just *do* it. Just write it yourself."

Finally, I think I must be satisfied with the following description of my purpose in writing this book. In the letter I wrote to Rhodessa Jones, trying to convey a sense of my purpose and my self—my credentials, as it were—I told her I was (am) a middle-class, white woman: "I am a teacher and a mother and a citizen. And in those three roles, I guess what I want to do is pass on some information—about what other people do to make places at the table for everyone—to make reality more nurturing, sentiments more constructive, to turn indifference into connection. I guess in a pretty old-fashioned way I believe in a common humanity and wish to find ways to express it—concretely." In order to express things concretely, I rely on quotations gleaned from interviews; I refer to academic discussions about the definition of public culture and the nature of theatrical representation. None of this is particularly cutting-edge; it's only that I'm living in a lucky, rich moment in cultural production, as we head into a new century. I grew up during the civil rights and feminist movements, and in the university where I was formally educated and at the college where I work now I have been taught by an increasingly diverse curriculum and student body. My education has been both utterly traditional and at the same time open to innovation. The Medea Project is not classical literature, it may never become canonical, but it references the classical and it also reproduces the sounds of people who walk our streets today.

It is that mixture of sounds, its hopes and its rage, that make it culturally vibrant and strong and which has attracted me and so many others to it.

I'd like to thank the following people who allowed me to talk with them, in person, on the telephone, or via E-mail: Idris Ackamoor, Barbara Bailey, Darcell Bernard, Fé Bongolan, Gail Burton, William Cleveland, Marcia Colhour, Edris Cooper, Michael Hennessey, Hallie Iannoli, Nancy Johnson, Stephanie Johnson, Paulette Jones, Rhodessa Jones, Andrea Justin, Denise Landrum, Karen Levine, Michael Marcum, Tanya Mayo, Agnes Marie (Aggie) Mercurio, Ruth Morgan, Pam Peniston, Francis Phillips, Sean Reynolds, Carole Robinson, Kary Schulman, Felicia Scaggs, Martha Stein, Kamilah Nyota Watson, and Angela Wilson. Their stories, the way they told them, their beliefs and hopes—these are what compelled me to write this book, and they often made me wish that I could find some alternative to the confining pages of a book and free them all to speak out loud to you, as they did to me. Despite the inevitable disappointment that some who know the project well may feel about all the missing voices, all the people I did not speak with, I trust that the voices I have quoted represent the extraordinary passions and eloquence of the amazing group of people who have made the Medea Project possible.

I am, once again, grateful to the largesse of Pomona College, which has always backed me to the hilt. Pomona College students Shauna Antley, Stacy Hammond, and Jennifer Tsai tirelessly checked sources, transcribed, and helped me with research. A Fulbright Fellowship to India midway through the writing gave me a chance to compare and contrast theater projects with similar aims. My friends Betty Farrell, Gayle Greene, Julia Liss, and Joanna Worthley read multiple versions of the manuscript. Abbe Blum, once again, proved herself to be my closest reader. Robert Dawidoff not only encouraged and advised me, patiently as always, but at a critical moment put me in touch with my very sympathetic editor at University of North Carolina Press, Sian Hunter. I am beholden to both of them, as I am to Michael Roth, who invited Rhodessa Jones to participate in workshops at the Getty Center in Los Angeles, and to Ellen Stewart, who had Rhodessa Jones lead workshops in Italy. I descended on both locations, and Ms. Stewart was exceptionally generous in allowing me to stay at her Umbria convent, where Rhodessa and I were able to continue our conversation about life and art (and the book).

Finally, *Imagining Medea* could not have been written without the cooperation of Rhodessa Jones. I'm thankful to her not merely by the way but because she went *out* of her way to encompass me with her generosity, wisdom, exuberance, and friendship. She enabled me to see my way through to finishing these chapters, and then to begin to imagine that there might be others still to come.

Imagining Medea

Introduction

Imagine a woman able to partake in a
social political cultural conversation. . . .
—*Rhodessa Jones, program notes,* Slouching Towards Armageddon

I begin with an image of a theatrical eruption that occurred in *Slouching Towards Armageddon: A Captive's Conversation/Observation on Race,* the fifth full-length public performance of the Medea Project. The audience is seated, waiting for the performance to begin, the stage is dark, and all of a sudden, hip-hop music booms out, the doors in the back of the theater are flung open, the audience twists and turns around to look, and what they see coming down the aisles of the theater is a long line of stamping, kicking, dancing women moving through the theater and up onto the stage. The women's boisterous entrance—not from the wings, where we might expect actors to enter, but from outside the theater—heralds the key act of the Medea Project: to make visible what has been repressed and oppressed. That which has been sequestered, kept out of sight, bursts out among us, so loudly and with such exuberant, menacing, energy that it is impossible to ignore. The women interrupt the normal boundaries of the theater, and they even manage to interrupt our view of each other as they parade among us. They have been let out and are now in our midst, invading the space usually reserved for the audience. What are we to make of them? Who are they? What will they say? What do they stand for? Are these women supposed to be mythical furies, or are they simply furious? Are they the elemental allegorical figures we see listed in the program, or are they the people with names like Darcell and Chelsea also found there? How will this theatrical event explain the interruption before us, and make us not only understand what we are seeing but what our connection may be to what is in front of our eyes? What have they to do with us?

Rhodessa Jones consciously directs these women to be "in their face," to "take it to the audience." She wants them to interrupt the comfortable passivity of an audience sitting in their seats, awaiting their entertainment. She wants the music *loud;* she wants the women to look *scary.* And she insists on making a connection between us and them. In her preperformance speech to audiences, she argues that these women from jail have *everything* to do with us:

> In the days of antiquity, theater included us all. It was a religious experience. I hope this project resounds back to that theater. This is not psychodrama. Word came out that one critic has said, "We've seen *The Medea Project.* Why see it again?" Well, the reason is, this is the voice of the people here, of women, and women are mad as hell. It's lawless out there. We ask the question why more and more women are going to jail; what's happening to our children. . . . This is theater for the twenty-first century. The evening news doesn't get it; it talks about African American men. But we want to take a global look, at all of it. If your life is so normal, give your seat to somebody else. Attempt to imagine the life of another; this is theater for American culture; it is rehabilitation, planting the seeds. If you think jail doesn't have anything to do with you, someday, just wait, a ten-year-old will be pointing an Uzi in your face. Just as we've seen AIDS touch us all, so will this violence.[1]

Her central claim is that theater is a religious experience, a place of communion, which includes everyone. Her use of Greek, African, and Asian myths and of folk stories is one way she insists on making her theater inclusive. Her theater also depends on bringing together people who normally wouldn't find themselves in one place at any one time thinking about what they have in common. She means her work to be a kind of education for the women who take part in the ensemble or chorus. Those women, like the young men in training in classical Athens, are meant to see how they can defend themselves and their children and their community from violence and to be able to distinguish between true friends and enemies within and without. Jones's theater, like the classical Greek, wants to make the audience the judge, reacting in horror to the violations of civilization and in sympathy with a critique of it.

When she convinced the San Francisco Sheriff's Department to release the women to perform in a legitimate theater space in the city, she changed more than just the location. The incarcerated are, for the evening, no longer hidden or silent. And for those few evenings, the work is no longer drama as therapy or arts as correction; it is no longer theater *only* for incarcerated women. It becomes theater about why some women end up incarcerated and some do not; it is about what should connect communities and what does not connect them at present. It calls into

"Up from Below," from Buried Fire. *Photograph by Pam Peniston, 1996*

question the boundaries of what is public and free and what isn't, and it exposes the violence that connects us all. Short of promising personal salvation, Jones has said she means her art to build bridges, in order to make even the most protected and privileged of spectators feel their connections with those who are not. Part of the drama is to make the audience ask questions: why *these* women, why are *more* women going to jail, and how does the incarceration of women affect society at large? Finally, Jones wants her theater to be a call to community, to thinking about what a proper community should look like and what sorts of social action would have to take place to bring that community into being.

It makes sense to begin with a description of the most visible part of the Medea Project, the public theatrical production, because the conversation can begin only when we can hear what hasn't been heard, see what hasn't been seen. But everyone who sees a live Medea production feels the tension between what they can see and what remains invisible. We know there are other women we will not hear from, because we are told at the end of the performance who they are. We also know there are numerous organizations that played a part in controlling the movement of these women back and forth and in and out, but they are not on stage. In the last Medea Production of the twentieth century, *Slouching Towards Armageddon: A Captive's Conversation/Observation on Race,* the theater workshops that led up to the public performance existed in and around many institu-

"Hear No Evil, See No Evil," from Buried Fire. *Grouped together on left: Edris Cooper as Ebon, the Black Angel; Tanya Mayo in nurse's cap; Nancy Johnson as Goddess Osun, in white skirt and bra; Fé Bongolan as Aswang, crouching. Photograph by Pam Peniston, 1996*

tions: hospitals, jails, halfway houses. Jones coordinated an impressive list of organizations of political and social power that promised to help the incarcerated women after the public performance is over.[2] But we know watching the evening's performance that we can't know who will and who won't profit.

Walking to the theater in which *Slouching Towards Armageddon* was performed, up Powell Street in downtown San Francisco, I wind my way through panhandlers, street people, drug addicts. I mostly don't look at them; I even hope they stay mostly invisible. And the irony grows, because I know I'm going to see performances by the very types I am now trying to avoid seeing. *Slouching* opened on 21 January 1999 at the Lorraine Hansberry Theater, a theater that produces African American plays and is located inside the gymnasium of the old YWCA, now the Sheehan Hotel. Seating 300 people, the theater was sold out every night of the two weekend runs.

The audience was racially diverse; there were African Americans, Asians, Chicanos, whites. A San Franciscan mixture of progressives and bohemians, old hippies and the young hip, gay and straight filled the theater. Various representatives from the jails came to the performances; the

"Dance," from Slouching Towards Armageddon.
Photograph by Stephanie A. Johnson, 1999

sheriff was there on the first Saturday night. Angela Davis came one evening. There were funders from local foundations; social workers and resi-
dents from the halfway houses some of the women live in; students, families, and friends of the women in the troupe; people from the theater
community in San Francisco; and the simply curious. Since 1992, when
the Medea Project first went public, Jones has worked to expand the network of people who make the evening possible. The shows have been ad-
vertised, reviewed, and celebrated in local papers as great entertainment
and as a socially worthy cause, so that now, when an audience gathers,
it feels like a reunion. Many in the audience are known to each other;
they are colleagues in the work place, or neighbors, friends, or friends of
friends. They are ready to be entertained, but they also participate—cheering, stomping, hissing, and rising to their feet to applaud at the end of
each evening.

There is no mistaking Jones's presence as the master interpreter, the
person who focuses the audience's attention, first in the program notes
and then in her opening speech. Her program notes for *Slouching* begin:
"On the eve of the millennium at the end of this century we are wading
thru the 'politics of personal destruction'; the very air is tight, soiled
and murky. We are inundated with voices complaining, shouting, argu-

"Curtain Call," from Buried Fire. *Photograph by Lorraine Capparell, 1996*

ing, threatening, patronizing, lying, yes, even crying. In the cities we are living in virtual lockdown! Rage reigns outside—the poor get poorer, our children choose exile, disappearing even as they dance, anesthetized with rhythm, rhyme, enshrouded in oversized fashion, gulping sugar, smoke and powder. We are all seduced into virtual reality. Armageddon beckons."[3]

Then Jones appears in front of the audience to give her customary curtain speech, a mixture of rage and celebration. The Rockefeller Foundation gave her money to develop this performance with women in the jail around the subject of race and racism. Race, Jones remarks ruefully, is, for the moment, a sexy subject. But it was a real challenge to have a conversation about race in jail, she says, "since, as a general public, we haven't had that conversation yet." She goes on, saying it was like opening up Pandora's box—all sorts of evil things began to creep out. Jones tells the audience that she started the workshop by asking the women two questions: what was their first memory of race; and, if they could take a pill and change their race, their gender, their entire being, what would they choose to become.

As the lights dim, Jones takes her seat directly in front of the first row of spectators, puts on headphones and begins to "direct" the show from this spot. Periodically throughout the evening she calls to the actors, "Speak out!" "Move it!"—snapping her fingers and generally acting as the protective mother/director. She never takes her eyes off the performers; that is her most visible connection to them. The stage set is simple. A big painted banner erected across the stage reads, "We the other People of the United States." There is a piano on one side of the stage, on the other is a bank of six or seven televisions at various angles. Throughout the show, clips from different television shows appear—news, Michael Jordan, sitcoms, as well as rehearsals from the Medea Project.

As a spotlight comes on, a rather short but solid black woman comes on stage. She is wearing a loose white shirt, baggy dark blue pants, her hair in dreads. Holding a big book, she introduces herself as the Mother of God. There are titters from the audience. One evening, she pauses, looks out, and says, "Surprised, aren't you? (Pause) Most people are. My grandson, Jesus Christ, he wasn't blonde either. He's short and brown like me." The audience laughs after each line, and she continues, "If you're praying to some blonde guy . . . that's why it's not working."[4] Now the audience is guffawing. The woman speaking is Sean Reynolds, social worker, Rhodessa Jones's oldest partner in the Medea Project. As the Mother of God, she introduces the gangster motifs that permeate *Slouching Towards Armageddon.* Many of the women in this Medea production are young; some are still teenagers. They are different from the habitual cons that the Medea Project used to see in the mid- to late 1980s. Some of these young girls, aged eighteen and nineteen, are in jail for more violent crimes—attempted murder, bank robbery. Reynolds reads some text, pauses, and ad libs in reaction to the audience; at the same time, she is interacting with the cast, who are making their entrance from the back of the theater down the two aisles on either side of the audience. Dressed in street clothes that mimic the slouching look of the multicultural, hip-hop gangster, the women move forward in fits and starts, until they are all on stage, black, white, one Filipina, threatening, posturing, surrounding the Mother of God. Reynolds says, "You don't scare me. *I*'m the Mother of God." Jones's warning about all sorts of evil being released from Pandora's box is before our eyes. They move offstage, swaggering, with attitude.

Reynolds follows them off, and the lights come up now on Paulette Jones, a formerly incarcerated woman (no relation to Rhodessa Jones), who sits at the piano. Like Sean Reynolds, Jones is black and grew up in the 1960s. She has a magnificent full-bodied singing (and speaking) voice and, like Reynolds, is able to play with and off the audience throughout the evening. In many ways, *Slouching Towards Armageddon* is Paulette Jones's showcase, though she has sung and performed in two other Medea productions. Here, she sits at the piano throughout, anchors the troupe through rap songs and cabaret tunes, and sings two of her own songs. The first, which she sings after the Mother of God leaves the stage, is a slow, sweet ballad she has called "Dancing the Dream." Gina Dawson, the choreographer for *Slouching Towards Armageddon,* dances lyrically to the music, with a silver veil over her face and a long white dress. People in the audience who do not know Dawson may not know how to read her racially. Her veiled self coupled with Jones's refrain, which says the dream is not about color but about love, seems to undercut any simple notion of identity politics. It's a wistful tune, a wishful song, that hopes to disentangle race from identity. It asks whether we can see beyond the color of someone's skin, see a "real me." Here, in this opening song, a more essential "me" is posited, beyond race, in the lyrics and the visualization of an indeterminable racial subject. The dream of peace—a song about peace—fades away as Dawson dances off. And abruptly, with a huge crash, a top-selling rap song pours into the theater, and the troupe of "gangsters," now dressed in various costumes of white, stomp onto the stage. As the song fades, they begin to fight each other, until they are pushed backstage by a black woman, Gail Burton, who comes forward to tell us Pandora's story. Burton, who grew up in East Harlem and went to Radcliffe, is a playwright herself. She wrote two versions of Pandora's myth to open and close the show. The Mother of God and Paulette Jones (or the Auntie of God) make jokes with her ("Zeus, Prometheus, Pandora . . . and they say *black* people have funny names"), as she gives us the standard version of the myth in black street language, with a saucy, coy presence. Zeus uses Pandora to revenge himself against Prometheus, who is not paying him proper respect. Zeus gives Pandora a box filled with evils (and one good thing—hope) to give to Prometheus, but he also gives Pandora an inquisitive nature, so he knows she will open the box and let the evils out. She finishes her speech:

> BURTON: So Pandora said, "Sure, you're right, Zeus. *I'm* not going to open your box. Your box is safe with *me*. Just let me have it." But Pandora had already been given that nosy nature, so y'all *know* she opened up that box. And when she opened up that box, all *hell* broke loose. The only thing left in the box was hope.
>
> MOTHER OF GOD: Keep hope alive!

The troupe now spills over the platform in character, each as a particular personification of Evil: Naughty, Vanity, Confusion, Desire for Power, Money, Pride, Misfortune, Jealousy, Slander, Revenge, Fear, Lust, Desire, Sorrow. They swarm and dance and mug until they form a lineup. Revenge steps out, and points at the audience: "Don't let me catch you sleeping." Jealousy shakes her finger: "*Don't* hate me because you can't be me." Misfortune stares: "Anyone feeling lucky? (Pause) I didn't think so." The audience laughs.

The incongruity of ancient story and contemporary talk create the joke and reinforce the questions about identity that the play raises from the opening moments. Are these allegories or signs of personal traits? Are they examples of our own internal evils that we know we each harbor, or external ones that we fear will attack us? Do these figures appear before us as objects of pity and fear, providing us with a cathartic letting out and letting go, or are they instruments of punishment, punishing themselves and also warning us that we are their next victims? It is in part the indeterminacy of these boundaries, the mixture of personal and allegorical identities, the permeable boundaries between the evils we see on stage and those we know are within us that sharpens our sense of connection.[5]

This opening of *Slouching Towards Armageddon* choreographs and sings the essential structure of the Medea Project: individual monologues, songs, and group dancing are juxtaposed; old-time wisdom, myths, and spiritual histories are brought into relation with contemporary women, who sometimes stand alone to tell their individual stories and sometimes sing and dance together en masse. The women learn discipline and coordination from the goddesses, and the goddesses are also changed, as their ancient rituals are modified, updated, and their classic stories are performed anew. There is a constant state of fluidity between the collective movements and individual stories; sometimes someone dances alone, and sometimes stories get passed around. Always there is the conscious use of space to signal who has been let out, or broken out, which serves to remind us that more women remain locked away, unseen. With no intermission, Jones knows how to vary the emotional tone and control the dramatic shape of the evening. It's the pacing of the show, the juxtaposition of inset plays, of music and dance, humor and horror, the mixture of classical references, children's folktales, and contemporary street stories that work to keep the audience riveted. The energy of the performers doesn't flag and neither do the audience's responses.

The audience's laughter at the wiseass jokes that the Mother of God cracks with the Auntie of God stops while they listen to one of the most powerful and ominous stories told during *Slouching Towards Armageddon*. Darcell Bernard (Revenge), an older black woman, steps on to a darkened stage. The chorus of women stand behind her with masks on, punching their fists in a slow rhythm, dropping to the floor behind her as Bernard slowly tells this story, each sentence distinctly spoken, with long pauses between each phrase:

It was hot as fuck outside. It was a beautiful day. I was walking up Haight Street and lo and behold, the devil . . . disguised. He had brown curly hair, he was light skinned, big green eyes. He was a good looking fella.

He said, "What's happening."

I said, "Hey."

He asked where was I going.

"To the park."

We started walking, stopped at the store. I bought a pack of Kools and a pint of Wild Irish Rose. We were kickin it. Then somehow money came up.

I said, "I got some food stamps."

He said, "You do? Give 'em here."

So I gave him a $50.00 book.

He said, "I'll be right back."

He came back quick with $40.00 cash.

I said "Wow" and gave him $10.00.

He said, "I'm going to go get some crack."

And I said, "Cool, but it ain't my thing."

He comes back and started smoking his crack while I'm drinking my wine. Getting a little hungry, I said, "Let's go to the new Burger King on Fillmore."

He said, "Cool."

We walk over to the Burger King, order, sit down and I see a friend of mine.

I say, "Hey, Nel. Wha's up?"

He said, "Hey, baby."

I said, "I'll see you in a minute." I finished eating and looked over at the devil.

And I said, "I'll see you later."

The devil said, "Can I talk to you outside for a minute?"

We goes outside and he sticks a gun in my ribs.

And he says, "Walk, bitch! You better not say a mother fucking word."

And I'm walking scared as fuck. He takes me up to the roof near the Kabuki theater. We get up on the roof.

I said, "What you want? Some head, some pussy? Anything. Just don't hurt me."

But he wanted me to fight him. And I did. And I got my ass kicked. He snatched my backpack. He cut my straps and tied me up. He made me suck his dick. He fucked me and then he cut my throat. (*Hands up to throat, head tilts, scar visible.*) He was smiling the whole mother fucking time. I can hear him going down the stairs. I jumped up and tried to untie myself. I could hear him coming back. I lay back in the puddle of blood.

And I said, "Oh god, please let this man think I'm dead. Don't let him kill me."

I could feel him staring at me and I'm scared and he walked up to me. And he pulls out his dick and then he pissed in my face. Then he turned around, he pulled down his pants and then he shit in my face. I could hear him walking away. I jump up. I went to the top of the stairs and untied myself. I looked down and he was gone. I see a whole lot of church people in the parking lot. I must have fainted. When I came to there was a black woman tying her scarf around my neck to stop the bleeding.

That day I walked with the devil.

There is silence, murmurs, someone is crying in front of me, and then the audience claps, somberly.

Another young black woman with a wristband on to alert us to her incarcerated status, Chenique Garret (Misfortune), eighteen years old, stands up and addresses her missing father. She has written him a letter that begins:

Dear Dad: I want to let your sorry ass know how I feel. I've been carrying your sorry ass name for eighteen years and you're not even around. Daddy, I miss you, but how can I miss somebody I don't even know? You know how fucked up my life has been because I never had a father figure? Did you know that at the age of twelve I started getting high, fucking older men, being abused and shit? Well, as you can see, I grew up pretty fast. I grew up without you. Just with mom, and half the time, I felt like she didn't want me either.

You know, I envy some girls when they talk about their dad this and their dad that, and when Father's Day comes around, shit, I'm really upset. I go spend my money, *my* money, on someone else's father just so I can feel happy. You know that I hate you. I hated you for not being there when I needed you the most. And you know what? I wish you could be in my life. But, you know, that's your decision. But if only you knew what you were missing.

If I were to see you, hell, I wouldn't know what to do. But I tell you what, that might be the happiest day of my life. And that *might* be the worst day of yours. I just have one last question: How do you like me now?

With her hands on her hips, striking a bold stance, she leads the troupe into the Medean "Kicking Dance." The women all move forward and thrust their legs up and out: boom, boom, boom. They fight back, then recede back into formation.

A white prisoner, Angela Wilson (Confusion), delivers a piece that speaks about her frustration at landing in jail. On stage, the troupe of women stand in a line with their hands interlocked. Wilson begins to speak from behind them, describing her rage at finding herself in jail as a kind of second jail, her "own personal lock up." Continuing to speak, she breaks through the line of women, recognizing herself at the end of her monologue as responsible for herself: "A killer I've allowed myself to be—of me. Here, all locked up in this place. Heart, mind, body, and soul, all agree, we can't wait, to be set free, of this prejudice against—me." Wilson's story about her "own personal lock up" contains images of her self that are contradictory. She shows herself to be a victim of prejudice but also a participant, a killer of herself as well. She is responsible for her lock up and not entirely responsible. She longs to be free, but it isn't clear from what: freed from the self that landed her in jail, or from prejudice (of what sort?) that locked her up? Remembering the sentiment of Paulette Jones's earlier song, which asks whether anyone can look beyond the color of a person's skin and see the real "me" beneath it, I find Angela Wilson's "me" inchoate, and I can't tell whether it's because I need to know more biographically or because she is, in some fundamental sense, still personally locked up.

Other women sing about being free. Chelsea Parnell (Slander), a very young black girl, sings a capella gospel songs in which she gives herself up to God and testifies: "Though in this life I've made mistakes / Only God can judge me now / Because he controls my fate." Wilson and Garret perform "Hair Rap," in which curling irons or perms hold out the promise of changing, at least, hair fate:

Our hair, their hair, your hair

If you're black and your hair is nappy, get a perm to straighten it really snappy.

If you're white and your hair is straight and stringy

Get a perm to curl to make it snappy.

Our hair, their hair, your hair

From stringy and straight to springy and great

Check it out.

The juxtapositions seem critical, but I'm not sure what other people would think, and here's where I'd be glad to partake in a conversation. Are these modes of control, God and a hair perm, equally powerful, depending only on what someone happens to believe or not to believe? Can we *choose* to look a certain way, and so *be* a certain way, or are we in God's hands? The production offers different ways of thinking about identity, and Jones refuses, as director, to rank them for us. Instead we are given different versions of the same story.

Toward the end of the show, Gail Burton appears again to tell Pandora's story, only this time from the goddess's sisters' point of view. And when the point of view shifts, everything changes. What was purely evil is now seen as good *and* bad. Out of the box, now described as a jar, come gifts for the world, not just terrors:

BURTON: Well, the last story I told y'all, Zeus's brother's, uncle's cousin's people told me. . . . But now Pandora's people told me this.

Number one, Zeus didn't make Pandora, because Pandora was a god herself. And at one time she was more powerful than Zeus. She was older than Zeus.

MOTHER OF GOD: I could have told you that.

BURTON: When Zeus and his crew took over the world, they made up that story—they were just trying to perpetrate that story on Pandora, they were trying to make everybody believe that nothing existed before them. Now y'all know better than that. Number two: Pandora was down with the Earth Mothers. Y'all know who they are: Gaia, Mother Nature. . . .

AUNTIE OF GOD: Don't fool with Mother Nature.

BURTON: She put me in mind of Osun. You know that girl.

AUNTIE OF GOD: We used to play together. Big booty Osun.

BURTON: Zeus told me she had a box. But these sisters said she had a jar.

And from that jar she poured all these gifts into the world for human kind. What gifts? Well, stuff like a pomegranate that became a lemon and then a pear. And then there were flowering trees with fruit and gnarled trees with olives. And y'all know what else she made? She made the grapevine.

AUNTIE OF GOD and MOTHER OF GOD (*singing*): I'm about to lose my mind. Heard it on the grapevine.

BURTON: She put her hand inside the jar and pulled out seeds and scattered them across the hillside, for illness and hunger and for weaving. There were minerals and ores and clays of all kinds. She rolled the jar down the hillside until everything was covered in her flowing aura. Chile, *everybody* bathed in the changing colors of her aura. She brings wonder and curiosity and wisdom, she brings healing and communal bonds, she brings justice and mercy, and loving kindness for all human beings. You know, it seems like Zeus made up Pandora. You know how it is when someone tries to bring down a powerful woman.

My mama used to tell me, "Look at the good side. Think positive." You know, if you stay positive and you think about Pandora you might consider her Mother Abundance. You got to take the good with the bad.

In this revisionary myth, Pandora is responsible for all that is good in the world, not just the bad. Good and evil seem to be a package deal. What kind of charge evil has depends upon who is doing the charging. We think we know what evil is, but maybe we don't see to the bottom of it, its roots, its connection to that which is good.

Sean Reynolds now addresses the audience and remembers the women who started rehearsing but did not make it to the end. Sally, who rehearsed up to the very last day, but then was told she couldn't perform in the theater because her crime, attempted manslaughter, was too serious; some who were released but didn't stay with the group; and the rest who dropped out while still in jail. Finally, each performer speaks an affirmation, "If I live and do not die, I hope I . . . ." As Bernard says, "have a career in fashion advertising," someone in the audience cries out, "You will!" The audience cheers and claps, perhaps hoping that vocal acclamation can translate hope to a reality. At the end of the evening, Jones has brought us back to wondering about the reality of these women's lives, and the distance between what they (and we) can hope for and what will come true. What was most powerful for me, after seeing my second live

Medea production, was not the swelling sounds of applause, which had so moved me while watching *Buried Fire*. Having seen more of the rehearsals of *Slouching Towards Armageddon*, I was moved by all that the audience could *not* know because they hadn't been there: the long road it had taken to get these women to this point. I was more aware than ever before of how little I really knew of each person in the cast, how imperfectly I could predict their futures.

The drama of the Medea Project lies as much in what isn't scripted as it does in the choreographed evening performance itself. One evening, in the middle of her speech about the Devil raping her, Bernard moves too close to the edge of the stage, steps into the lights, and falls off the stage, crashing to the floor. Jones rushes up to her, asks, "Are you all right, Darcell?" And she answers, from the floor, flat on her back, in a drawl, "Yeah, I'm all right." "Can you go on?" "Yeah, I can." She is helped back up on stage, stands for a minute, says, "Now, where was I?" The audience roars. And then she just moves right on. It's amazing concentration for a thirty-seven-year-old woman who has been doing every conceivable drug (in her words) since she was in junior high school. One man in the audience that night said he thought the moment had been rehearsed, just part of the show. The second night before the end of the run, Bernard is released from jail. But at 4:00 in the afternoon she isn't where she's supposed to be to get a ride to the theater. Nobody is much surprised not to see her. And then an hour and a half before the curtain, she strolls into the Lorraine Hansberry, receiving cheers and applause and gets to work. She is there for the next performance as well. But she doesn't show up for the first Saturday meeting after the show closes. Even in the glow of the affirmations, "I hope" and "You will," surely everyone wonders what will happen after, whether the performance of the Medea Project will affect the performance of life. A month later Paulette Jones hears that Bernard is strung out on heroin.

The form of the Medea Project itself forces everyone to think beyond the performance, to wonder whether the performers are following a script, whether the story they tell is true, whether the telling of it will make a difference next time the same plot is encountered. We may wonder how much hasn't been told, and we may wonder where they are now. Darcell Bernard told me that on her way to the theater that first afternoon as a free woman, she walked through downtown, past all of her friends offering her all kinds of drugs to celebrate her freedom.[6] She could very easily have decided to join them. That day she said no.

Rhodessa Jones thought Garret, of "Dear Dad," had made the most progress of all the women in the group. Garret and Parnell, both under twenty, sucked their thumbs whenever there was a lull in the rehearsals. Garret, who was so sullen at the beginning of the process, toward the end seemed more often just sad, and at one last rehearsal, cried about her missing, fucked-up family. Three days before the production opened, she could barely speak her letter to her Dad. She had to read it; she couldn't remember it. She had no attitude. Her affect was flat. I thought this was hopeless, that the performance would be a debacle. But Jones kept working with her; she made her stand with her hand on her hip for the last line: "How do you like me now?" When she was forced to move a certain way, her reading became more intense. By the opening, Garret did thrust her hips and remember her lines. She made the audience listen, commanding their attention. Whether her family (the ones there, the father not) were changed by what they heard, whether she herself was, once the public performance was over, I don't know. But I did see an almost miraculous transformation from a girl who sucked her thumb to a young woman who stood in front of 300 people and spoke her mind.

The fierce questioning of what constitutes the "real" identity of these women, the core "me" that Paulette Jones and Angela Wilson allude to, occurs in each of the Medea Project's works. What do race, class, family, gender, desire, and education have to do with it? *Slouching Towards Armageddon* was to focus on race, but race was just one subject used in exploring the reasons for an incarcerated self. Who is agent? Who has agency? Who is in control of their fate? Who speaks of freedom? Of being seen? Of being desired? Bernard tells me, and she told Jones, that she didn't think her story about being raped by the Devil had anything to do with race. She thinks of herself as lucky and as a survivor. In fact, Jones thinks Bernard's story *does* have to do with race, at least in part, and so do many others in the group, though that disagreement was never voiced in discussions. It was a hot day in August and there were lots of people on the street outside Burger King. No one saw her walking down the street with a gun held up to her back. No one cared, no one heard, no one looked. Outside on the streets, in a neighborhood used to violence, Bernard is not visible. She's held hostage even before she gets to jail.

The artful presentation of these stories in *Slouching Towards Armageddon* seems to offer a promise of personal salvation for the actors and a demand for social change to the audience. When Bernard tells her story, she becomes visible, and we cannot bear the thought that she will be silenced again. But, of course, she may be, and we may remain silent too if we see her, or don't see her, on the streets outside the theater. Jones is funded now not only for the workshops she conducts in jail, but because she intends to bring the women center stage, to make the private rehearsal go public in a professional manner. And then, once it goes public, in spite of its label—"Theater for Incarcerated Women"—it isn't only a theater for the incarcerated. It becomes theater for people who want to see the incarcerated visible, safely available. The project continues to garner funding in part because Jones is able to pull off, over and over again, a polished, rousing public production in spite of the obstacles.

She does not overpromise. Although some participants may harbor illusions about salvation, Jones entertains no such fantasies. She often tells the women, "This ain't no *Dreamgirls*. . . . I don't delude myself that I'm making a hell of a lot of difference with this. . . . I don't expect these women to get out of jail and go right out and find jobs and stop smoking dope and suddenly become successes. But what this has done is light a few lights. And light is always better than darkness, you know what I'm saying?"[7] Jones always distinguishes between fantasies and reality: "There's a lot of lost children, women who have no idea where they really are in the world, just the ideas they get from TV. . . . We play with fantasies in our workshops. But when somebody goes, 'After I get out I'm gonna be a hairdresser in Beverly Hills,' I say, 'Wait a minute. Let's get real. How are you going to pay for a ticket there? How are you going to get some training?' They can't wait around for miracles."[8] The Medea Project is interested in an investigation of the plots that lead to imprisonment— the causes for addiction, rage, recidivism—in hopes that by asking certain questions, the women might not count on miracles but instead plot a different course. But Jones knows that the traditional plot won't change for most of the women unless more people participate in its redesign. The Medea Project, in its most far-reaching conception of itself, means to make us not only recognize that we share common plots but to find ways for all of us to change them by becoming more socially active citizens.

There are, obviously, many ways to tell the story of the Medea Project: Theater for Incarcerated Women. One could organize a book about the Medea Project around the (to date) five theatrical productions, creating an expanded production history, of the sort begun above, but I don't believe it is possible to duplicate, even approximately, the experience of a performance. As Peggy Phelan has argued, "Performance cannot be saved, recorded, documented, or otherwise participate in the circulation of representations *of* representations: once it does so, it becomes something other than performance."[9] Thus, in the rest of this book, rather than try to recapture the experience of the public performances, I focus instead on how the plots or myths or driving metaphors that differentiate each production link specific social concerns with artistic expression. Though the public productions are aesthetically interesting in and of themselves, to restrict this account to a discussion of the public performances would not fully encompass the project's long-range trajectory, its pedagogical aims and political aspirations, that is, on all that comes before and after the public performances.

It would be relatively simple too, as these things go, to explain the making of the Medea Project heroically, to write a biography of its founder and artistic director, Rhodessa Jones, making her the hero, describing her singular beliefs and her experiences. There is no question that the making of the Medea Project could not have happened without her. It would be difficult, everyone concedes, to find someone with her combination of talents so as to duplicate the project somewhere else. Her African American heritage, her background as a performance artist, her feminism, her blues, energy, sweetness, wisdom, and rants have made her one of the most charismatic divas of the postmodern performance art world, a performer and director who dismantles the traditional borders between performance, theater, therapy, high and low art, in order to rethink the meaning of community in a multicultural nation. There is no sense in downplaying the importance of individuals—Jones, in particular. But to make her the hero leaves everyone else playing the role of acolyte or follower, with fewer lines, weaker parts, diminished voices. That is decidedly not the sort of theater Jones makes.

Rhodessa Jones is the connector who links incarcerated women with artists, the guards from the San Francisco jails with ushers in theaters, directors of private foundations with the elected sheriff of San Francisco, and then translates their ways of talking and beliefs, negotiates among institutions and rules, to create theater in public that aims to do more than entertain. She is an artist who speaks with a sense of a mission, not as religious leader or heroic savior or patriarchal (or even matriarchal) master/mistress, but rather, I think, in the language of Kobena Mercer, "as a connector located at the hyphenated intersection of disparate discourses."[10] Jones is an artist, a social scientist, a political activist, and a public intellectual, who performs each role for different audiences. She is adept at crossing over—in the 1960s, as a black woman in a white feminist dance troupe; since then, as a performance artist who also teaches children and adults. She has long worked with difference—different disciplinary structures, people from different cultural backgrounds—and her performances incorporate many different artistic traditions. Her voice is unmistakably powerful, her rants loud and clear. But her voice does not overpower others. Instead she makes it possible to hear those who in some other show would have been only part of a chorus at best, or not heard at all. In the intersection that is the space of the Medea Project, people try on other parts, become articulate in ways they may never have been before, think about and act out what it would be like to take off down a different street, work out a different ending. To write a single biographical history would not be faithful to the many biographies Jones means us to hear.

As a scholar and teacher of American studies, I was intrigued by the sounds of the Medea Project. Different voices reflected different communities and different discourses: of rehabilitation, punishment and discipline, social work, aesthetics and salvation, commercial viability and tourism. It was these sounds that I wanted to capture. The Medea Project depends upon the collaboration of many organizations: the jails, public and private foundations, halfway houses, theaters. In the Medea Project all sorts of people stand in close proximity who might never have otherwise, and all get a chance to sound off, to make their mark: San Francisco sheriff Michael Hennessey and assistant sheriff Michael Marcum; social worker Sean Reynolds, MSW; executive director of Cultural Odyssey, Idris Ackamoor; director of Artists-in-Residence in San Francisco County Jails, Ruth Morgan; and, over the years, the women who make up the performing Medea Project troupe. All of these people are skilled at speaking for their own institutions, but they also see the great benefit of collaborating with strangers. The Medea Project inspired me to continue to believe that the arts can serve social concerns and that the academy can also encourage, even facilitate, social activism as an intellectual and moral imperative.

In the theoretical language of the early twenty-first century's cultural criticism, the Medea Project is a quintessential "crossover" project—interdisciplinary, multicultural, and hybridized. It occupies an interstitial space, between social work and art work, among individuals and institutions and disciplines and discourse that allow for certain kinds of actions and constrain others. Nowhere is this more apparent than in the jails themselves, where the disciplines of violence and punishment hold sway. From jail, society's most restrictive site, the Medea Project creates space to move physically, emotionally, and theatrically—to reconfigure the discipline and particular habits of survival of the streets to the customs and surprises of the theater. Its strengths and its limitations come from the very different groups who participate—artists, social workers, guards, prisoners—and who have, sometimes, very different measures for judging the project's effectiveness.

In fact, what I think people find is that the usual standards they rely on for judging do not accurately reflect the effects of this project. For example, if theater critics evaluate only the quality of the singing, the dance steps, the formal integration of myths and contemporary stories, the lighting design, and costumes, they recognize that they are not getting at what is unique about the performance, its back story, its intensity. Critics ask whether what an audience sees *is* art, or is *good* art, or whether this is some form of victim art and thus beyond criticism.[11] Guards ask whether the prisoners are more dissatisfied or more confident. Funders want to know how many lives have been saved or the percentage who return to jail. None of these questions yields a description of this project that accounts for the interaction and intermingling of art and social work. It is precisely the way in which the project collapses such distinctions that marks its vitality and seems worth paying attention to.

In order to chart the effective communicative power of this particular community project, which owes everything to its hybrid cultural formation, to the multiple communities it brings together, I feel it is important to describe the various kinds of participation it demands. Rather than represent this still-in-process project in terms of either a straightforward theater history or a biography or a series of biographies, I have situated the Medea Project in three sometimes overlapping fields of practice that frame the sorts of participation that occur. If, as Gillian Rose has argued, the basic act of participation in community arts projects is seen as a transparent good, that the basic process is to produce *more* process and *more* participation, I hope that by scrutinizing particular practices of participation I will be able to evaluate and analyze at least some parts of participation's efficacy.[12]

Autobiography

The first form that participation takes, and which is perhaps most central to the project, is the expression of autobiography, the telling of one's own story. Many of the theatrical techniques Jones developed for the Medea Project are aimed at enabling and showcasing autobiography. That the incarcerated women's experiences have to be acknowledged, understood, related, and heard is a key principle of this feminist theatrical project. That everyone has a story to tell, that everyone's story is worth telling and is more amazing than anything heard on *Oprah,* is a constant refrain. However, though the Medea Project begins with honoring experience, it would be limited if that were all it did. Instead, Jones finds theatrical ways to interrogate the personal, surrounding the contemporary with the mythical, providing more texts, and thus context, for these women, so that each individual's story is not isolated but always seen in relation to others. Practically, the project knows what theorists have argued, that autobiography alone neither guarantees new insights nor changes behavior. As Joan Scott has argued, experience is *not* transparent but is "at once always already an interpretation *and* something that needs to be interpreted." [13] The Medea Project wants women's stories to be told, but it also recognizes the importance of interpreting those stories, of making connections from the personal to the social. If inner feelings are discussed separately from their relationship to power, rules, discipline, money, and means, then "discussion of . . . 'inner' self and feelings replaces rather than leads to a discussion of links to the 'exterior' and ways to transform it." [14] A move from personal autobiography to the contextualization of the self in history or mythology is apparent in the title of the project itself. Jones insists on using art and world culture as points of comparison and contrast to the personal.

Critical Thinking

Secondly, like other forms of liberation theater, or theater for development, the Medea Project loosely uses Paulo Freire's pedagogy of the oppressed in the course of its workshops, though not explicitly in the productions themselves. [15] Freire's "conscientization," critical thinking through dialogue, is a key practice for the Medea Project. As Freire argues,

> True dialogue cannot exist unless the dialoguers engage in critical thinking — thinking which discerns an indivisible solidarity between the world and men and admits of no dichotomy between them — thinking which perceives reality as process, as transformation, rather than as a static entity — thinking

which does not separate itself from action, but constantly immerses itself in temporality without fear of the risks involved. . . . For the critic, the important thing is the continuing transformation of reality, in behalf of the continuing humanization of men.[16]

It is not only that people must develop an intellectual awareness of their place in history, but they must find ways to *act out* that consciousness. This is, of course, a tall order, for anyone. Liberation theater workers have been pretty hard-nosed when they evaluate the success of their own theater work to perform this sort of critical thinking. Honor Ford-Smith, director of the Jamaican feminist theater group Sistren, has argued that although her group's work validated popular culture and developed in the women a sense of self-worth and although "the process of the drama improvisations taught the language of the theater while, at the same time, allowing people to reveal and reflect on their own experience," it "did not teach people how to theorize about their experience, nor did it teach them how to teach."[17]

Talking, even critical talking, is not a sufficient pedagogical goal for Freire or for liberation theaters like the Medea Project. Talking is only a means to an end, which is to liberate the oppressed. Reflection doesn't necessarily lead to the sort of critical thinking that would allow people to take social action, to reproduce the act of teaching, or to reproduce some part of the project elsewhere. As Ngũgĩ wa Mĩriĩ has said, "In terms of the whole concept of Theatre for Development, where the emphasis is dialogue, you have to be very careful because it can also be a means of mystification of the problem—that once you have discussed it you have actually solved the problem."[18] The Medea Project insists on dialogue and attempts to develop critical thinking. But no one on the project is naïve enough to think that talking will have solved anyone's problem. They are all too aware of the necessity of changing social conditions, aware too of the limited power of the theater to directly affect the "transformation of reality."

Reimagining Community

The third important practice of participation is the Medea Project's attempt to redraw the boundaries of community. In workshops and productions, the Medea Project interrogates what community means, the boundaries we can cross over and those we cannot—as women, men, of a particular class and race, nationally and locally. It establishes connections between groups that otherwise might not come into contact and, by imagining communities different from those we have at present, presents itself as a radical or alternative geography, what Homi Bhabha calls "a third space."[19] Critics have become suspicious about the use of the concept of "community" for radical politics, since, as Doreen Massey writes, the concept depends upon distinguishing between members and non-members, inside and outside, "another way of constructing a counterposition between 'us' and 'them.'" She goes on to argue for a new conception of place:

> [one that] can be imagined as articulated moments in networks of social relations and understandings, but where a large proportion of those relations, experiences and understandings are constructed on a far larger scale than what we happen to define for that moment as the place itself, whether that be a street, or a region or even a continent. . . . If places can be conceptualized in terms of the social interactions which they tie together, then it is also the case that these interactions themselves are not motionless things, frozen in time. They are processes. One of the great one-liners in Marxist exchanges has for long been, "Ah, but capital is not a thing, it's a process." Perhaps this should be said also about places; that places are processes, too.[20]

Insofar as the Medea Project inhabits a place on the map, it is in this sense of being a meeting place of social interactions, not static and not homogenous, seeking other connections in its mission to transform the boundaries that now exist between the imprisoned and the free, to chart a course from jail, through the theater, to a center for women on the outside that could be an alternative home and school.

All of these practices—the autobiographical, the critical thinking, and the reimagining of communities—impinge upon each other. All are filtered through a theatrical medium, and all can be evaluated as effective tools in the service of this practical and utopian project. Jones mostly refuses overtly political goals:

> I would refrain from saying what the politics are, because then it becomes a school of thought, and it isn't that. I didn't come with any politics other than theater saved my life. You can be in my dream if I can be in your dream. This is what I know, sister. This is how you make bread, this is how you make community, this is how we can take care of our children, this is how we can

live in the world as women. It's very homespun, it's very much mother wit. I'm not the intellectual, academic one. That was Sean. I don't think Sean set herself up to be lofty. But Sean set herself up to be the didactic teacher. She was also guerrilla warfare for both of us. I don't think I would dare talk about the politics of it. It would become dated in a way. You can't trust politics. Politics implies a certain kind of order. And basically, at heart, I'm a sort of anarchist. I do think there's a way we can live together, there's a humanistic, very simple way to live together, if we can remember that we are all part of a human family. *It's about women saving their own lives through the creative process.* I guess for me that's the bottom line.[21]

Sistren director Ford-Smith concurs:

> Often theater, poetry or dance will be expected in a highly simplistic way to carry responsibility for articulating and enacting political positions. In spite of the fact that it cannot do this, cultural work strives nevertheless to be connected to the political and to violate the parameters of the term political. It aims at change or consolidation through the revelation and understanding of forms of oppression and exploitation, forms of affirmation and celebration. It combines an experience of pleasure with personal spiritual, political and economic experience. It can confront areas of experience hitherto hidden, and in so doing it will disturb rather than effect change, create insight rather than measurable action.[22]

The Medea Project does disturb, and people will testify that it creates insight. Ford-Smith is right when she suggests there are limits to what art can do, but what the Medea Project causes us to imagine is the way artists, connected to other institutions, could effect change and take measurable action. I believe that the success of cultural projects in the United States will depend increasingly on the ability of performers like Jones to translate back and forth for others, to be able to make common cause across disciplines and institutions, to integrate the techniques of the imagination with the practicalities of finding the money for a new address and safer homes.

In the following chapters, I highlight certain cultural intersections: autobiographies and classical myths; scenes of dramatic instruction, refused and taken; prison statistics and singular ex-prisoner voices; institutional constraints and communal imaginative hopes. In Chapter 1, "A Counter Epic: Making the Medea Project," I describe Jones's background and the beginnings of the project, when Jones transformed a jail work-shop into the first public Medea production. Jones made a brilliant con-nection between the myth of Medea and the stories she heard from the women in jail, though the women initially denied any similarity between Medea's anger and revenge and their own lives. Jones explores the way certain plots still constrict, while showing how narratives, telling one's own story in relation to others, may release different endings.

The second chapter, "To Be Real: Rehearsing Techniques," focuses on the pedagogy of the theater, the theatrical and antitheatrical techniques Jones uses to investigate, remember, claim, and reproduce women's pri-vate lives for the public. In workshops and in the public productions, Jones focuses some of the drama on women's bodies, and audiences have had a range of responses, from "The Medea Project is just into titillation" to "The Medea Project is all about men bashing." I am interested in the way Jones combines humanist and postmodern techniques, the ways in which she and Reynolds share in the pedagogy of liberation, through the theater and through discussions of current events, making the politics and cultural work of art inextricably intertwined.

In Chapter 3, "Prison Discourse: Surveying Lives," I briefly survey the history and current polemics surrounding prisons in the United States—seen by some as the problem, by others as the preferred solution. Most discourse about prison relies either on statistics or on representative anec-dotes. I find both unsatisfactory as analytical tools. Instead, I turn to five once incarcerated women who performed in the Medea Project and speak about themselves "before and after." As the core of the project, these women appear in the center of the book, a sort of ground zero. They speak for themselves. I don't attempt to interpret their experience but offer each woman as she described herself for me in an interview. I think that their strong self-presentation refuses any simplistic solution and yet also com-pels readers to think further.

The fourth chapter, "Community Work: Imagining Other Spaces," ex-plores the real communities that surround the project—local San Fran-cisco history, foundation practices, the ideas of a progressive sheriff, and halfway houses that teach self-esteem—and ends with utopian visions of what the Medea Project could become: more than a theater, a project that in yoking together institutions, artists, and individuals from different communities transforms the nature of community itself.

Jones walks a fine line, and perhaps this is a line worth paying attention to as we watch arguments swirl around government funding for the arts today. She doesn't claim that art can save all lives (though she says it saved hers); instead, she says she is teaching some people the skills to save their *own* lives. To give these women the means to control their lives differently is certainly one of the purposes of the Medea Project. The artistic service—the individual epiphanies for those on stage and those who watch in the audience—I take always to be a possibility, and I do not underestimate its power. Indeed, for me, the fierce ambition that underlies all the Medea Project's contingent and contradictory relations is the belief that art transforms—not only individuals but communities as well.

But this ambition is the hardest to realize. If what people hope is that the theater can resolve racism or spring everyone from jail—the answer has to be no. No single cultural institution (or performance) can be expected to do that. It may even be a dangerous trajectory to argue that the social work that art does is more important than its aesthetic value, because people will expect some way of quantifying the production: how *many* lives have you saved? I will argue that the arts do provide *social* services, though to be most effective they must be woven into other equally important social services—ones that provide housing, education, jobs. The Medea Project depends on many different institutions, any of which may cease to invest, and on particular individuals, who may shut down, burn out, move on. Practically, the Medea Project has worked extraordinarily well in certain arenas and less well in others. As a public theatrical event, the Medea Project has inspired local enthusiasm and appreciative audiences, but it has not managed to institutionalize itself within the jails, depending from year to year on different grants to be able to begin another workshop. In medias res, it is not clear that the project will be able to sustain the partnerships it has that make the public performances possible, or to create new partnerships that would support programs for formerly incarcerated women, or to institutionalize itself by training new directors, teachers, and staff who can continue the work or duplicate it in other jails or in community centers. However, by making visible what our society has not thought worth saving, producing a public event that is self-consciously always questioning what it means to be a public, the project moves beyond the theatrical to inspire the audience to think of more creative and useful intersections that will help protect and educate everyone who inhabits our worldly public sphere.

CHAPTER I

A Counter Epic

Making the Medea Project

> *I would be nothing more than a memory or a bitch with a bad*
> *attitude if I hadn't found acting. . . . Yeah, theater is my religion.*
> *I've been baptized in the applause and it saved my life. But if you're*
> *blessed enough to climb up on the platform and say, "Over here!*
> *Everybody look at me!" then you damn well better have something*
> *to say.*
> —*Rhodessa Jones, quoted in Snider, "Just Say Rho!"*

In Rhodessa Jones, the creator and director of the Medea Project, the women in the project have a life story they can use as a counter against the traditional, predictable, plots usually attached to women of her class and her race. In certain ways, Rhodessa Jones's life conforms to the lives of many of the women she has met in jail: African American, born into a poor family, an unwed mother at an early age, with no college education. And yet she is always aware that she has escaped their fate. Jones was born in Florida in 1948 to a large African American family of migrant laborers. She is the eighth of twelve brothers and sisters. She remembers living in migrant camps, the sounds of Saturday night dances and music, watching performances that seemed like vaudeville. One of her brothers was a great dancer, other family members sang, she was a comic. In the 1950s, the family settled on a farm near Rochester, New York, where the schools were good. Rhodessa and some of her siblings started a singing group; another brother, Bill T. Jones, kept dancing.[1] Someone was always reading: her father, Zane Grey; a brother, D. H. Lawrence and Henry Miller. Both her father and her mother were strong presences in the family. She describes the lack of tolerance for loafing and whining: if she was sitting around, her mother would hand her a broom; if she did something her father thought was wrong, there wouldn't be time for an explanation. She recognizes her parents' influence in the way she directs:

Rhodessa Jones. Photograph by Diane McCurdy, 1992

I am a terrible taskmaster. I'm really hard and I demand a lot. I really do. I'm very demanding. I think I take after my father. He was a wonderful, sweet, benevolent daddy, but also, my god, if you did something wrong. He didn't talk to you, he went and got his belt or his switch, and he came and got you. There was no warning. You could be playing and he would say,

"Come here. *You.*" And it wasn't going to be, "I have to talk to you." No. He would pick you up and go *Whack. Whack, whack, whack, whack.* "Now don't do that again. If I ever hear you doing that again you'll get that again. You understand?" And that would be it. My mother would rant for two days, but my father was scarier. He would just tear you up. And there was no crying. "I don't want to hear no crying. Because you should have been crying when you were doing it." Whatever it was. I think, on some level, I'm like that inside. I don't beat up on people physically. I'm hard, but I'm also very tender. There *are* people who just push you.

I was not allowed to act up in my mother's house. There was no acting up with my mother. No petulance, pouts, storming. No. And there wasn't any talking about it. "You pull in that lip. Get it together." And she also believed in work. "Go do something. You feeling sad? Bad? Go in there and clean up that kitchen. Go clean out the basement. Work." My mother said, "If you won't work, you'll steal." And my father said, "If you're going to be a thief, you better be a damn good one. Because if you get in trouble, I can't help you. I am a poor man." It becomes a part of you. I'm not saying that's always good. But the other side of it is I learned I could wield a mighty sword. At the same time, I would never cut your head off because you're my family. I couldn't do this work without these people letting me manipulate them, letting me mold them, letting me challenge them. I couldn't do it without people trusting and believing in me.

It's like Harriet Tubman. You pull out the gun and say, "We're going on. We're doing this or I'm going to kill you." And at a point you don't get to quit. You don't get to quit after a point.

Now fifty, Jones exudes both warmth and discipline, a respect for keeping busy and hard work, and no self pity. She is filled with stories about her mother and father, their complicated relationship, the responses of her sisters and brothers to the family. While her mother believes her sons must be protected and respected, her mother expects her daughters to be caretakers, and Rhodessa Jones, because she is an artist, is seen as someone who has lots of free time to take care of others. It isn't a Norman Rockwell family, by any stretch of the imagination, but Jones understands the strengths and roles everyone plays with a kind of wry bemusement. Her family is big and her own attachments have been various and multiple. She draws strength from her love stories and her family; they seem to justify the vibrant, charismatic, philosophical person she has grown into. She is someone who *likes* to stop and ask people for directions, at which point she can be warmed by a stranger's generosity, but not surprised by a racist response. At least part of the power she exudes in the Medea Project comes from the way she inhabits the role of grand diva *and* simple country girl at the same time. She is always aware of herself as a leader, director, but also part of a family. Her power isn't simply unidirectional; rather, she understands that people must give consent: "they let me manipulate them, let me mold them, let me challenge them." The work she does simulates a family, but the Medea Family is a strictly voluntary one.

At sixteen, Jones was pregnant and gave birth to a baby girl. She had grown up with the whole range of popular cultural female role models. Some of them provided her with alternatives to motherhood:

> *Cosmopolitan* was my Bible. Helen Gurley Brown. She was my hero. She had an afternoon talk show on TV, and wrote *Sex and the Single Girl*. There was something about her whole rap that attracted me. It was my secret life. I was going to take up the mantle. I was going to be beautiful, sexy, exciting. I remember Jacqueline Bisset said, "If I ever had a kid, I'd put it on my hip and I'd give it the ride of its life." I identified with these women. Marilyn Monroe. I always felt she was incredibly funny. I remember sitting in the back of my boyfriend Dickie's Fairlane convertible and hearing that Marilyn Monroe was dead and feeling sad about that. It was right up there with hearing Barbra Streisand first sing "People," and hearing the news about Malcolm X dying. I remember exactly where I was when that happened. When Sam Cooke died, I was very pregnant. My daughter was born a month later. I wept so. I wept for myself. What's going to happen to me? Because this was not what I planned. I couldn't formulate it, but I know I was thinking that. In every bit of my body. Looking at the women in my family who were married and thinking, "I'm not going to do this." They were saying, "Who do you think you are? You're already saddled with a kid." But my brain said to my body, "No more. We're not going to get pregnant any more."

Helen Gurley Brown, Marilyn Monroe, Barbra Streisand were women who signaled to Jones not complacency and domesticity but cosmopolitan experience, a wider world than the one her sisters lived in. Her brother, Azel, who was working in a bank and also writing plays for the Living Arts Theater, a commune in Rochester, introduced her there, and she saw at once an alternative to the way she had been brought up. Men cooked along with the women. Everyone helped put together performances. Made up mostly of young white people, the Living Arts Theater was a place where racial and gendered expectations could be exploded. The experimental theater she found at an early age helped her to define difference against class, racial, and gendered expectations.

At the same time, she met and fell in love with a young Irish man, Dennis John Patrick Riley. When another brother, serving time in Attica, was injured during the uprising there, in reaction, and in the peripatetic ways of the sixties, Jones and Riley planned to move to South America. They got as far as Costa Rica and stayed for a year, but when her daughter became ill, they moved to San Francisco. Her brother Azel was there, and together with their brother Bill T. they formed a theatrical troupe called the Jones Company.[2] At the same time she was dancing with her brothers and sisters, she also joined the feminist collective, Tumbleweed, run by Teresa Dickinson, a former Merce Cunningham dancer. Tumbleweed's style was very athletic, improvisational, and political. And as the only black woman in the collective Jones got a fair amount of attention:

> I remember going with Tumbleweed to Portland, Oregon, to Reed College. And being the only black woman in this very feminist audience who had come to see these dancers. Teresa was very macho. We flew through the air. We were gymnasts. Teresa Dickinson was one of the first women to talk about strength in women. I remember looking at magazines with Teresa, and Teresa would say, "Yeah, Rhodessa, but she has no strength. She might be beautiful but look at her frame, the spine." She was that kind of teacher to me. I'd always been very strong but I'd been taught to be ashamed of my muscular arms, my skinny body, my skinny bone and muscle body. Which is part cultural too, because I come from a culture where you're supposed to have a little fat on you. My mother would say, "You need a little of cushion on your pocket." Which means you should be a bit plump around your vagina. "The softer the cushion, the better the pushin,'" was what the men said. This is the kind of stuff I used to grow up hearing. At the same time I met Teresa, who said it is better to be strong. "A good dancer is a dancer with a sense of carriage and a sense of alignment which has to do with the strengthening of the spine, thus the strengthening of the stomach muscles so that the back is strong." We were doing gymnastics. We were doing calisthenics. We were doing rope work. We were learning how to use our own natural weight as a part of body building. This was long before it was fashionable to have a great butt and great shoulders.

Also we were contact, improvisational artists, so we were lifting each other, which was totally provocative for young women who were coming out of the closet, young women who believed in a certain kind of woman power. We were amazons. We really were.

At the same time I was the only black woman. So whatever I said, people were hanging on every word. And I didn't know a lot about the dance world. I did not have a degree from an art institute. The dancing I had done had been in the fields and in my backyard and in the jukebox room with my brothers and sisters. And that was very natural. As an African American girl growing up in the late 50s, 60s, you had better learn how to dance. Also I worked in potato fields. I worked in orchards. I got in a lot of trouble in ballet classes. I thought I was being mistreated. Teachers expected with the frame I had that I was just a slouchy, lazy student. Because obviously, they thought, I had a lot of ballet training. I couldn't have been that strong and with that form without it.

I remember in those days being on display all the time. That was very life affirming for me. I was someone. I was something. People wanted to hear what I had to say. And I did have a different voice. My experience was very different. I had already known a lot of life. I had a daughter. What was I? Twenty-three, twenty-four? My kid was already eight years old. I was beautiful. I didn't comb my hair. I had dreads before dreads were popular. All of those things. These were the germs, the germinations of my political artistic ideas which have flowered.

Out of this mixture of feminism, of dance collectives, of her body formed in the fields and by popular music, she began to tell her own life story. The only black woman in Tumbleweed and the only woman who still was dancing in her family dance troupe, Jones moved easily between and among different groups. It was her difference that interested others—her black race, her hair, her body—and together these began to be her subject.

But she wasn't making any money. In order to support her daughter, whom she was raising by herself, she began to work as an erotic dancer in the San Francisco district known as the Tenderloin. There, the business of sex was transacted, in her case, through storytelling. As she stood or sat in a glass room, the men would speak their sexual fantasies to her and in order to keep them dropping quarters into the box she would respond as they wished her to, dancing or talking, anything to keep them pumping the money in. The fantasies were often violent and racially ugly, though there were sweet encounters too. Listening to their stories, reading Anaïs Nin, Virginia Woolf, and Doris Lessing at the time, and thinking about her responses, she began to write the stories and her thoughts down. The writing became her first solo and full-length piece, *The Legend of Lily Overstreet,* work that got her recognized as a serious artist in her own right. "After I made *Lily Overstreet,* I became a bona fide artist. I had a place in the culture," Jones has said.[3] In *Lily,* she reenacts, sometimes naked, the things she said in that glass box and what was said to her. In the reconstituted performance in the theater of the initial performance in the peep show, her body, as an instrument of control, is centrally staged. Jones has said that for her, "The subject matter is always sex and women as sex objects. I seem to always come back to these issues."[4] *Lily Overstreet* questions the border erected between art work and sex work. The audience in the theater is forced to wonder whether what they are seeing is different from what Jones performed in the club. Are not both paying audiences voyeurs, or is desire altogether uprooted from those sitting in the theater? Has her subject changed because her audience has, or has she changed the subject in the way that she stages it? *Lily Overstreet* does not deny the primacy of experience, but in dramatically restaging it, Jones creates a new self as subject, one who engages the audience in the project of thinking about how we create ourselves and others through our various and multiple desires.

During that initial run of *Lily Overstreet* in 1979, Rhodessa met jazz musician and theater visionary Idris Ackamoor, who was developing a performance and production company called Cultural Odyssey. They became partners and, though no longer in a private relationship, they continue their working partnership as codirectors of Cultural Odyssey.[5] Like so many artists who came of age in the 1960s and created alternatives to mainstream commercial theater—artists like Joseph Chaikin, Robert Wilson, Richard Foreman, Amiri Baraka—Jones and Ackamoor had to create an alternative organization to make space for their work and that of other artists. Ackamoor remembers that when he first met Jones in the 1970s, "Rho was doing stuff that no performers—particularly no black performers—were even thinking about. . . . The subjects she was tackling, the way she got so far out there on stage, I hadn't really seen that and it excited me. I knew there was a kindred spirit."[6] They began to tour nationally and internationally, creating a body of work that included works with music composed by Ackamoor.[7]

Jones came of artistic age in the late 1960s as a feminist artist. Her work over the last thirty years falls under the rubric of what has been loosely called "performance art." Critic and performance artist Coco Fusco has described this genre as "ephemeral, time-based and process oriented," one that "incorporate[s] the body as an object and as a subject of inquiry, and explore[s] extreme forms of behaviour, cultural taboos, and social issues."[8] This description fits Jones neatly. From *The Legend of Lily Overstreet* to her more recent *Hot Flashes, Power Surges, and Private Summers,* to the work she has directed in the Medea Project, Jones uses personal memories to investigate the barriers between life and art, infiltrating the boundaries around cultural taboos, rewriting the legends. Jones has focused almost all of her performances on an investigation of women, most particularly female icons—from the unknown, herself as an erotic dancer, to the well-paid rock goddess, Tina Turner. Given her status as insider to popular culture and outsider as a poor, black, formally uneducated woman, her performances have provided instances of how to measure different cultural desires and possibilities within the utterly familiar sounds of mass culture and stranger notes from abroad.

In all of her performance pieces, Jones has been drawn to more voices than just her own. She has never been a cultural separatist but is rather a great sampler, mixing and infusing her work with many artistic traditions—African American, the European avant-garde, myths from around the world—as well as different media—dance, video, storytelling. Jones never seems to have gone through the stage that many artists of color did: what Coco Fusco, quoting Stuart Hall, has called the "imaginative recovery of a singular, unifying past" that made their work seem authentic and therefore valid. Like so many performance artists now who practice a melange of styles, Jones has always moved "back and forth between past and present, between history and fiction, between art and ritual, between high art and popular culture, and between Western and non-Western influence." She is one of those artists who "reflect the hybrid experiences that shape so much of contemporary life."[9] As a performance artist and as a feminist, Jones promotes a hybrid aesthetic and hybrid politic. She has always been drawn to the juxtapositions of cultural forms rather than to discriminating between pure signs of culture, and has felt closer to an anarchic philosophy than to the seeking of first principles.

This is why, I think, that when the leading historians of feminist theater argue that performance has gotten more complex since it has moved from an early interest in pure expressions of essential womanhood (in the 60s and 70s) to later performances of socially constructed subjects (in the 80s and 90s), they cannot accurately account for the hybrid quality that exists in Jones's work from the 60s through the 90s. Rebecca Schneider writes:

As women artists became more difficult to ignore, feminist theory and practice gained in complexity, and as theory and practice gained in complexity,
women artists became more difficult to ignore. If the 1970s feminists had, in
an effort to establish a feminist voice and a feminist stronghold, largely been
seeking a "true" or positive or essential image of "woman," by the mid-1980s
artists were able to declare that the "woman" they sought was a cultural construct, a strategic moment, and could move to the more materialist notion
that identity is produced through the machinations of representation. Inter-
secting with poststructuralist theories in a powerfully burgeoning amalgam
of French and Anglo-American feminisms, artists in the mid-1980s could
better deal with the messy terrain between the essential and the constructed,
aiming with a firm theoretical base beyond "essential" woman to analyze how
and why meaning and its engenderment is produced. This shifting of emphasis away from essentialized female nature toward a radical interrogation of
both engenderment and nature motivated and gained motivation from the
general politicization of aesthetics at the backbone of critical postmodernist
inquiry.[10]

Schneider describes early feminist performances of the 60s and 70s as producing essentialist portraits of a true and positive woman, in contrast to
the more complex deconstructive performances of the 80s and 90s, where
every experience of identity is open to interrogation. But Jones's early and
late work cannot be so sharply distinguished among theories and practices. I am suspicious anyway of the "over time theory gets more complex
and thus better" argument, especially so when such an argument is im-
plicitly applied to art. Art and theories of art obviously change over time,
but I'm not at all sure they improve. It is clear that certain easily distinguished styles of performances become available for women (and others),
and thus harder to ignore. At the turn of the twenty-first century, feminist
performance and feminist criticism of performance encompass a range of
methods and beliefs, from the traditional understanding of "the play's the
thing that mirrors real experience," to a postmodern questioning of any
"real" identity being possible except that which is always performed.[11]
But Jones's work mixes up the very terms—essentialism and constructed-
ness—that Schneider distinguishes so thoroughly.

Even in the early days of Jones's work with Tumbleweed, which could
be considered an essentialist feminist dance collective of the 60s and 70s,
where the women sought to define a stronger, more positive ideal, embodied by flying young women on trapezes, Jones recognized that at

least one of her roles in this troupe was to demonstrate that there was no *single* womanly body. She looked different, her experiences made her different—a mother of an eight-year-old, the only black woman, wearing dreadlocks before anyone else was. People hung on her words because she was different, and Jones played to her audience. Her identity was more than pure woman; it was also black and a single mother. Jones was self-conscious of her differences, and through a silent dialogue with her troupe and audience, she created a powerful performing identity out of the differences she combined. If this example of early "pure" essential feminism is tainted by Jones's self-conscious construction of multiple identities, so *Lily Overstreet*—a perfect example of constructed representation, in which Jones performs for one audience the character of Lily who performed sexually for men—is markedly single-minded in its political insistence that audiences are essentially responsible for whatever degradation or desire is generated in their seats. In both the overtly "pure" essentialist work of Tumbleweed and the self-conscious performance art of *Lily Overstreet,* Jones combines critical practices; she exhibits the way her body has been constructed and managed, but she does so in the service of a powerful, autonomous, feminist, performing self. Jones cites her own experience and then demonstrates how her audience participates in the makeup of her identity, in the desire for her difference, or in the celebration of her similarity. She makes us feel that experience matters, and that we participate in creating that experience.

Because she always honored the many voices and influences upon her, Jones did not pass through a single identity politics phase (either black, or feminist, or black-feminist), as did many of her performance artist counterparts in the 60s and 70s. However, she would never argue that experience is not an essential part of her kind of performance and politics, only that her experience is multivalent, that her identity is a product of both what she experienced and how others experienced her. It is important that she marks her own coming of age, her bona fide sense of herself, her finding a place in the culture, when she makes her first successful performance piece, *The Legend of Lily Overstreet.* She repeats the mantra in many places that theater saved her life. She feels her identity most deeply expressed when she calls herself a performer. But if this begins to sound suspiciously postmodern in an apolitical sense, if she sounds like a performer who *only* shows off her ability to perform multiple constructions of her self, this is not the whole picture either. Because in all of her work, Jones insists on creating a performance space that calls out to audiences to respond to questions: How are we responsible for creating the very experiences and identities that she performs? What filters our own desires and definitions of good and evil? What institutions shape us and swing us, constrain and free us?

As theorists in the late twentieth century have tried to find ways to bridge humanist beliefs in the validity of experience with the postmodern belief that the subject is socially constructed, Jones's particular dramatic mix of form and beliefs can be seen as a practical example of such an amalgamation. Critic bell hooks has noted the unease of some black feminists with the critique of essentialism, but she has argued that one can give up a narrow, constricting form of essentialism and still retain "the authority of experience." She says further, "There is a radical difference between a repudiation of the idea that there is a black 'essence' and recognition of the way black identity has been specifically constituted in the experience of exile and struggle." [12] Liz Bondi distinguishes between a type of 60s and 70s essentialist feminism that equated experience with authenticity, and which therefore could not be questioned, and the 90s "postmodern" notion of identity as process-oriented, performative, and provisional. But she goes on to argue that both these positions are too extreme for an effective progressive politics. Like hooks, she believes that experience must be given its due, acknowledged as valid, because without an acknowledgment of personal experience, it is hard to know how to judge the inequities and oppression that exist in the world. But experience must not think of itself as true, authentic, and therefore impervious to questions and critique, because without critique and dialogue, there cannot be exchange and mutual learning. Identity, Bondi argues, may not cohere as a "real essence, nor in the realm of a received mythology, but in the realm of a context-dependent creativity." [13] I believe that this "context-dependent creativity" is the space that Jones's best work inhabits, as she both honors experience and questions how social conditions and the individuals in her audience are responsible for creating the context in which she creates and performs our intersections.

Though some critics may believe that liberal humanists are simple-minded in their belief that men and women are free individuals capable of mastering the universe, it seems important to note that Jones holds such a belief, but not simple-mindedly. In her work she demonstrates, at least sometimes, that women *can* master the universe. She also understands the ways in which the discourse of the universe masters her too. This is more than just strategic essentialism. Jones doesn't just choose to move from one position to another depending on what she believes will work best in any situation. Instead, she entertains deeply held contradictory beliefs: faith in the possibility of mastering, alongside the knowledge of how power works for and against such mastery. These beliefs allow Jones to inhabit a space of creation that is dynamic, perhaps even contradictory, alive to complexity and simplicity in the same space and the same body.

In her continued devotion to the intersection of social activism, feminism, and the arts, Jones remains faithful to the times during which she first began to perform—the 60s and 70s. Teaching and working on community projects paid the rent long before her performances could. She has benefited, as have other performance artists, from money that private foundations and the government have given to artists to support community art projects. In prisons, hospitals, mental institutions, and community centers, artists have created new work.[14] For Jones, working in "community projects" began in 1978, when she was funded by the Comprehensive Employment Training Act and then by the California Arts Council, to teach drama in various high schools and art in elementary schools. Almost ten years later she received an invitation from the director of the Artists-in-Residence program at the San Francisco County Jails, Ruth Morgan, to work in the jails, teaching dance (or aerobics—the stories differ), and she accepted. Jones's predecessor was a woman named Jamie Miller, who was a professional belly dancer, so it wasn't as though the staff at the jail were not willing to be experimental with the people they hired. But both Miller and Jones *had* to experiment, because neither knew exactly what they were supposed to do or what they could do, what was expected of them, or what they could expect from the women in jail. Of her initial visits, Jones remembers:

> We had a radio; we had a beatbox; we had these tapes the women liked; and we had gym shorts, because Jamie had gotten the women gym shorts. And all this stuff was left over at Harriet Street, right around the corner from 850 [Bryant Street]. I'd go over, pick it up every morning, and go in and try to make something happen aerobics-wise.
>
> They said, "aerobics." I said, "What the *hell?*" First of all, I wasn't an aerobics teacher. And then you look at the women, and everybody's bored. Everybody's pissed off. The diet just sucks. Nobody wants to do anything but sleep. The deputies would make them get up, would round them up. A lot of women came because they got to walk past the men. But a lot of them would just want to sit and talk and listen to the radio.

And I started to create routines for myself. I would start to do dramatic things. Tricks. And then I started to talk. The young women were fired up because they remembered tumbling and handstands and cartwheels from gym, from cheerleading practice. And they started talking about that.

They'd say: "I used to be able to do that." And then they started to ask me how old I was.

And I asked them, "How old are *you*? What do you mean you *used* to be able to do that? How old are you?"

"Oh, I'm twenty three."

"Oh," I said, "I'm forty." And that just really. . . .

They like, "She *forty?!*" The older, harder cons, they just thought I'd go away, the ones who were back in jail to be back on their way to prison. But they became more intrigued because I made it my business to talk to them. I made it my business to interact with these people. Because first of all, they were mostly black women, and the ones who weren't black, they were women. I am from a woman's community. First and foremost. I'm a womanist. And what that means is that I cannot help but identify with female-based things: family, home, children.

And they all sort of got it. They were fascinated. They liked Jamie too. But I was a black woman. And I could talk that talk. I could throw in that vernacular. It's a whole way of talking. Of getting down with them. Talking about the real. Talking: "Don't bullshit me." And talking about their problems. Talking about why they went in.

Saying, "Why are y'all here?"

And some woman would say, "I just did six years for so and so. I was out for six months and then they busted me down."

I'd ask, "Why? Don't bullshit me. I don't want you to tell me what you think I want you to hear. Just tell me."

And they'd say, "Is you the police?"

And I'd say, "Well, no."

"Well, who are you?"

"I'm an artist."

They'd say, "What's *that?*"

And that's a real interesting question. It still is an amazing question, which is why I'm still doing the Medea Project. What is an artist in that context? How can an artist truly affect it, given that we're suspect? It's a powerful challenge to take what I know as a live transforming thing. That is what art has done for me. That is what theater has been for me. For this African American woman. It has changed my life totally for the better. It really did.

Finding a place to tell my story. Finding a place to feel this sinew, the muscle, the strength, the power of this body, this voice.

When that woman, Regina Brown, said to me, "Are you the police?"

"No."

"Well then, who *is* you?"

I thought, "Good question." I'm still trying to answer. What can an artist do?

What is striking about Jones's history in the jails, is that the community work so directly affected the growth of her own artistic development. From the beginning she used the site as a place to explain by demonstration what an artist does. She very early on saw a way to create her own performance piece, *Big Butt Girls, Hard-Headed Women,* which was a compilation of voices of women she first heard in the jails, and then, pushed by the painful revelations women had about their childhood, she made her own autobiographical piece, *Blues Stories.*

Jones was first struck by the language she heard in jail.

I wrote down the language that everybody said. I used to love to hear them. People in jail are great performers. They are bullshit artists. They are poets. They are very colorful. They really learn to survive by their wits, and part of it is language. You got to find out how to go in and grab people, which is the genius of a great comic, of a great dramatic actor. It's the same thing. You've got to be the shaman, the magician. You got to make us believe whatever you want us to believe about you.

And so I used to watch people, and if they knew I was watching, they'd get to talking about their life. All this energy and language and movement and who can top who. Sometimes they had the most intelligent retorts. I watch TV, MTV, and I watch commercials, and I watch how they're selling things in this culture, and it's language lifted right out of African American culture. So much more beautiful is jail culture. Like the term "being on vacation." Which is like, you've been to prison. Something as simple as that, but when they're talking to each other, all of this is very real and very vivid. So I used to watch them taking on other personas to survive: the dyke in jail, the femme, the old con, even the crazy people, the fat girls.

I thought, "I want to make a piece that speaks to the recycling of this language. I want to open the doors of this jail with a performance." I didn't know what I was going to do because they told me I couldn't record the women, so I had to go home and write down the things I heard. The women knew what I was doing because I started to say, "I'm going to make this show about you all."

You say to people who aren't involved in theater, "I'm going to make a performance about you"—Joe Schmuck, lower-middle-class, or lower-class people—they don't know what it means.

The women in jail thought, "Yeah, sure."

But then, when I said, "Who is this?"

They were like, "That's Regina! That's Mama Pearl!"

"Well, is it? How can I make it better? I really want to change into this person. Tell me how to do it."

There's a mime exercise. One person gets up on the floor and takes a shape and people get to come up and readjust their body. And this is what I allowed them to do to me.

They would say, "Well now, Regina really poked out her mouth."

And I'd say, "Well then, come up and pull on my mouth." All of a sudden, they were touching me, they were engaged in this artistic process and then I would go through the same line.

"You sure sound like Regina. That's how Regina sounds."

"I'm an actress, y'all." That was really deep. All of a sudden you have a little bit of light about who I am, about art, about theater. I'm an actress. This is what I do for a living. I guess on some level I'm a social scientist, but I didn't tell them that. I talked about transformation, that's what I loved about theater, and at the same time I talked about how theater had saved my life. All of a sudden people are engaged.

And I'm coming back and they want to see what I'm going to do now. "What you going to do today? What you going to do?"

"Oh, that gym teacher, she ain't no gym teacher, she's an actor."

I mean that's why Anna Deavere Smith is killing. Anna went out and got real people and said, "Y'all remember these people." And with her craft and with her PR and her budget, she's killing across the country. Audiences are saying, "Brilliant!" Clapping. We in theater, I think a certain "we," the innovative, cutting edge, have always been interested in people's voices.

Jones transformed herself into the women she heard in jail. By performing the transformation and by asking the women to help her make the act more real, she included them in a particular artistic process—an exploration of voice, mimicry, and life story. She had already performed this sort of theater with Idris Ackamoor in *I Think It's Gonna Work Out Fine*. When she was invited in late 1989 to the Women's Theater Festival in

Boston to make a piece about her work in jail, she presented an early version of *Big Butt Girls,* consisting of monologues of women in jail. Back in San Francisco, she was asked to show *Big Butt Girls* to inmates who were about to take part in the work furlough program. Seventy men were sent to the performance, but no women. At this point, she was moving from the jail at 850 Bryant Street, in the heart of San Francisco, out to the jail in the suburb of San Bruno, where she was asked to teach a theater class for men and women. According to Jones, it didn't work.

> That was a real flop because the women just didn't behave themselves. They didn't give as much with men around. Which is why I say now I want to work only with women. Women are shape shifters in their own right, and around men they get very nuts. Anything you set up, they can find a way to deter it. I remember the turning point for me with men and women was this one woman, Rosa. She was a Cuban woman who jerked off this guy under his coat. They learned early to sit under the cameras. Then she went back to the dorms and told everybody that she'd jerked this guy off. And then I get it from a deputy. I got a little note implying that I was allowing lascivious behavior to go on in this heterosexual environment.
>
> I just asked, "Well, could somebody tell me what this means?"
>
> And then I think it was maybe Deputy Sergeant Marcia Colhour who told me: "Well, the idiot's been telling everybody in the dorm."
>
> So I just went off. I said to them in the dorm, "To tell you the truth, *I* probably would be the girl under the camera too if I were in jail, but I damn sure wouldn't tell anybody. You don't get to do it again. We might have jeopardized the whole program. The only ones you're fucking with is yourselves, you *realize* that? Those guys don't give a *shit.* You know, that guy wouldn't look at *any* of y'all on the street. Those men don't care about y'all!" They had never heard anybody talk like that.
>
> The deputies were like, "God. Who is this?"
>
> And the women were like, "Daaang." But they all returned.

When Jones was asked to come back to teach another class, she proposed that she work only with women. The administration agreed, and a social worker she had met at 850 Bryant Street, Sean Reynolds, helped funnel women into her class. Reynolds became a key supporter of Jones's work in the jail. She has performed in each of the *Medea* productions and is a key adviser. When Reynolds told Jones what she believed—"All art is so-

Sean Reynolds.
Photograph by Keba Konte, 1994

cial work. And I think that social work is an art"—Jones thought right away, "*Boom.* This woman and I have some common ground on which to stand. . . . Sean mentored me. She was so fucking fierce. She taught me that it was about how are *we* going to change ourselves, our culture, how we relate to men. It was a 'we.'" Reynolds was already holding workshops with women in the jails when Jones came up with the idea to work exclusively with women. Both of them independently had seen how crucial it was to get the women to talk about their own lives and what mattered to them. They often shared classes together, teaching a mix of theater, self-esteem, and parenting workshops during the day.

Since Jones had heard about a production of *The Merchant of Venice* at the women's prison at Framingham, directed by Jean Trounstine, she had been thinking about having the women in San Francisco put on the classical play *Medea.* Jones had met a woman in jail who had killed her baby because her husband wanted the baby but not her. But when Jones handed out various versions of *Medea* for them to read, she realized that nobody was reading it. People were drawing on the books or putting them down or leaving them behind. Performing the classic in a classical way just was not going to work. And yet she felt certain that the story *should* mean something to the women. One day one woman who was usually in the workshop was in lock up for disruptive behavior because she had found out that the father of her kids was in jail and the kids were going to be put in foster care. Jones remembers Reynolds came in to report this and asked: "What's up y'all? What the fuck's going on? What is it that makes us leave our children?"

We were talking about parenting. Then I told the story about Medea. We hadn't planned it that way, but I started to tell them about Medea and they went off and said, "The bitch was fucked up for killing her kids."

"Uh uh. Ain't no man gonna make me."

And then I was saying, "Hey! What are the ways we kill our children?" And everybody was like *What?!* Or they were crying.

Sean was always good at, "Oh, honey, please. This is not the time to be crying. OK?" I was always the good cop. She was always the bad cop. But we knew we were on to something.

Because it stopped them all. Because all of a sudden it's like, "You're not with your kids. Your baby is somewhere right now dying of a broken heart. That's real, you know. Children miss their mamas." And of course their first reaction is everybody is crying their eyes out.

I said, "How are you different from Medea? At least she put her children out of their misery. She didn't leave 'em with Jason. She took 'em out. You know? And it was an act of love. Something like the slave mother who bashes her children's brains out so they wouldn't be sold. There's something liberating about a woman saying, 'This I can do.' At the same time, I agree, Medea was fucked up because she was angry, and the children got it. But if she couldn't be with them, maybe it was better that they were not left alone in the world amongst their enemies, as she said."

I thought we should really stop and examine the myth of Medea. Women had a very hard time blaming their mothers, on the one hand, or looking at the abandonment of the father.

So I said, "Tomorrow, I want everyone to write down something."

The girls said, "Write? You mean like rap?"

I said, "Yeah, sure. Do me a rap."

And one girl said, "Well, I don't like rap. I'm religious."

So I said, "Write me a parable."

One girl said, "I like love songs."

I said, "Fine. Write me a love song." So that's how *Reality Is Just Outside the Window* was born. It was their response to the story of Medea.

And so the women began to write their own pieces, stories, dances. It was the women who began to recruit the mechanics class and the GED class from within the jails to become an audience for their work.

All of a sudden there was a troupe mentality. All of a sudden there was an "Us." I thought, Wow! Just us performing. This is ours. And it wasn't about drugs, it wasn't about rocks, it wasn't about alcohol. It wasn't even about men. It was something intangible, a concept, an idea, and it blew my mind. When people would leave jail, they'd say, "Well, Rhodessa, you just can't be bringing other people in. You got to let us help decide who is going to be in the group. Who gets to be in the play." Because people would be leaving and going home, and we'd have to recruit other people to be actresses. It was like "Whoa! What is it that I stumbled upon here?" And then they're claiming something. They made this. Women as nurturers, as keepers of the flame. It isn't necessarily the man who digs out the space in Stone Age times. I think it was the woman who went into that cave and made sure that there was light. They were doing this again.

At that point, Jones felt the need to bring in artists she knew from the community to see what was happening and get their professional points of view. Jones was wondering whether she could or should have the women perform in public. She thought the women were doing amazing work, but she was in the middle of it and needed to have outside corroboration. She invited Brian Freeman of the performance art troupe Pomo Afro Homos; Ellen Gavin, director of Brava: Women in the Arts; Dean Beck Stuart from Theater Artaud; her friend Andrew Brown, a psychologist who works with drug addicts and street people; and Teresa Dickinson from Tumbleweed. They watched a performance and all were very supportive. Now she had a core group to help her think about how a public performance might happen. Gavin ended up being one of the coproducers of the first *Medea* public performance, *Reality Is Just Outside the Window.* Dickinson started working at the jails. But no one really knew what a public performance would mean or how it would come about.

Jones knew that she would need some help from actresses on the outside because some of the incarcerated women could write the stories but could not act them on stage, either because they were too shy, or their stories were too painful, or because they had left jail and vanished. At the Center for African and African American Art and Culture, where Cultural Odyssey's office was located, a friend of Ackamoor and Jones, Lester Jones, was teaching a theater class. Jones visited and invited any of the women students who were interested to come to her apartment to talk about working at the jails. From the beginning, Jones knew she wanted a record of the meeting and asked another friend, Kathy Katz, to videotape the proceedings. Jones was widening the circle of participants.

She knew she wanted other women to work with, but she also wanted to maintain control. Already there were people telling her how to transform what she had started in the jails.

> Everybody was happy about and impressed with the work I had shown them in jail, but then they started telling me what had to be done to make it palpable for the *real* stage. "Now, Rhodessa, that was nice. But we want John Malpede to come in and show you how to *really* work with marginal people. We think you should do this. We think you should do that." *I* wanted to do the script. *I* was going to do the script. I was going to do the script *my*self. It's easy for everybody to come in and tell you how to do it. And everybody is excited because it's new, and at the same time the inmates get confused if they see white people arguing with me.

Jones is a generous collaborator, but she is also proud about her work as a director: "From the beginning, it has been mine. *I'm* the one that walks the floor. Oh, *yeah*. I take full responsibility. See, *always* Rhodessa puts the show together. And the shape of the show is mine." Finally she went to ask for Sheriff Hennessey's support to take the women out of jail for a public performance. There was some precedent for this in the jails; other groups had performed outside. And the sheriff had always supported various arts projects. He gave Jones permission to go public.

Jones's great capacity to communicate her beliefs and passions have attracted other equally talented people to work with her. A group of highly skilled designers, actresses, and choreographers have worked with Jones throughout the history of the Medea Project. Set designer Pam Peniston, lighting designer Stephanie A. Johnson, costume designer Rene Walker, writer and actress Edris Cooper, and actress Tanya Mayo have been instrumental. Jones had already performed with Cooper in the San Francisco Mime Troupe, Peniston was recommended to Jones by Brian Freeman and had been designing shows already for Cultural Odyssey. Mayo she had known since she was a child. Other members of the core group—Fé Bongolan, Nancy Johnson, Gina Dawson, and Hallie Iannoli—came to know Jones and the Medea Project through the informal women's/art community in San Francisco. Jones has said how much she cherishes the dedication of this group. Their mixture of professionalism and commitment to working with women ensures the project's creative strength. Over the years, other members—Andrea Justin, Barbara Bailey, Felicia Scaggs, Libah Sheppard, Angela Wilson, Nikki Byrd, Paulette Jones, Dorsha Brown, Joanna Perez, and Veronica Arana—have been stalwart supporters and performers. Peniston recalls:

> The first year there was a tremendous amount of energy. Things seemed to grow like a weed almost. It was so exciting. . . . Whatever it took. Whether it was going to be we were going to be paid $1.25, which is kind of what happened (laughs), or what. Because for these shows the team spends a lot more time than we would on a conventional show. . . . I mean, normally a set designer comes in, meets with the director, meets with the other designers, produces a design, it goes into construction, paints the design, the show goes up, the show opens, you go away, you come back and strike. And instead, five months before the show ever got started, I was going into prison, into the jails, and I worked two or three times a week with these people and got to know these people.[15]

The realization that the private would become public, and that a mixture of "outside" and "inside" people would create the public performance, demarcates the real coming of age of the Medea Project. But even in its maturity, the Medea Project contains a multiplicity of goals, as diverse as the individuals who participate in it. For some it provides entertainment; others mean to politicize prisoners and thereby change the system; a few may use it as training for professional advancement; all see it as a way to stretch the imagination and to support the expression of women who have not been listened to. It is an opportunity to explore certain plots, listen to narratives, converse, and create.[16]

Remastering the Medea Myth

CHORUS: *Legend will now reverse our reputation;*
  A time comes when the female sex is honoured;
  That old discordant slander
  Shall no more hold us subject.
  Male poets of past ages, with their ballads

Of faithless women, shall go out of fashion;
For Phoebus, Prince of Music
Never bestowed the lyric inspiration
Through female understanding—
Or we'd find themes for poems,
We'd counter with our epics against man.
—Euripides, Medea 418–28

When Jones insisted on staging *Medea* in jail, when she named the project after the classical Greek legend, she was claiming that this ancient story had everything to do with women in jail in the United States in the late twentieth century. The Medea story is about a woman held subject and her struggle to break free. She is made a subject by her great passion, her love for Jason, and then through her ferocious desire for revenge, she becomes her own subject, a terrifying example of a woman who refuses to be mastered, except by her own desires. In the Greek play by Euripides, Medea seems sometimes to speak for herself and sometimes as a representative for all women. Jones knew that Medea's story was relevant even when, or perhaps especially when, the incarcerated women initially resisted seeing any connection. She knew that the ambiguous qualities of the heroine and the choices before her were subjects that these women were uniquely qualified to address. How could a woman kill her children? How could a woman not *be* with her children? These were some of the questions they grappled with. Medea is full of rage, and so are the women in jail. Like Medea, these women are seen by society as outsiders, barbarians. Like Medea, they have committed crimes, and crimes have been committed against them. They too have broken taboos, transgressed laws. They are women who are ruled by their passions, who are self-destructive, and who destroy others. Their lives, like that of Medea's, contain examples of courage and debasement intertwined. And, like Medea, many of the women are master storytellers. Storytelling can be a con game, a trick used against one's foes. It can also be the beginning of a different drama—a way to imagine, if not live out, a new life.

There are many ways in which this classical Greek tragedy continues to resonate in our culture, in both the particularities of its plot and the nature of Western drama itself. So much of Western theater has to do with the expression of transgression and the struggle for control. Froma Zeitlin, in her work on classical Greek theater, argues that the emerging practice of theater in the West came to be associated with female attributes: the stage divided between the public domain and the inner sanctum of the home, the physical body coming forth from the private home to the public stage; the plots that turned on cunning, wit, disguise, role playing, intrigue, deception—these last characteristics so strongly associated with the female and ones that Medea uses to exact revenge and escape punishment.[17] But certainly one of the paradoxes of Greek culture and of the origins of Western drama is that while the Greek tragedians wrote spectacular parts for women, they bore little relation to the lives of actual women living at the time. The starkly different male and female cultures—corresponding to the public world of the market and war, a world for male citizens and warriors, and the private household world of women and servants—relegated the practice of drama to men. Men wrote the plays and acted all the parts; it is disputed by scholars whether women were even allowed to view them. Nancy Rabinowitz argues, "Even though relations between the sexes are central in tragic plots, the actors and writers were men; the theater, like the agora and the assembly, was a male space. The representation of conflicts between men and so-called women was, therefore, constructed from a masculine point of view."[18] As Zeitlin argues, women are portrayed not only from a masculine point of view in Greek drama but in order to bolster male subjectivity: "*Functionally* women are never an end in themselves, and nothing changes for them once they have lived out their drama on stage. Rather, they play the roles of catalysts, agents, instruments, blockers, spoilers, destroyers, and sometimes helpers or saviors for the male characters."[19] The Greek theater, for all its attention to female characters, then, used them to point out what was appropriate and fitting *male* behavior; even Medea, Zeitlin claims, who "comes closest to demanding an equivalence of the feminine self to the male," formally functions in the plot as a vehicle to punish Jason for breaking his sacred oath to her.[20]

The modern Medea Project reorients the dramatic spectacle so that women are no longer merely catalysts but instead become protagonists of their story. Role playing here aims to make women masters of themselves by telling their own story. Euripides himself reminds us in *Medea* that it is men who have controlled women's "reputation." The chorus complains that male poets have always slandered women: "That old discordant slander / Shall no more hold us subject. . . . / We'd counter with our epics against man" (418–28).[21] To "counter with our epics against man" is exactly what Jones's Medea productions mean to do. By allowing these women to speak their own rage, Jones believes she gives them the opportunity to become their own protagonists and find a different ending.

The ancient world of Greece and Rome—in poetry, drama, and philosophical discourse, in vase paintings and wall murals—was fascinated by Medea's composite, contradictory character. Medea is a foreigner and yet like all Greek women (or all Roman women); she is utterly human, but also, as Circe's niece, she is sometimes depicted as having the powers of a witch or sorceress; she acts heroically, like a man, and demonically, like a woman; she acts with reason and good cause out of love, but she is also depicted as angry, vengeful, mad.[22] Her complexity continues to haunt the Western imagination. From at least the eighth century B.C. onward, different versions of the myth exist, but a core story and certain features are always recounted. Medea's story is embedded in the quest of Jason and the Argonauts. Jason has been told to go to Kolchis, according to Herodotus an Egyptian settlement on the outskirts of Greek civilization, (making Medea not only foreign to the Greeks but, perhaps, in the language of today, a woman of color), to take back the Golden Fleece and thus reestablish his family as rightful leaders.[23] Medea, the daughter of the king of Kolchis, is always depicted as the barbarian, the outsider, a woman from far away, who falls in love with the Greek hero Jason; she helps her lover win the Golden Fleece, betrays her family in doing so, and leaves with him for his home. Sometimes she is said to have been ensnared by Aphrodite, but sometimes, independently of any supernatural intervention, she simply falls in love. Like so many other historical or mythical women in the ancient world—Helen of Greece and then of Troy, Io, or Europa—Medea is an object of exchange, a diasporic woman.[24] When she helps Jason steal the Golden Fleece from her father, and leaves with him on his voyage and his adventures, she burns her bridges to home. Trading her father's protection and familial status for her husband's, she becomes dangerously dependent upon him.

Once she leaves Kolchis, different episodes in her life are recounted, and the shape of her character changes as she moves from Corinth, to Athens, and Medes, a city she founds. In some versions she seems heroic; in others, evil. After she dies, one story has her marrying the hero Achilles in the Elysian Plain, a place where only the privileged find rest. There are other stories in which she causes her brother (or half-brother) to be killed and ones in which she tricks the daughters of King Pelias into killing their father, assuring once again Jason's fortune; in Athens, she almost manages to trick Aegeus into killing his own son.[25] Sarah Johnston points out that usually heroes fight against monsters, but it is unusual to find a hero and a monster "encapsulated within a *single* mythic figure." Says Johnston, "Not only does [Medea's] checkered career allow authors and artists to explore the opposing concepts of self and other, as she veers between desirable and undesirable behavior, between Greek and foreigner; it also allows them to raise the disturbing possibility of *otherness lurking within the self*—the possibility that the 'normal' carry within themselves the potential for abnormal behavior, that the boundaries expected to keep our world safe are not impermeable."[26]

Euripides's *Medea*, the play that caught Rhodessa Jones's attention, focuses on the most infamous episode in Medea's life, the moment in Corinth when she kills Jason's about-to-be-new bride and, most horrifically, with her own hands kills the children she had with Jason. It is the Euripidean Medea that has been the most famous, perhaps in part because Euripides has yoked together in his play the most disparate parts of Medea's character, the most human and inhuman, forcing us to make sense of her actions, to reconcile her various legendary selves. It is a commonplace to say that in Euripides' treatment of the Medea story, he initially creates a sympathetic character. As Euripides' play opens, Jason has won the King of Corinth's daughter's hand in marriage, and Medea is beside herself with rage and jealousy. The nurse warns everyone: "She'll not relax her rage till it has found its victim!" (93). But when she first appears, moving from backstage, figured as her home, to the front of the stage and into the public space of Corinth, she tries to portray herself as worthy of sympathy:

> Women of Corinth, I would not have you censure me,
> So I have come. Many, I know, are proud at heart,
> Indoors or out; but others are ill spoken of
> As supercilious, just because their ways are quiet.
> There is no justice in the world's censorious eyes.
> They will not wait to learn a man's true character;
> Though no wrong has been done them, one look—and they hate.
> Of course a stranger must conform; even a Greek
> Should not annoy his fellows by crass stubbornness.
> I accept my place; but this blow that has fallen on me

Was not to be expected. It has crushed my heart.
Life has no pleasure left, dear friends. I want to die.
Jason was my whole life; he knows that well. Now he
Has proved himself the most contemptible of men. (214–27)

Her speech here is calculated, a mixture of truth and deception, because, of course, events show she does *not* accept her place, and though her heart may be crushed, she does not die. She makes sure that others do. She knows that as a stranger she must appear to conform to local rules, but she is stubborn. And so she begins to scheme:

Come! Lay your plan, Medea; scheme with all your skill.
On to the deadly moment that shall test your nerve!
You see now where you stand. Your father was a king,
His father was the Sun-god: you must not invite
Laughter from Jason and his new allies, the tribe
Of Sisyphus. You know what you must do. Besides—
[*She turns to the Chorus.*]
We were born women—useless for honest purposes,
But in all kinds of evil skilled practitioners. (400–407)

Medea acts like a born woman, a skilled practitioner of schemes. But Euripides also has her, in the context of ancient Greek culture, acting like a man.[27] Her father doesn't give her to Jason to be married; she chooses Jason. She knows she will be tested, and her models are her father and grandfather, a king and sun-god. She moves from the crafted humility of her opening speech to the heroic language of the warrior:

Let no one think of me
As humble or weak or passive; let them understand
I am of a different kind: dangerous to my enemies,
Loyal to my friends. To such a life glory belongs. (805–8)

In this play, the glory she finds for herself is of a horrible sort. She plots to have her own sons deliver poisoned gifts to the King of Corinth and his daughter, and then, not satisfied, decides to kill her own children. With this act of filicide (and it seems to be an act that Euripides added to the many legends of Medea), Euripides created a woman who steps outside the boundaries of human civility. She is no one we want to recognize:

I understand
The horror of what I am going to do; but anger,
The spring of all life's horror, masters my resolve. (1079–81)

The question of who is master and what masters whom is foremost in this play. Euripides makes it difficult to know, just as he makes it hard to recognize right from wrong.[28] Was she wrong to love Jason and help him win power? Wasn't she justified in feeling betrayed by him? At what point does Medea's desire to be master, to be her own subject, cause her to become a monster? We are no longer sure who is victim and who victimized. Euripides created a woman who not only transgresses the proper role of a woman, deciding for herself whom to marry and whom to kill, she escapes our better judgment too. As she takes off in her chariot at the end of the play, she flies beyond our human understanding, beyond the pale of civilized behavior (even though she's headed to, ostensibly, civilized Athens). Her performance disrupts boundaries of right and wrong, of borders, and laws. Medea is loose in the world, not disciplined or punished in the way we might expect, not, in the end, under anyone's control. How to take hold of one's own subject, to control one's own plot, not to be written over or cast out, not to be a victim nor to victimize others, is the exercise of the modern reenactment of *Medea*. The complexity of the Medea myth—an example of female agency, but agency gone horrifically awry—propels the Medea Project into a dynamic quest to develop a counterplot and alternative, transgressive endings.

Reviving Medea

MEDEA: *They should never have fucked with me. Look, look how they treat me,*
a black woman doesn't have anything and no representation. Look how I'm
treated, much less my kids. This world isn't for them. Maybe in another life.
—Edris Cooper, "There Are Women Waiting: The Tragedy of Medea Jackson"

The first production of the Medea Project, *Reality Is Just Outside the Window* (1992) was an ambitious amalgamation of theater and art installation. Jones wanted to reenact the Medea story but also to include the women's stories in their own words. She asked Edris Cooper to write an adaptation of the Medea story that the women would perform in the course of the evening. Cooper called the inset story, "There Are Women Waiting: The Tragedy of Medea Jackson." Pam Peniston constructed a set with steps for the chorus, hanging empty window frames everywhere around the stage, enclosing air. In addition, Jones wanted an artwork installation effect. When audiences entered the lobby, they had to wend their way through chain fences, with pictures of life in jail attached to them. As the performance began, there were two "mud women," who were up on the higher deck of the theater painting themselves and the walls with mud, covering themselves with feathers. To begin the show, they came down through the audience to the sounds of Marvin Gaye's "Mercy Me," singing "Things ain't what they used to be."

Jones had seen a production of *Medea* at La Mama in New York the year before, in which Medea had been chained to the wall, ranting and raving as the audience settled into their seats. She wanted the same madness at the beginning of the play. Teirrah McNair, a professional actress, wrote an opening monologue for the performance. McNair's mad rant plunges the audience into the violent juxtapositions of language—classical reference and street talk—that mark the sounds of the play that follows.

HCTIB (*written and performed by Teirrah McNair, dressed in African garb*)
Do you know what BITCH is backwards? I said, do you know what BITCH is backwards?

It's HCTIB. Now from one computer to another. If I'm talking to you, you are programmed too, aren't you? No, she didn't say that on nationwide TV in front of her Mama. There goes the train. Now, where was I? Oh yes, Bitch is a 20th-century response to an overabundance of microwaves in the environment. Seen most profoundly in the development of such products as instant grits and tampons, a product that will not hold water, let alone anything else. Use of the term "Arrogant Woman" is a clear sign that one has more respect for dog doo doo's doo than for your mama's mama. We didn't used to talk like that. And if we did, Queen Mama would say, "Come here, sugar spoon. Bring your little head over here, sugar spoon, so Queen Mama can go whoops up side your head. And if Queen Mama hear little sugar spoon say that word again, Queen Mama going to have to put your little sugar spoon head on the chopping block." And YAAAAA! (*mimics chopping a head off*) Oh, the head bone connected to the neck bonnnnne.
(*calls out*) Eve! Nephertiti! Medea! Come on down. It's power stripping time!
"Queen to bitch." That's bridge talk for women's progress through the ages. And the answer is double the double standard.
"Don't wear no drawers to Master's house, you crazy?"

"And ain't I a woman?"

"Oohee baby, you sure look good tonight. Woof! Woof! Woof!"

"What we have here is a failure to communicate."

(*sings*) If you loved me baby, you would do what I tell you to do.

If you loved me baby, you will do what I tell you to do!

If you loved me baby, you would do what I tell you to do!

(*exits chanting*)

This hybridized speech encapsulates all of the Medea Project's concerns. Women's progress through the ages may be illusory. The call to "Queens" of the past—Eve, Nephertiti, Medea, Sojourner Truth—is a reminder of their powerful struggle against the Master. The Master's language denigrating women—"Queen to Bitch"—is crystal clear. "Oohee baby, you sure look good tonight. Woof! Woof! Woof!" Language between men and women has failed to communicate. The sign of love is obedience, nothing more: "If you loved me baby, you would do what I tell you to do." Language altogether has degenerated over time, it seems. "Bitch." "We didn't used to talk like that. And if we did, Queen Mama would say, 'Come here, sugar spoon. Bring your little head over here, sugar spoon, so Queen Mama can go whoops up side your head.'" How can these women find the proper language, powerful language, to negotiate or command respect? One way is to take the most common words, like "Bitch," and make them strange, spell them backwards, remember different ways of commanding: a Mama who would not let her children be disrespectful, a Mama who wouldn't say, "Bitch" but would give a "whoops up side your head." McNair looks backwards to the ancient goddesses and the not so distant ones, to grandmothers who spoke differently, when a slap wasn't simply violence but an education.

McNair exits, and an adaptation of *Medea* begins. Edris Cooper has said that she "fully embraced" Euripides' version of the Medea myth:

> I did not attempt to reinvent anything other than putting the language in San Francisco street jargon. I just tried to look at it through proletarian eyes, not actor educated on Greek symbolism, etc. hoorah. I just tried to break it down. My simpler goal was to reduce every speech into three sentences or less. I was aware that every part was to be played by women so the parody embodied women's views of men. Lastly, I was feeling rather Medeaish and put upon by men so I emptied my mind of all the bad language I had been fed by the men in my life.

We, recognizing ourselves as flawed characters, had no problem accepting Medea's moral contradictions. I think women are more complex characters, therefore more vulnerable to contradictory lives. We operate equally at times through our heart, our head, our body, our instinct. But ultimately, I think the work was not very close to Greek thought. The adaptation immediately became specifically African-American and San Franciscan.[29]

The African-American sound of the language is the most powerful part of the adaptation. It is full of "bad language," street talk that both energizes and shocks in its familiarity. The location is San Francisco, though that is a superficial feature and could just as easily be changed to Los Angeles or New York City, any urban American place with the sounds of the black inner city. Though there is a loss of strangeness and even nobility, the contemporary dialect sets out a clear and palpable sense of anger and the desire for revenge.

"There Are Women Waiting: The Tragedy of Medea Jackson" [from *Reality*]
(*Written by Edris Cooper; music by Carole King, Carolyn Franklin; performed by Jeannette Tims as Singer, T. McNair as Jason/Nurse, Edris Cooper as Medea, Angellette Williams as Creon, Dorsha Brown as Aegeus; with The Home Girls of San Francisco, Belinda Sullivan, Tanya Mayo, Nikki Byrd and the Ensemble. Dressed in street clothes; the ensemble moves downstage in a line; music plays; Rhodessa Jones, down in front on the floor of the theater calls out, "Work it!"* "Energy!" *They strike an attitude; and then break into another.*)
SINGER *sings "Natural Woman" with back up from* ENSEMBLE, *who also sign.*
"When my soul was in the lost and found . . . you came along to claim it. . . .
Now I'm no longer doubtful, for what I'm looking for . . .
Baby what you done to me—you made me feel so good inside . . .
You made me feel like a natural woman . . ."
Enter NURSE *with two* CHILDREN; *they stand on the edge of the stage observing the action.*
NURSE: (*Eating barbecue. All words in capital letters spoken by* CHORUS *as well*) Chawl, why in the hell did them collegiate ass niggas have to take they slummin' asses down to Haight Street. Like they don't got enough crack houses in Daly City? Medea wouldn't have gotten in alla that shit. Killing up all them people. Gave up going to SCHOOL to be with him, where he want. Gave up her TIME to work and spend money on him.

And gave up her KIDS because he couldn't stand the COMPETITION and she even gave up her EARS because she couldn't stand to hear the truth. And gave up the rich black nectar of the goddess to the basest of men, MEN. Now she down here in the Fillmore and he sleeping with a white girl! After all she did for him. Now y'all, you know she is pissed. She just sit up in the house crying. Girlfriend don't wanna go to the club, the movies, chawl, she wouldn't even go get no cue-bob with me. Something's up. Shit, you know how sistah is when she gets mad. Sheeit!

MEDEA: (*offstage*) Motherfucking bastard! (NURSE *covers kids' ears*) You Clarence Thomas, David Duke, Wilt Chamberlain, William Kennedy Smith . . . looking ass nigger! Son of a bitch motherfucker, I hope your dick falls off!

NURSE: There she go again!

CHORUS: Word! (*children giggle*)

NURSE: All right she gone catch y'all laughing and y'all gone have a knot upside your head.

(*To audience*) See, Medea's mother raised her to be too sedity. See me, myself, I don't expect nothing from nobody, just to leave me the hell alone. Don't expect no shit and you won't get no shit.

CHORUS: (*Circle around* NURSE, *chanting*) Don't like, don't want, don't love.

MEDEA: (*offstage*) Awwwww—shit!

SISTERS 1, 2, 3 *hurry on stage.*

S1: Girl, is that Medea hollering like that?

NURSE: Who else?

MEDEA: (*offstage*) I hope a bolt of lighting strikes me dead. Or the roof comes crashing on my head.

S3: Pitiful chile.

MEDEA: (*offstage*) Just kill me nigger, go ahead and kill me. Fuck! I hate this world and I hate niggers.

S2: Girlfriend, please, you gone kill yoself with alla that grieving you doing. I don't know why; 'cause he slept with another bitch? Please!! That nigga ain't done nothin' every other nigga done done. Shit, he wouldn't worry me. Get a grip!

MEDEA: (*offstage*) Some support. Y'all are shit. *Loudly wailing.* Nobody understands. Jason, I'ma get you and that bitch! After all I've done for you.

NURSE: Girl and she means that shit too, O.K.?

The CHORUS *and the* NURSE *all snap together*—A chorus that snaps together caps together.

S1: Girl, she need to talk to somebody. Bring her out here so we can give her the news, baby. That's what the sisters is for, girl. Laying on hands and all of that. Hurry girl, for she hurt somebody.

NURSE: Girl, I'll try, but you know she might cuss me out.

S1: She ain't gonna cuss you out. Bring her on over to my house. We'll listen to some Anita Baker; that always helps me out. All she needs is to be rubbed the right way.

S2: Girl, I don't know about you.

NURSE *exits;* CHORUS *ad lib until* NURSE *returns with* MEDEA

CHORUS: Hi, Medea.

MEDEA: Look, I know y'all been out here just reading me to the tee. I know you think I am stuck up, but I am just tired, O.K.? Tired, tired, tired. Of niggas and of life. The man who was everything to me turned out to be the basest of men. Y'all women; you know how it is. Look how we're treated. First of all, we always doing everything for our men and in return, what do we get? Fucked! And most niggas feel that's payment. I did everything I was supposed to do. I cooked *dinner*, I cooked *rocks*, I even cooked in *bed*. But you know it's hard to find a good man with a job that won't beat you, that won't fuck around, and that'll be nice to your kids. If you get a good man, all the bitches is backstabbing. And if you get a fucked up man and leave him, everybody talks about you. Shit, better just be dead or turn gay.

S1: Word! (*snap, approaches Medea*)

MEDEA: Shit, it's not fair. A man get upset and he can go out and kick it with the fellas. But a woman—shit you ain't got nobody, you can't trust no bitch.

S2: Girl, please, you been reading too much Shaharazad Ali. You shoulda been looking out for you.

MEDEA: If only you could seen; we were really good together. We was making money, cleaning up. We could have got out of the coke business, and retired, and traveled.

CHORUS: On the slow boat to hell.

MEDEA: Like Bonnie and Clyde, or Donald and Ivana.

S2: Girl, please, they white. You are trippin. You shoulda asked somebody and got a clue. There ain't never been shit here. People round here just like all the rest of us—all out of work.

MEDEA: And thank you for the news this morning, Miss Thing. Well shit, alla y'all know each other. I'm not from around here and y'all ain't really been all that charitable.

S3: And you have?

MEDEA: Wait, I'm sorry for that, but we got to stick together. Men always talking about how hard they got it, how hard they work. Shit, let me see one of them have a baby. Then they'll appreciate us.

CHORUS: O.K.? (*snap*)

MEDEA: Look, y'all gotta hang with me. Just one thing I ask. If I figure out how to get this bastard, you will keep the tee for me?

CHORUS: Girlfriend, won't no tips pass from these lips.

MEDEA: Cool . . . fuck with me, shee—it. I'll show that nigga. I'll slap his ass so hard he'll wake up and his clothes will be out of style.

MEDEA *opens her mouth to start loud talking when* S1 *stops her*

S1: Girl, chill, here comes Creon.

CREON *enters*

CHORUS: Hi, Creon.

CREON: Look at you, woman, lips all poked out like you a madwoman. I think you are. And before you mess around and do something foolish, I'm kicking you outta my house. You and them damn kids.

MEDEA: Oh great Creon, where the hell am I supposed to go?

CREON: Woman, that's not my problem.

MEDEA: Why, Creon, why are you putting me out?

CREON: Cause you crazy, woman, and quite frankly I am afraid of you. Look how you fucked up Pelias, not to mention your own brother. Now you do that to your own, what the hell's keepin' you from doing that to me? I heard you threatening me, and Jason, and my daughter.

MEDEA: Everybody holds these deaths against me without hearing my side. If I hadn't fucked up Pelias, Jason wouldn't even be around for your daughter to enjoy. With all that shit he talked, Pelias was gonna kill his stupid ass. Here I am helping his ass and I'm the bitch. Look, Creon, I'm not crazy. I only did that shit because I love Jason. I don't have nothin' against you or your daughter. Hey, she got eyes just like me. I'm not stupid. I have nowhere to go and I have such a nice home here. It'll kill me but I'll be cool, count my blessings and keep to myself.

CREON: You talk a good line, Medea, but I gotta watch my back. You're outta here.

MEDEA: Creon, please, I'm on my knees.

CREON: Well, you can just get up.

MEDEA: Where will I go?

CREON: Women, that's not my problem.

MEDEA: God don't like ugly.

CREON: He ain't too fond of pretty neither.

MEDEA: Creon, please, I got problems . . .

CREON: You ain't never lied.

MEDEA: Then Creon, have a heart. . . . (*Creon laughs*) You a cold motherfucker Creon. Well, all right then, but let me ask one favor before I go. Please.

CREON: Oh lord, what now?

MEDEA: Please, just give me one day to get my things together. I gotta get the kids together. You know Jason ain't gonna help. If not for me, think about the kids. You gone turn them out, naked and with nothing?

CREON: I am too kindhearted, I tell you. O.K. woman, I'm gonna give you one day to get your kids and shit together, but I'm here to tell you so you'll know. If the sun rise on you and them damn kids, you'll wish it hadn't, cause I'ma play your evil game, O.K.?

MEDEA: I get it.

CREON: (*walking*) Don't try me woman.

CHORUS: Girlfriend, where you gonna go? You up the creek.

MEDEA: Please, who do I look like, Sally or her sister, Suzy? Girl, I ain't got time to be bumping gums with that bastard for nothing. I'ma get that crackhead bitch and that basest of baseheads Jason. That jackass gone let me stay one too many days. I'ma fuck they asses up. I just don't know whether to burn them butts up as is fitting or if I should cut off Jason's nuts, or slice a hole in her titties and stuff 'em. I got to be cool though, cause they got lots of fire power. I ain't goin' out like that. Fuck it! He done fucked with the wrong bitch now.

CHORUS: Jason will be back tomorrow sayin' he sorry. (*snap*)

JASON *enters*

JASON: See Medea, a hard head makes a soft ass. You just had to show you ass, now you outta here like last year. You could've had everything Medea, if you just hada acted right. I was taking good care of you. I'll give you $150 on your way out. I still care for you and the kids.

MEDEA: $150! Just keep that shit. I don't want it. Nigga please, you never gave a flying fuck about me or the kids. Throwing me a coupla dollars pretending to be somethin'. You ain't giving me nothin' I cain't get at 170 Otis. Fuck you. I saved *your* life, I showed *you* the game. You wouldn't have *nothing* if it wasn't for me. Shit, I was love sick for coming here with you. And you ain't got no shame for how you treated me. Answer me this. Where in the hell am I supposed to go? I ain't got no friends left, thanks to you. You are an asshole Jason, and you need to step off the curb with that shit. You low life bastard.

JASON: Woman, who asked you to give it all up for me? I can't help it lady if I got it like that, hey? And you need to clean up your motherfucking mouth. You used to be a lady.

MEDEA: (*yelling at his back*) I am a lady, bitch, I still got plenty a pussy, don't I?

Enter AEGEUS *in drag*

AEGEUS: Shake it but don't break it, wrap it up and I'll take it.

MEDEA: Aegeus, girlfriend, what's up?

AEGEUS: What's up with you announcing your goods up and shit. Gimme some.

MEDEA: I know you can do better with it than I did.

AEGEUS: Girlfriend, tip to the tee.

MEDEA: You know he's goin' with that other bitch.

AEGEUS: So what.

MEDEA: She's in my bed.

AEGEUS: Oh hell no.

MEDEA: O.K.

AEGEUS: Girl cut the nigga loose, that's all. Shit, dicks a dime a dozen.

MEDEA: But I can't go out like a ducker sucker motherfucker.

AEGEUS: Well, then don't. I got it girlfriend. I got a sister I know would be glad to hole up if you know what I mean.

CHORUS: O.K.! (*snap*)

MEDEA: Thanks, baby, but I got a plan, O.K.?

AEGEUS: Word girl, get him. Be slick, O.K. (*Exits*)

SI: O.K.! (*snap*) Girlfriend, that queen is your friend. Now he's gonna hook you up with a lady friend. Taste the life baby, and you'll wake up if you know what I mean.

MEDEA: Girl, I ask you again, who do I look like, Sally or . . .

SI: O.K., O.K., impart the poop. Come on and listen y'all.

Lights dim as the CHILDREN *exit.*

MEDEA: Now, I'ma lay it out and I'm telling you, don't sleep on this cause I am serious. I'ma get them bastards and good. Word, I'ma send for Jason and play up to him real sweet. I'll plead the case for the kids for him to let them stay.

CHORUS: Witcha so far.

MEDEA: Girl, please, do you really think I'm gonna leave my kids over here in this mess? For them to be treated like dirt, mistreated, and abused by her? NO! I got a wiley plan. Check this shit out. *She pulls a vial from her pocket.*

CHORUS: Girl, what's that?

MEDEA: Crystal, baby, pure and sweet as it was in '66. This will make that bitch turn her face inside out. I will send the children bearing gifts to offer to get on her good side to let them stay. A beautiful teddy and a sexy g-string, soaked in crystal.

The CHORUS *stands there looking at her with their mouths hanging open.*

CHORUS: What??? Crystal???

MEDEA: That's right baby. And PCP and heroin and some new shit they got in 1992 most folks don't even know about yet. When they get back from delivering the deadly gifts, we are going to celebrate with some Jim Jones Koolaid.

The women stop laughing and stare in horror at MEDEA.

MEDEA: They should never have fucked with me. Look, look how they treat me, a black woman doesn't have anything and no representation. Look how I'm treated, much less my kids. This world isn't for them. Maybe in another life. I know what I have to do. Nobody shall despise me or think me weak or passive. I am a good friend, but a dangerous enemy. For that is the type that the world delights to honor.

Silence

s3: Eloquently put my sister, but you cannot kill your children.

MEDEA: You don't see the injustice that I see. It's the only way.

s3: Medea, this may not be much of a life, but they deserve a chance at survival.

MEDEA: Look, this talk is tired. Now go and get Jason please and I will expect some solidarity, sisters!

CHORUS: *Sing Franklin song.*

"Medea think, think Medea. Think about it Medea.

You gotta think, think bout what you trying to do to me. . . . Freedom . . . Think."

JASON *enters.*

JASON: Watchu want Medea.

CHORUS: *hums "Natural Woman" under* MEDEA'S *speech.*

MEDEA: Jason, you know, I've been thinking about how I've been acting and about how I could always count on you to put up with me when I acted like a bitch. I just get jealous, you know. It's hard for me to face that I fucked up a good thing. You have been really good to me, letting me stay here and all and I should really thank you and your wife. But you know I am what I am. I didn't know what I had. Today, no worse a woman.

JASON: Yeah, well, you a bitch, Medea, but you got some sense. It's only natural for you to miss this dick. I forgive you but you still got to go.

MEDEA: But Jason, what about the kids? I don't feel comfortable you know, they're boys and they need a man around. You see, I'm discovering some things about myself, you know . . .

JASON: Medea, I *knew* you was a dyke! That's why you can't appreciate no man. That's O.K., Medea. It's all right, Medea, it's all right. I will ask Creon if the boys can stay. No need for them to suffer and be confused.

MEDEA: I hope it's O.K. with your wife. But she is a woman and she should understand. I'll send them over with a peace offering for your wife tonight. You can pick them up in the morning. I'll be gone.

JASON: I can persuade her. *Grabs his dick.*

MEDEA: Just let the kids bring the gifts over. They are beautiful and expensive. She'll love them.

JASON: Don't spend too much Medea, you gone need the money.

MEDEA: They say that gifts persuade even the gods, and gold is worth more than ten thousand words. And to save my children it is worth it.

JASON *exits with the kids bearing the gifts. Chorus sings "Do right . . . all day woman."*

CHORUS: Go on girl, eloquently put. But you are in serious trouble.

CHILDREN *return.*

MEDEA: Did she like the gifts?

They just stare at her. Sounds of hell start softly and swell throughout. MEDEA *takes the* CHILDREN *and begins to walk up some stairs with them.*

VOICE: *repeats as* MEDEA *walks up ramp.* At the bottom of our news tonight there has been a new animal aimed in the direction of falling off the face of the earth. Yes, young, black teenagers are reported to be the oldest and the newest creature to be added to the endangered species list, to the endangered species list . . .

The CHILDREN *are represented by puppets now. The real* CHILDREN *observe. When she reaches the top she bellows over the noise.*

MEDEA: No, by the unforgetting dead in hell, it cannot be! I shall not leave my children for enemies to insult and if die they must, I shall slay them. Who gave them birth? Happiness be yours but not in this life. Your father has stolen this world from you. I can delay no longer or my children will fall into the murderous hands of those that love them less than I do.

She drops the puppets. A scream (the sound of glass breaking). Medea is lifted up (or given wings), and throws herself into the women's arms. She is bathed in an eerie spotlight.

VOICE OVER: Medea Jackson. We have a warrant for your arrest.

CHORUS: Oh well! *snap*

WOMEN: Oh well, Medea's dead.

ALL: How'd she die?

WOMAN: She died like this.

ALL: She died like this.

Exchange repeated four times, each time a different freeze is assumed after last line. Black out.

Cooper follows the plot of *Medea* until the end, when she writes the chant, "Medea's dead. . . . She died like this." The Medea Project insists that Medea is, indeed, dead, so that, I think, a different beginning might be imagined. Women are now in charge of retelling the story. This death chant offers not just a cathartic experience, a purging of the terror, and of our pity and fear of the Medea principle, it also activates us to think about different ways we might tell her story.[30] As Burton retold the Pandora myth in *Slouching Towards Armageddon,* so Cooper twists the final moments of *Medea.* Both Burton and Cooper freely rework myth into a new narrative, and the new narratives operate as modes of contestation, what George Lipsitz calls forms of "counter-memory . . . a way of remembering and forgetting that starts with the local, the immediate, and the personal." Says Lipsitz:

> Counter-memory looks to the past for the hidden histories excluded from dominant narratives. But unlike myths that seek to detach events and actions from the fabric of any larger history, counter-memory forces revision of existing histories by supplying new perspectives about the past. Counter-memory embodies aspects of myth and aspects of history, but it retains an enduring suspicion of both categories. Counter-memory focuses on localized experiences with oppression, using them to reframe and refocus dominant narratives purporting to represent universal experience.[31]

Retelling the Medea myth by focusing on the local and immediate, the adaptation begins the work of reframing master narratives by making room for hidden histories. All of the women participating in *Reality* go on to tell their own stories, which haven't been heard before. They are still alive, liberated at least for the moment they are on stage from what has been Medea's fate, her plot's purpose to punish Jason, to act as a catalyst, an instrument, in *his* story, but not in her own best interest, not as her own agent. The great task would be to turn a tragedy into a different genre altogether, a counter epic, making Medea stand on her own, for herself. These Medeas revise and rewrite history.[32]

In the women's monologues and skits that follow the Medea adaptation and make up the whole of *Reality Is Just Outside the Window*, we hear powerful stories of physical abuse, poverty, and abandonment. Their experiences of reality are searing. To tell them must be a sort of purgation, and hearing them certainly acts to demystify the audience. We understand more fully some of the reasons why these modern Medeas act as they do. But the telling of a story, even a counter-epical retelling, cannot, in and of itself, save anyone from continuing to live, once they've left the stage, within the same horrific plot. Other influences must invade the boundaries of the self. As Jones reminds us, theater saved her life, and so did all those other examples of women and men who broke with tradition and constraints. Medea is vulnerable to barbarisms perpetrated from without and from within because she is so alone. She needs to listen and learn from a reality that exists beyond her self if she is to escape her fate, wrest control, become her own agent, construct a different ending, become a different subject.

After the first production received great acclamation, the cast was elated. Jones recalled:

> I had no idea. Sean and I look back on the first one, *Reality,* and it was so much like the colored ladies auxiliary church function.
>
> There's never enough money for the works of passion or love. You're doing it. I think my relationship with Idris suffered incredibly, fell apart, because that's what I was doing. I was on fire with it. It was one of the greatest things I'd ever done. I was so proud of myself. And it wasn't bullshit. It was socially important. It had to go up, regardless of whether I had any money or not.

The core group, almost immediately, began to think about how to sustain the project, to find a way to push the boundaries of *Reality* and make the Medea Project more than a single staged performance. Peniston recalled:

The first one [*Reality*], you forget, was just one weekend. One incredibly sold-out, packed, you know, "maybe this will work, maybe this won't, but we're going to do it anyway," outrageously, successful weekend. In some ways it was a tremendous letdown for us when it was over. So I can't imagine how it was for the women who had to return to their lives in jail. We all really were worried. I remember Tanya, every year, making sure that there were groups of people who would go into the jail for a few weeks after, at least to try to touch base with these women and see if there was anything *we* could do personally to alter what was happening. . . . One thing we all felt committed to: we can't just end this kind of thing because it's just been so big and so important.[33]

The women organized a fund raiser, to raise money for longer workshops. Jones was committed to further work, and quite clearly the women inside and out were eager for more contact, as were the audiences. There were more "themes for poems," more counter epics to write and direct, and there still was plenty of "discordant slander" holding women subject. Theater may have saved Rhodessa Jones's life, but it might not be enough for these women. Some of the incarcerated women who performed in this first play were empowered but not yet freed. The questions still lay before them: what it meant to be Medea, to become Medea, to kill Medea. Who else might they become as they represented their lives as drama?

CHAPTER 2

To Be Real

Rehearsing Techniques

> *I love women. In all their incredible, magical terror. Because*
> *women can be horrifically difficult, wondrously vulnerable, incredibly*
> *surprisingly strong. I love all of that. I love the shape of women,*
> *the curve of women, I love their temper. I love how they act. I do.*
> *And I love being a director because I get to say, "OK, OK. What's*
> *going on?" You know? It isn't like I have a wife or a girlfriend.*
> *It's a very different kind of a thing. I have an army of women who*
> *get their turn to be flipped out and I think they know it. You have to*
> *enjoy the company of very wild women or it's no fun.*
> —*Rhodessa Jones*

In this chapter, I focus on the ways in which the real is rehearsed, the dramatic techniques Jones uses to build a production and educate her troupe. Much of what I catalogue here is reproducible, the artistic components and the educational philosophy, though the particular rhythms and style of the individuals are not, of course. But it is in the interplay of the reproducible and the originality of the individual that the project exists and evolves. The Medea Project concentrates its energies on the wilderness of the female gender, its construction, destruction, and its various performative styles. It acts in interesting ways that straddle the humanist and posthumanist divide. Using the language and belief structure of a materialist world, Rhodessa Jones will command: *"Be real!" "Claim it!" "Work it!"* Or, she will begin to rant when the women aren't paying attention: "When I ask you to hold your tits—these boys wouldn't *exist* if we didn't have these tits and this womb." Her imperatives acknowledge an everyday reality and the stake these women have in owning it, as well as how much they've lost by not; she makes the women touch their bodies as the site that generates being and meaning. But the great strength of the Medea Project is that Jones believes in the category of the real and interrogates it

"Rehearsal Planning." Rhodessa Jones (kneeling, third from left); Fé Bongolan (seated on chair, fourth from left); Nikki Byrd (on floor, fifth from left); Edris Cooper (crouching behind water bottle); Sean Reynolds (wearing glasses, white turtleneck); Tanya Mayo (striped shirt); Gina Dawson (stockings and leather jacket). Photograph by Ruth Morgan, 1993

at the same time. Embedded in the command to "Be real" is the director's artfulness in commanding the women to be *more* real, to *say* what they know to be true more forcefully, to *touch* their tits and see what happens, to *feel* womanhood come to a point. She never forgets how to appeal to what may be empowering in our common sense and apprehension of how women are shaped by their bodies, but she always knows how to critique the assumptions we have about the ways things "just are."

The rehearsal process, during the workshop months that precede public performance, focuses on talking about "it"—the experience of being women, gender, sex, their bodies. How they talk about "it" (the various names for sex, the vagina, pussy, cunt, tits and womb, and dicks and the question of who puts what where) and how they perform it (dancing, kicking, legs spread, their ability to bend over and roll, their reluctance to touch)—those discussions and, more importantly, the exercising of the body seem to rock the foundations, shake up the territory of the real, material world. Bodies matter. The question is, how is it possible to matter differently, move more powerfully, and happily.[1]

"Rehearsal Movement." Rhodessa Jones in center. Photograph by Ruth Morgan, 1993

Jones insists, indirectly through her direction, on the necessity of both categories: the real and the real rehearsed. When she isn't satisfied that a performance is powerful, making connections, she lets the performer have it. "Anyone can be on stage," she screams at Fé Bongolan, who has performed for years with the troupe. "*I* never went to a drama school, you just have to *feel* your story." "We practice so it gets easier," she tells the cast. Easier to be real? Easier to *feel*? Feelings, indeed, may take work. They may even need to be rehearsed. The verb "rehearse" in English is derived from the Old French *re-hercer,* to harrow—the act of using a tool that works like a rake, leveling and breaking up plowed ground, covering seeds, rooting up weeds. It isn't a requirement that every woman in the Medea Project tell her own story, because Jones does not intend to create a straightforward documentary, or even a confessional, autobiographical theatrical experience. The "real" category that she speaks of may exist in a personal story, but it also may be embodied in a myth that belongs to everyone. In either case, the real never exists inviolate or isolated. Through the workshop process, Jones expects the women to swap stories, to reenact their own and those of others, to reshape their pasts and presents. As Jones sees it, the defiantly imaginative and unreal space of the theater, a space that collapses time and genre, historical and mythical realms, allows the participants in the Medea Project to experience an alternate reality, one that can be changed, lived through differently. The category of the real is not somewhere outside the theater, in the lives these women have led, waiting to be accessed, brought forth on stage. Rather, a new category of the real is established, even if only provisionally in the space of the workshop and public performance, a reality in and during which the women act out different versions of powerful stories.

The long workshop rehearsal process of the Medea Project is always physicalized. Rhodessian theater, Jones says, is about taking a certain stance, hips thrust, elbows out. "I am not interested in demure," she tells them. "Take it to the audience," she demands. Take the everyday violence, the beat and the language, and dig deeper, thrust that hip *more*. But some of the rehearsal process takes time out from the physical altogether. Jones will stop everyone to take the time to reflect on the process itself, to allow the women to express and exchange views about their feelings, their sense of the conditions facing them.

If Medea was alone, and therefore vulnerable, Jones works hard to find ways to practice community: "I remember them fighting on stage. They did not want to help somebody out. They get scared and they don't have a sense of community, they don't value or understand the nature of being together, which is why I ask other actors to come in, to help me cement that idea of an ensemble." In this rehearsal process, she fundamentally teaches how to work in an ensemble, how to listen to others, how to move in synchrony. Together with Sean Reynolds, Jones offers the women information and skills. But they are Freirean teachers too; they expect these women to interact with new people and new ideas, in order to form more critical opinions. Medea could see only one side of her story. The pedagogical thrust of the Medea Project is aimed at uncovering the connections between an individual and the system of power. Jones and Reynolds believe that critical literacy—understanding social context, moving with others and not alone—will transform the oppressed and apathetic into people who believe they can think and thus act for themselves and also for others. The Medea Project wants to revive community. Jones and Reynolds cultivate defiance—cutting, leveling, breaking up, tearing out weeds. Through conversation, critical reflection, listening to others tell their stories, and moving their bodies, women take the material ground on which they stand—their bodies and what has happened to them—and work it, cut it, break it up. The best work is harrowing, but its most important effects are always delayed; one breaks up the ground the best one can and hopes that the crops will grow.

Myth

There are artists in my group who are always trying to get me to be linear.
ABCD vs. . . . . They don't always get the large picture. The idea that it's a
moment. I want to create a moment. You can make any associations you want to
make with it. There is a narrative. Because to name things is the intention to
make things. And I feel like things continually open up. They move circularly.
—*Rhodessa Jones*

Up to almost the last possible minute, Jones keeps the pieces of a production in her head. Some parts will be cut or moved from first to last
place. The written program might get put together the night before the
opening performance. This doesn't mean that Jones isn't naming things
or making things as she goes along or that she doesn't have a larger picture in her head; it just means she wants to keep things open, provisional,
for as long as possible. She has certain ways of structuring original material, rhythms of juxtapositions she will adhere to in each production,
but as she interacts with each particular group of women, she absorbs
what unique things they have to say and throws into the mix the rich bank
of associations she carries with her.

One of the visible recurring structures of the Medea Project, an organizing principle, is the use of a myth that influences the look of the set
and the costumes and which can be read as a thematic conceit. In a perhaps uniquely postmodern twist, the literary classical reference (Euripides' play) reverts to its original oral story as Jones initially tells it to the
women, and then it becomes literary again when Edris Cooper rewrites
and updates it for performance. The myth is invigorated as a cultural
story, modified to respond to contemporary sources of anxiety. Each core
myth grows out of issues that come up in the workshops. The Medea
myth, we have seen, came to Jones's attention because a woman inmate
had killed her baby, and other women who were in jail for other crimes
had also, in effect, abandoned their children. The Greek myth, rewritten
and performed, can be seen as structuring the monologues that follow:
riffs on betrayal, abandonment, anger, too much love—the emotions that
make up the classical and the modern Medea. In the second performance,
Food Taboos in the Land of the Dead, the production Jones loves the most,
she had asked the question: what were women putting in their bodies
or in their mouths? Many of the women from the outside who had performed in *Reality Is Just Outside the Window* came back to work in the

next production. They had been talking about AIDS and the importance of using condoms with women in jail, but the women from the outside turned up pregnant, or were having abortions, or had a case of herpes. Jones remembers asking Sean Reynolds, "Why do you think they're doing that? Why do you think the women on the outside are getting pregnant and having abortions?" She recalls:

I was getting messages in very weird ways because everyone was trying to hide it from me that people were having miscarriages. These were my actresses who supposedly had it together. Sean and I wondered what the hell was going on. We were talking about AIDS, we were talking about condoms. And we got people having herpes attacks. "How'd you get that if you were using condoms?"

I was struggling with people inside and outside around authority, around the mother image. I was focusing on the lack of self-esteem and a lack of politics around women's lives. It's just easier to be male identified. Even my work with young girls, I still hear the same thing, "Oh he's so cute. That's my boyfriend." So I really wanted to do a piece with women and their bodies and the whole idea of being conscious of what we open up and take inside of ourselves.

The name, "Food Taboos," was in this collection of myths that Fé has. At the top of one page was the category, "Food Taboos in the Land of the Dead," a whole area of myths about food and death. I said, "That's it!" The critics said it was some New Age idea. It wasn't New Age at all. Out of that came Demeter and Persephone, the seeds. Demeter and Persephone was my favorite myth. Because it's how we got the seasons. When I was very young I had this beautiful picture book. And I remember this picture of this girl going through the fields and this dark man with a skull. He was lifting her up and it was the most impressionable image. I must have been in the sixth grade. It made me understand this is how we got the seasons.[2]

Jones was fired up and ready to create a powerful artful piece. *Food Taboos* may be the most visually exciting of all the Medea productions. It was probably the most physical and the most surreal. It had just about everything in it, including the kitchen sink, which the goddesses sat around at the opening and close of the show. There were a multiplicity of associations here, of the most intense sort, of heaven and hell on earth. Jones had just come back from Bangkok:

I believe that heaven and earth exist right here. We walk amongst the clouds and we are in the pits of hell at the same time. In Bangkok, it's four o'clock in the evening and there's so much smog, with the putt-putts and the cars. You have these incredibly filthy canals and then these elegant people. You look at these incredible gold-leaf temples which are flickering in the sun. Temple demons that are ten feet tall that are made out of semiprecious stones. And you walk into the Temple of the Reclining Buddha and every-where there are gold-leaf Buddhas and, I mean, they're huge. They're huge. And there are lines and lines of them encased in glass, with a different ex-pression on their faces. And you're moving through this, and you might see somebody with no legs. Now all this is going on with a flock of school girls with beautiful faces, and there's another parade of monks in robes of saffron. I believe heaven and earth exist side by side. If we're going to deal with reli-gion and spirituality, it's all here. Thus it must be moving through all of us all of the time.

In *Food Taboos*, I wanted to do the beginning of life. Spring at the edge of the world. I wanted to deal with imagining the first morning on earth. And everything was giving birth. That's what I was thinking of. Sean did an open-ing story called "Once Upon a Time Called Now"; it was a story from my family, a story my grandmother used to tell us when we were little. I think Gina Dawson had heard it too. Because it's mythology. I told it to Sean. It's an Abiku myth, an African myth about the reluctant souls who are born but don't want to be here.[3]

Something I'm always looking for is myth around life, birth. Myths from different cultures. . . . I also really wanted to play with goddesses in this show. This is when I thought, "The hell with it. We're just going to have our god-desses up in the good kitchen." And a descent into hell.

Food Taboos featured stilt walkers and women swinging on trapezes, and Jones worked with many of her most powerful collaborators—Nikki Byrd, Edris Cooper, Gina Dawson, Tanya Mayo, Fé Bongolan. The ex-travagant movement and mixture of goddesses in the kitchen dispensing wisdom and whores strolling the streets gave *Food Taboos,* Jones believes, a layered frenzy, a hellish beauty.

For me, as director, the visual is very important. It creates the painterly idea that I have as a director. How do I make this beautiful, phantasmagoric? Somebody who can't speak English, they can still sit there and feel things.

And in part, my use of the stilt walker and the trapeze artist should hearken back to something very primal. Chagall is one of those artists that I love. I love his flying cows and his brides. I love some of Dali's work. To me, it just takes you back. I love the impressionists. They are fantastical. The trapeze, the stilts completes the spectacle. The work is large and full of movement. I bow to Greek theater. I bow to the modern spectacle. Mnouchkine's pieces out in football fields. Pina Bausch. All those people influenced me.

I think stilts are magical. They're about heaven and earth, paradise lost, paradise regained. The spirits walk amongst us. The goddess walks with us. And spirits stalk the stage. And I love them visually. It's just a whole other level in which to work. And Kathy Katz was so good at it. She was doing it with Terry Sendgraff, the woman who created "motivity," a dance technique, in Oakland. Terry has this theater; she teaches trapeze. Tumbleweed, the dance collective, became Terry's first Fly by Nights. Fly by Nights were the first women she trained to use trapeze as dance. She was our teacher. Terry worked with Barnum and Bailey. Terry has one breast and she's the strongest woman I know. And moves so beautifully. So Kathy, who was working with Terry when we were working in the jails, was really excited about stilt walking. I said, "Wow. Let's use it." This was a woman doing it, a white woman doing it. And my experience had been that stilt walkers were mostly Chinese acrobats, or French clowns, or African dancers. And they're usually men on stage.

I was criticized by various artists of the African American community that I had it all wrong, that you can't have stilt walking with a white woman. When people want to take a swipe at me, they say, "Why you dealing with African mythology and have a white woman on stilts? come from Cameroon." But stilts also come from China. They also come from Europe.

The point is, I'll use anything that speaks to me. And many people have. Many kinds of art have.

Jones takes the power and privilege and right to use anything that speaks to her. She is criticized with dehistorisizing, but she believes that art crosses borders and that myths do as well. Her sensibility doesn't lend itself to linear, historical ways of thinking. Instead she subordinates cultural specificity and historical difference to universal mythologizing. The stilts and myths help create the phantasmagoria, a word she uses to describe the mysterious and beautiful effect she wishes to capture on stage, juxtaposed with her sharp eye for the degradation she finds in the present.

For me, the myths, the mélange of material, have always distinguished this project. No doubt because of my literary training, I *expected* them to be important, critical for everyone. *I* wanted the myths to make the difference, to be the key, because they were *my* association with the project, a literary association, but they weren't operative for everyone. As I was trying to establish the quality of difference of the shows, based on the different myths, I asked Felicia Scaggs, one of the women from jail who performed in three of the productions what the Medea story meant to her. Her answer brought me up short:

FRADEN: What did you think about the Medea story in the first play?
SCAGGS: I didn't really trip on that story. I always wanted to be an actress. I always wanted to be on a stage doing something. You know what I'm saying? That was just a way—all those people going to be seeing me. This is what I want. I want these people to see me. I want to get that applause. I just clicked right with the show. It was lovely.
FRADEN: Have the shows been different experiences for you? Have the stories been different?
SCAGGS: For me, [the stories are] almost the same kind of thing, basically based on the same theme. [There are] different people. Every year it's somebody different, and no one is the same and everybody has different problems. Everybody has to express their selves differently. That's what makes it interesting too. But for me, it's . . . it's basically just like the same. But I enjoy it. I like it a lot.[4]

For Scaggs, the myths were all the same, "based on the same theme," but the *people* were different, and had to express themselves differently. For her, the experience of the different shows has been similar, because for her it was always about performing, being on stage, being seen. *That* was lovely. What I began to see was how the work of the rehearsal process, like the finished production, was utterly contingent upon personal difference and personal associations. As I outline in this chapter the various techniques that Jones uses—the incorporation of myths, her reliance on exchanging information, her techniques for exercising the body—I am also aware that people connect in different ways to different parts of the process. As with all performances, not one is exactly reproducible, and, as with all works of art, the range of interpretive associations are as varied as the various people who engage with it. The rehearsal process can seem real in a different way to each woman who participates.

Education

We in the Medea Project create a circle of consciousness.
—Rhodessa Jones

In theory, the disciplines of education, therapy, and art can clearly be separated, but in the jails, in practice, different professionals with different degrees may find it difficult to separate drama's ability to educate from its ability to provide therapy. Role playing can be used by a drama therapist or by an actor or by a teacher to help a client/actor/student experience empathy for others and articulate other points of views, creating art for others and personal insight. Though there may be trained drama therapists working in jails, most of the people who have developed theater workshops in the jails (like Rhodessa Jones and John Bergman, for instance) have been professional actors or community organizers, and what differentiates them is how explicit they are in separating the work of art from the work of therapy (or rebellion).[5] The Medea Project is now known to be a public theater project, the process culminating with the public theatrical performance. But the particular blend of dramatic education that Jones has developed from her work in community-based, feminist theater makes it important *not* to separate education, therapy, and art. She deliberately mixes them up, the education and therapy folded together into what she has called "creative survival."

While the project can be said to culminate in the public production, complete with myth and music and stilts, by focusing on the rehearsal period as an *educational process,* such linear descriptions of the Medea Project become inadequate. To understand the place of the individual within the culture, to make that associative and always critical leap, Jones believes that everyone involved in the rehearsals is taking part in an education, a leading out, bringing up, rearing, training. In the Medea Project, rehearsing and educating are both conceived of as strenuous tasks, and they are absolutely intertwined and ongoing. Education doesn't stop after the rehearsals are over and the performance occurs. Even after one graduates, as all teachers know, a good learner keeps on learning, while bad ones may never have started, or may have plagiarized or pretended or only memorized, but did not fully realize. Teachers never can be sure when or exactly how education works—what a student learns, remembers, or finds useful. The transmission of knowledge (and power) may be delayed, or it may be refused, or it may operate in ways not intended.

Accurate assessments of acquired knowledge are harder to come by in this model, because the women are not just taking in facts and figures but are finding new ways to act. Jones does believe she has specific information that can be transformatively useful for the women to know. But she is very much in the Freirean school of educators: she refuses to operate as a bank, a receptacle of treasures from which women make withdrawals. Instead she understands her role is to help women to become actively engaged in shaping their own educations, framing their own questions and answers.

During rehearsals the women are interviewed and then asked to interview themselves as subjects: what do these women know, what have they experienced, what kinds of critical reflection do they have on their life? What story can they tell that rivals a classical myth? Jones has said that their stories are so much more powerful and real than anything they hear on Oprah or would read in a Danielle Steele novel, more terrifying than anything sung in the latest hip-hop song. But their stories are rarely easy subjects to release, and the women are often reluctant to tell them. Once having told them, they may be even more reluctant to critique them. Nevertheless, Jones believes accessing the personal story and then, most critically, *responding* to the story—creating a dialogue—is essential to the education, the leading out from prison.

> It's long-term work to have workers in the jail, doing the kind of thing that we do. If only there were more people who were having this kind of discourse with these people, this exchange, expecting this kind of relationship, expecting people to form opinions, have relationships with each other. I think that it's a new model. You're not going to get results tomorrow.
>
> Somebody in the system had to realize that something is not working. I think people delude themselves. They think that if they slap an adult on their hands, hold them somewhere for six to twelve months, they're not going to come back to jail. Given their crimes and the reasons that they're there: poverty, sickness, all that stems from pain and loss and lack of self-esteem— they think they're not going to come back? And in the course of time, nobody—their captors, the gatekeepers, the keyholders—gets them to tell their story. They don't exchange with people who are there.

The Medea Project demands that women tell their story, and they promise an exchange of stories. While it sounds easy, the results show that it isn't for everyone.

The Medea Project is anchored by Jones and her co-teacher, Sean Reynolds. It would be impossible to reproduce the exact combination of personalities that form the backbone of the Medea Project. Jones and Reynolds together are a formidable pair. Reynolds's background as social worker, writer, and activist dovetails perfectly with Jones's artistic life work. Both are superb talkers; Reynolds is sharp, fierce, statistical, while Jones rants in a more mellow tone. Reynolds is an African American woman who grew up on the South Side of Chicago. Like Jones, she feels were it not for role models, a good education, and a little bit of luck, she could have ended up like the women she is working with in jail. Reynolds has channeled her rage and wit into mesmerizing performances. She is a big, strong, smart, tough-talking woman who is not afraid to take on authority *or* the women she is trying to help. She has worked as a health educator in the city/county jail system as a part of the Department of Public Health. Her job there was to provide male and female inmates with information on sexually transmitted diseases, birth control, sex, and AIDS education. When she realized the women just weren't showing that much interest, she had to begin to think about how to get them to pay attention: "I realized that there were a lot of things missing in my performance, in my presentation, and their level of reception. So I had to figure out some ways in which to reach a captive audience. In addition to talking about AIDS, I started talking about drugs, I started talking about sex. I guess I *have* been interested in performance, because I can remember coming home sometimes saying, 'I was really *on*.' And I would tell them, 'This is a great job, the greatest job in the world. I get paid a very decent salary talking about drugs, sex, and music.'" Both Reynolds and Jones are consummate performers, no more so than when they are *acting* real and everyone knows it. Jones and Reynolds talk about each other as good cop/bad cop; they know that some women are more drawn to Reynolds's tough love, others to Jones's nurturing. Many of the women in jail themselves are fantastic storytellers, when it comes to telling stories *they* know. They also know when someone is just marking time. "Your average Jane in the Medea Project is used to being programmed, institutionalized, and getting over by saying what she needs to say with buzz words," Bongolan notes.[6] They especially recognize and appreciate a great performance, and those who remain in the project are not intimidated by the consummate duo of Reynolds and Jones.

Sean Reynolds describes the startup of each workshop this way:

At the end of August, beginning of September, Rhodessa and I go into the jail to interview women who want to be in the Medea Project. Women are told what they can expect and what we expect. What we expect is that:

- they will come and participate in each workshop (held two to three times a week);
- that they will be honest;
- that they will bring stories from their own lives to share;
- that they leave the bullshit in the dorms;
- that they make a commitment to the process and see it out till the end.

They are told that the workshops will culminate in a public performance. Usually at the first meeting, seventy-five or so women show up. By the second meeting that number is halved. By the time of the actual performance we have between six to twelve women.

Why those numbers? Because women are sent to State Prison; women are locked down for disciplinary reasons; women get released from custody and don't come back (even though they are invited back and can be cleared to work inside the jail); Rhodessa or I ask them to leave, usually because they aren't serious. Women leave on their own because they can't hang: the work is too physical; they would rather stay in the dorms and keep shit going; they don't want to be honest about themselves; they are too lazy.[7]

It isn't easy to count on anyone. There's a lot to learn, and high expectations. The women are expected to voice opinions and *do* things, and most of the women aren't used to doing either. For those who remain, a certain degree of trust develops; a kind of alternative family may be created. Even when the teachers scream and yell and rant, the women listen to what isn't being said as well as to what is. Women are paying attention to them, focusing *interest,* having expectations, and many have never had this combination of discipline and mothering. The ones who stay are able to listen and can rise to the expectations that Jones and Reynolds have: that, as damaged as these women are, they can think for themselves; they can exercise the mind and body, talk, listen, and defend their choices.

Jones means to give everyone an equal chance to perform, by leading with their own story. This is an important principle, this equalizing the forms of participation, creating the circle model of the classroom rather than student rows with the teacher's desk elevated in front. Says Jones:

We weren't talking "Y'all vs. Us." We were talking about *us.* And that was very new to them. Because we weren't playing that role of "*You* people get it together." But all of us have to. What about *our* children? And I think it struck chords in people.

We in the Medea Project create a circle of consciousness. I think the people who lead other sorts of therapy groups in jail haven't dealt with their own shit. They do not go there where it's "us." It's "y'all." "How *y'all* going to get yourself together?" I think we all got to be willing to say, if it didn't happen to me directly, I knew somebody. I've seen people from the outside have the light come on. When people finally say out loud, "This happened to me." One night, one girl from the outside said, "I prostituted myself for hash when I was in college. I had sex with guys I didn't like for drugs." All of a sudden people were saying this stuff out loud. And it was a place to begin. I could be wrong, but I don't think that other counseling programs get that intimate. I think there's a real boundary of us and them. And I think that's about training and how people see themselves in relationship to it.

You got to get in there and wade in the shit. You've got to be willing to say, "My experience has been this." Not that it's always going to be like hers, but you got to give her room to talk about that experience. At the same time you got to be there when she breaks down.

A lot of times it's race. There's not a black person leading it. That's not to say that we can't all share in it, but how much of my experience are you going to be able to understand and appreciate? And it's not your fault. But the culture has not set us up that way unless you been doing it a long time and you love the people and made it your business to go home with me, to talk with me outside of work, to invite me inside your house.

Erasing the border between inside and outside is clearly an important principle for the Medea Project. Jones goes on, "We were belly to belly with those people. And it was very exciting to me as a politically minded artist. You better be in the world, doing something, making a difference, instead of standing around in one place. We were in jail with women who looked like us. What are you going to do?" What Reynolds argues is that "what is important is not 'erasing' borders (which certainly exist) but crossing over them, being able to learn from each other without compromising your own standards." Jones and Reynolds keep rocking back and forth, emphasizing both their differences in power and knowledge and their cultural similarities to the incarcerated women. Jones and Reynolds have voluntarily landed in jail, but they can leave at the end of the day. The incarcerated cannot. Reynolds believes that "what is different about 'us' and 'them' is not differences in power and knowledge." She explains:

Rhodessa and I are pretty much like most of the African American women in jail. It is more the difference between the "privileged" and the "undeserved," with us being part of that privileged African American class who—because of timing, luck, nerve, and education of a different sort—did not wind up in jail.

The average age of the women with whom we worked was about twenty-eight or twenty-nine. Whereas Rhodessa and I are the direct beneficiaries of the civil rights movement, by the time these women came along, the times had changed. I am of the first generation of African Americans born in the north. The expectations for me were much different than the expectations for those born post-hippie, post-drug, post-Vietnam, post–urban riot, where a greater emphasis was put on television rather than books.

Regardless of how much Rhodessa and I might like, admire, respect, have fun with, attempt to impart information to incarcerated women, it is important for us to remember that, regardless of the circumstances which brought them to jail . . . they are, in fact, in jail. And many of them are in jail for good reasons, i.e., selling drugs (maybe to your kids or my kids); using drugs (maybe while pregnant); attempted murder, mayhem. A lot of that is serious business. . . .

The thing about the women in jail is that, yes, they have visits. But I'll tell you something. And I knew it. I knew it when I worked in the jail. And I knew it when Rhodessa came into the jail. Let's face it, the women are not used to seeing the likes of us. Let's face it. I walk into the jail. And I tell them first off, I'm a lesbian. Right?

And they say, "No, you ain't really a lesbian."

And I say, "Yes, yes, I am. What do *you* mean, 'not really'?"

"You have a degree, Sean?"

"Yeah."

And they'd say, "You just went to Europe?" I remember when I went to Europe, I brought them back money from Holland. It might sound trite, but they'd never seen that. They didn't know that there's different kinds of money in the world. They didn't know that here's two black women who were talking about going to Europe.

They *did* know that here are two black women not being bothered.

Here are two black women, strong, tough, going places, and not being bothered. And they are not Oprah, not black beauty queens, not women on television or in the movies, but women who are right there in the same room with them, neither one of them rich nor particularly famous, talking *to* them about things they had never seen, like money from Holland, but talking about it in the language they could understand. What might be unique about the Medea Project and hard to reproduce, though not impossible, is the creation of this complex relationship—a crossing of borders among the women inside and outside and an all important acknowledgment of their differences—in terms of power of movement and choice, the luck of having good role models.

When one thinks about what is easily reproducible in the Medea Project, one can certainly outline the kinds of subjects Jones and Reynolds bring up—self-esteem, drug abuse, dysfunctional families, battered syndrome—these are all standard topics for American women in the late twentieth century, crossing class and racial lines. But Reynolds points out that the *remedies* for such ills have *not* crossed class and race lines:

> If we talk about that which crosses class and race lines—i.e., lack of self-esteem, substance abuse, dysfunctional families, battered women's syndrome, then we must talk about the ways in which all of the above has affected different races and classes and why the remedy for such ills has not crossed these class and race lines. It is the standard to incarcerate undeserved people of color regardless of the ways in which we have been affected by societal ills. This has not happened with other groups.

> It is true that the Medea Project brings to the table a dialogue about the ways in which women are all incarcerated. However, what makes the work of the Medea Project profound is that the members of the core group work with women who are not theoretically or metaphorically incarcerated. Rather the Medea Project works with women who are in the "been physically removed from anything and everything that may have been dear to them, locked up for an indeterminate period of time, put behind thick steel bars with no windows to look out of, having to shit in front of everybody, subject to more abuse because some of the women who are locked up with you have psychological profiles similar to Charles Manson, can't find a job when you finally get out because you're wearing a convict jacket, having to go back to that same man who kicked you in the ass and got you locked up in the first place" kind of jail.

> They are there because they have been locked out of the process that would have given them at least a modicum of control over their own lives . . . education.

Reynolds's pedagogical stance is clear. She wants the women to become informed, critical thinkers. Reynolds recounts how the deputies wouldn't let the women watch the Anita Hill/Clarence Thomas hearings because they said the women wouldn't understand it:

The real reason, however, is more complex than that simple explanation. The deputies, unbeknownst to many of them, were directly cooperating in the institutionalization of the incarcerated women and of themselves. Instead of encouraging the women to watch the hearings, the deputies were more interested in the soaps and thus encouraged the women to be more interested.

At first the women in my group, approximately thirty, resisted even the idea of watching the hearings. I asked them if they knew what was going on with the Supreme Court nominee and not only did they not know, they didn't care. Mind you, these women are in jail, and the majority of them are African American, Latina, and Native American, and they are not interested in who sits on the bench in the highest court in the land.

They either didn't have an opinion about sexual harassment or they sided with Thomas. "That bitch is trying to set up a black man!" I would counter that Hill too is black. "She probably mad cause he wouldn't give her none!" Do you have any idea how frustrating comments like this can be? I knew what I was going to do. Since I was already taping each televised hearing for my own use, I decided to treat the hearings like a soap opera. In essence I serialized the Supreme Court hearings and for one hour each day we watched and then we discussed what we had seen, just like watching *All My Children*.

Whereas when we started this process the women had either no information or incorrect information, or information born out of sheer stupidity, when we finished, to a person, everybody knew what was going on. Some women still believed that Anita Hill was not telling the truth. But the purpose of the experiment was not to *sway* people's opinions; it was meant to provide them with the information so that they could *have* an opinion. Versus speaking in jailhouse sound bites and not taking responsibility for their own lives and the lives of other women, i.e., not participating in their own institutionalization.

To be institutionalized means that you no longer know the difference between taking advantage of and using. And knowing the difference between those two things can, in fact, save your life. Institutionalization requires the cooperation of everybody in jail, not just the inmate.

Many people I talked to believed that incarcerated women were more vulnerable and harder to work with than incarcerated men. Reynolds notes the differences she's seen between men and women in jail, how good the men could look and how broken the women were. She blames the hard life they've lived before they got to jail and the particular ways women are managed once they're institutionalized.

It's hard ground. The women can be street smart, gifted with great language, but they are not only ignorant about the world, they are sometimes passive. Their brains have been fried by drugs and abuse, their sources of information are television, advertisements, popular culture. They're addicted to drugs, men, and don't know how to take care of themselves; they have little physical or psychic mobility.

I've met women who had sexually transmitted diseases I've had to go look up. And I consider myself relatively sophisticated and a health worker.

I'd say, "How do you get this?" And these are twenty-year-old women. "How long have you been fucking?"

I'm a big woman and I would meet women who would say, "I can't touch my knees."

I'd say, "Hold it, if *I* can bend over and touch mine and I've got all this in the middle. . . ."

Men are exposed to so much more in society. In every dorm at the San Bruno jail there is Nautilus equipment. Some man in each dorm knew how to work the machines, and a group would always use it to exercise. Every morning, the men would look at the newspaper, read the sports page, and because there was nothing else to do, go on to other sections, talk to each other about the news, the army, drugs, women, while the women watched TV, did their hair, their nails, and used the Nautilus equipment to lean on. They tended to be overweight and depressed.

Up until recently, there were very few programs available to incarcerated women. Whereas men participated in the culinary academy program, where they could learn to be cooks, women were stuck in the dorms doing each other's hair. Men were in printing classes; women were sitting in dorms watching soap operas. The rationale provided by the institution for the difference was that the women were doing what they wanted to do . . . the women were not as motivated . . . the women didn't understand . . . or the women provided too much of a distraction for the men.

Reynolds challenges these women to think about what words mean, to ask and begin to answer, "Why are we here?"

REYNOLDS: I can remember one day, I said the word, "Pussy."

And the women said, "Don't say that, that's a bad word."

I said, "What do you mean it's a bad word? What do *you* call it? You are grown. You're a convict. You ain't in here for jaywalking. What do *you* say?" You know, I'd say, "Come on, we have to redefine our lives. I think 'pussy' is a great word. I say it all the time. I think it's a better word than 'illiteracy.' I think it's a better word than 'bitch.'"

We didn't talk about theater when we first went into the jail. We talked about life. And that's why we had such a captive audience. And I know the women would say, "Come on, you got to see them. Rhodessa and Sean. You ain't gonna believe them."

We talked for months. We talked for months. "Who are you? Why are you here? What are your dreams?"

JONES: We don't have that kind of time anymore. But we learned that that was vital: to talk.

REYNOLDS: "What do you think about when you wake up in the morning? Going to sleep would be easy, but what is waking up like? What about that man there? What is he doing for you? Why are you here? You talking about your family was fine, and yet you say you was smoking reefers when you was kids. Something wasn't right." You know. We *talked.* In the dorms, where I did my classes, with men and women, right up above us, two stories up, there is a window where people [the deputies] are looking down and listening to you. Sometimes I would get so outrageous, I would start laughing.

I would look up and say to myself, "Yo! Hey, they ain't said nothing, so I'll just continue." Sometimes I would get so over the edge. And I knew, even for *me,* it was over the edge. You know? Even for me.

JONES: I think there's also a method to that kind of madness. At least one of the things that I really learned from watching you, is about responding: "Come on, come back with something, because that isn't going to work with me."

REYNOLDS: I'll tell them, "You're not going to play the dozens with me. You can't win. And then you'll go away somewhere crying. We're not equal. The relationship is very unequal. I can leave here and go home. I get paid. You're sitting here. You're an inmate. You're a convict. You've been labeled." So it's a very unequal relationship. I think it's my job to balance it. Please, don't get me wrong. Not every inmate loves me.

JONES: No, they don't. Not me either.

REYNOLDS: I passed around a sign-up sheet for people in my class. One woman, instead of putting her name down, wrote "Fuk you." I looked at this sign-up sheet.

And then I went to the board and said, "OK. Somebody has written 'Fuk you,' and that's all right. I understand. You have a right to say that. This is America. For anyone who wrote this, this is how you spell 'Fuck.' So next time you write, 'Fuck you,' please spell it right. It's just learning. You can say 'Fuck you,' 'Kiss my ass,' call me a 'black bitch.' I might be wrong. I'm not right all the time. Challenge me. Have an idea. Please."

You know, if you're going to insult somebody, you have to know how to write it. You don't want to leave that door open for me. And people would say, "That's what I like about you." My ideas are my ideas. I mean, there's a foundation here. I would get the women to ask why do you think that way? *Why?*

JONES: That's the process. Getting them to talk about it. Give me some answers for these whys.

REYNOLDS: I have women in my class who would refer to themselves as "Negroes." And none of them were living at a time when African Americans were calling themselves Negroes.

I said, "Where did this come from?"

They said, "I just think it's a better word."

"Why do you think it's a *better* word? Why do you now think we have different words?"

I have one woman who told me, "Because maybe they didn't come from Africa, maybe they came from Frenchland." At which point I brought in a map. To show them where Frenchland is. I had people talk about geography. I asked people if they could go anywhere in the world, where would they go. And they'd say, "Fresno."

I'd say, "Hold on, look at this map. This is why you have so many conflicts, you don't know who the hell you talking to. You believe it because some ignorant person said it. Or it's what you've heard on stupid-ass TV."

I remember one day talking about masturbation. And I was telling the women how important it was to masturbate. I remember it was a Friday. I said, "OK, by Monday when I come back here, I want all of you to have had an orgasm. How many of you have not had an orgasm?"

Their little hands would creep up. Everybody would start laughing.

"Who you laughing at? You had one? *Tell me how it feels.*" And then I came to find out, 98 percent of them have never had orgasms. Which was not surprising.

I told them, "When you can do this for yourself, *(a), you can tell somebody else how to make you feel good; and (b), you won't need 'em.*" This is the point at which women have to arrive in my mind.

Independence for a lot of people means a lot of different things, but we're talking about a group of people who have no clue.

Reynolds directs the women back to the body. How can they give themselves pleasure, not through drugs or a man or clothes, but using one's own hands, one's own mind? Rehearse that vagina. Work it. Practice doing it to yourself. Once again the Medea Project moves between different types of subjects and associative styles: they praise the outlaw, the woman who can show her anger, who seems independent of cultural norms, but they also want her to know how to spell "fuck" correctly. Depending on which line of instruction one focuses on, the Medea Project can sound like a traditional uplift program, talking from wider experience to people with less, or it can sound Paulo Freirean, a pedagogy of the oppressed in which people circulate information, analyze it, form their own opinions. In bringing the Anita Hill/Clarence Thomas hearings into the jail, Reynolds decided this was important for the inmates to be exposed to. She saw it as a way to begin a dialogue and develop informed opinions. The women in jail are all too often apathetic, passive, and, as Reynolds notes, ignorant about the world. Her goal is to empower these women to recognize the myths and social conditions that oppress them and consider how they might change them, to become freer, to become women who are not bothered.

Independence may be a deeply specific cultural value; it may ultimately even be illusory or relative. It means, as Reynolds points out, a lot of different things to different people. But there is no question that these women are imprisoned in multiple ways. They are in jail; they are poor; they are mostly colored in a racist society; they are women. We can say they are in jail because of their class, race, gender, the accidents of fate and history, and/or we can blame their characters. One can rant at history and power, but if a racist, sexist culture isn't likely to change any time soon, it may make sense to begin an intervention by interrogation, sharing information, a map, foreign currencies, senate hearings. The Medea Project always ventures forth into that wilderness of gender in order to find a way to rehearse the nature of character differently, and thus, perhaps, influence culture. The Medea Project starts with the body, experimenting with using it differently and not letting it *be* used in exactly the same ways, and moves the body to critical thinking, first by having the women acknowledge what they don't know and then by encouraging them to think about where they can go to find out what they may need to know.

Just as important as asserting one's individual independence may be configuring a more self-conscious and invigorating kind of dependence. Many of the dramatic techniques that Jones uses in rehearsals focus on *relationships* among and between subjects. From collaborations with other artists and through her own development as a solo performance artist, Jones has amassed a collection of theatrical techniques that she brings with her to the jails. In the years she has worked inside the jails, she has learned that incarcerated women need to work on working together and they need to be able to claim their experience, as well as to see how their experiences have made claims on them. The techniques that follow are ones she makes for incarcerated women as they move from the workshop environment to shaping a public performance. Many of the exercises demand physical cooperation among the women and allow for opportunities to tell their stories. The exercises make the women remember painful moments and, as they react to them by acting them again, kicking back, repeating dirty secrets, Jones believes a healing can begin. The techniques are a mixture of therapeutic cure and art. Most of the exercises that follow are designed to help the group pay attention to each other while giving them the skills and confidence to rehearse their story.

The Rant

When people see public performances of the Medea Project, it is hard to miss seeing Jones. As the director, she sits on stage, or just below it, with headphones on, following the script, calling out to the performers from time to time, keeping the beat. She recalls:

> Jack Carpenter, who was the production manager at the Artaud, would watch our rehearsals. I would be yelling at these women. They were terrified of what I'm asking them to do. All of a sudden we're in a theater. Jack is the one who came up and said, "We'll have this chair here for you on stage."
> I said, "Oh no, I'm not going to be on stage during the performance. . . ."
> And he said, "Aren't you? I thought that was part of the play."
> I said, "That's *not* how it's *done*."

"Women Are Waiting: The Tragedy of Medea Jackson," from Reality Is Just
Outside the Window. *Rhodessa Jones at left, at desk, directing from on stage.
Photograph by Pam Peniston, 1992*

He said, "But when you're there, and even when you're not talking, they
know where to focus."

And then my friends from New York saw *Reality,* and they informed me
the Polish director Tadeusz Kantor always worked with national groups of
people and also sat on the stage. It made total sense to me. Because I love
to be with them. I *am* an extension of them. I too must go the distance.
So it's like, why should I leave? I'm asking them to go up there and expose
themselves and some of them can do anything if Rhodessa is watching. I'm
the conductor. I'm beaming and smiling when they're cooking. To be the affirming energy out there, mouthing "Yes, you're wonderful." That's just as
important as yelling at them "Stay in the play."

Even Jones's rants are a kind of affirming gesture, and they have become her most theatrical trade signature. She throws them regularly, and
women either accept them or drop out because they are too much for
them. The rant makes for this highly theatrical scene in which the director seems to lose control, gesticulating wildly. She looks like she has "lost
it," but after witnessing a few months of a rehearsal workshop, anyone
can begin to see that these rants, as delivered by Jones, may seem spon-
taneous but are absolutely planned and purposeful. One can even begin

to predict fairly accurately when they're about to occur. They are most often inspired by a nonresponse she gets from the women. The point is to make the women focus on the business at hand, their own performances or the performances of other members of the group. Jones delivers the rant in the language, she says, of the "gangster mother," in language they understand. She has given these rants now so many times that the rant has become a necessary part of the Medea Project, and a crafty performance piece in itself.

Many of the inmates are used to hearing the high-decibel range of ranting—from parents, boyfriends, foster parents, cops, guards, drug-addicted companions. They are good at tuning the voices out, refusing to listen, absenting themselves. They have to begin to hear the difference between Jones's rants and the ones that do them no good. Some don't and leave. The ones who stay always smile when asked about the rants. They hear behind the words a kind of caring; they're being held accountable. Jones's tone is a mixture of disappointment and respect; it is not meant to be disdainful or punishing. But it is nevertheless fierce, because the resistance to doing the work is sometimes as great as Jones's expectations.[8]

The following rant is transcribed from the video *Open the Gate: The Making of Cultural Odyssey's The Medea Project: Reality Is Just Outside the Window,* made by Kathy Katz.[9] Jones has stopped the rehearsal because she doesn't feel the women are focusing on the material, in this case, "My Mother's Shoes," a piece about a mother who knows her child is being sexually abused but doesn't move to help. The camera pans from Jones standing, pointing her finger, to the women, silent.

And I think that there are women here, that know what this is about. And if you don't want to deal with it, then that's too fucking bad because we have to! This is about some little girls who are possibly being molested. And her mother comes home and finds her. That's what this is about. Some motherfucker was finger fucking her while her mother was at work. That's what this piece is about!

Brandy! You stand there looking at me like you never heard this before. Did you read it? That's what it's about! It's about the dirty little things that happen to us long before we have any control over it. And that is part of the reason a lot of us are here in jail now. Because we are so fucking mad and we go out there and do things that destroy ourselves. That's what this piece is about! The other one, "My Mother's Shoes," is because my mother did nothing when my father was molesting me. That is what we are talking about here. It may not happen to you directly, but I feel like everyone of us has a dirty story to tell. And it's time to start telling them so we can get on with our lives.

Yeah, when I ask you to do the baby stuff, yeah, it may be painful and full of shame if you don't know where your children are, but at least live it! Let the audience see you be women with children! You are not animals! They got to remember that you are mothers too. It is a lot about examining what our conditions are as women. Because this whole fucking society wants to pretend it's not happening to us. And that we're just born bitches. We're *not* born bitches! A lot of fucking shit happens to us. And it's allowed to happen because men do it and men run things. And we allow men to do it. A lot of this work is about this. A lot of this quiet stuff is about the intensity and the awful things we live with that we don't tell anybody. That's what interests me.

When I saw the film *The Boys in the Hood,* I thought it was a great film, but I thought, "What about the girls in the hood? What about us?" When I ask you to hold your tits—these boys wouldn't exist if we didn't have these tits and this womb. Yeah, we need the dick, but it's the tits and the womb that keeps us trying. It's what keeps you all fucked up about being in jail and not with your kids. There's a pull there. It is the flow of life. When I ask you at the end to mention your mothers, your grandmothers, your children's names, I want you to honor them.

I'm not trying to get in your business because your business is right downtown. I could go downtown, push a button, and know your business, if that's what you are concerned about. It's about *you* looking at your business. And how you're going to change your life. I'm not going to pretend that everyone will walk out of here and not do drugs, not steal, not do whatever. But I'm hoping that it will affect you in a way that you will say, "My life means something! I am important, just who I am. I don't need a fancy car. I don't need a nigger with a lot of diamonds and a lot of rocks. I'm somebody. . . ."

Let's get on. Let's move on.

Actress Tanya Mayo recalls the circumstances surrounding that particular rant:

The rant that you see at the beginning of *Open the Gate* was three days before the show. I was performing a piece that Dorsha [Brown] had written, called "My Mother's Shoes." Everyone is just going through the motions, so people get kind of spaced. Partly because it's really real. It's really hard. All of a sudden somebody is talking about *me,* not word for word, but a lot of people's mothers' shoes never moved. So the women think, "I'm just going to space out. This is a hard topic and I'm just going to zone out." So that's what happened. Sometimes because they can't deal, and sometimes they just really space out because they're using all their energy they can to not space out, but they do anyway. So that rant came out of: "You have to do justice to their words. These are real people's words. This is not Shakespeare, saying, "This is a really good story about Romeo and Juliet." It's somebody's real life and it's really painful, and you have to give that back to this piece."

The "This is not *Dreamgirls*" rant got added onto this year with "What's going on? Are you waiting for Mayor Willie Brown? Do you think he's coming for dinner tonight?" rant. Because people were getting so spaced out. You gotta realize that these women are drug addicted or drug exposed or alcoholics or products of an alcoholic environment. It's like, "*Hello?* Wake up! Are you fried? What's going on?"

A lot of people come in to rehearsal initially kind of like, "Oh, yeah. This is just a way to get out of the dorm. Anything to get me out of there. But *what?* You want me to *do* something? You want me to pay attention? You want me to *perform?* You want me to act? You want me to think? People don't ask me to do that very often. I'm a black woman. I'm poverty stricken and I'm on drugs. And you want me to *think?* Aren't we going to get into trouble?" All this subconscious stuff that over the process has to be chipped away at. What Rhodessa does so well is get to the social crutch of why that's happening, and put it out on the table. She takes pretty much every opportunity to teach a life skill, to teach a social value, to teach a moral.[10]

Of her rants and their aim, Jones herself says:

So much is just getting people to focus, getting people to stop being so angry. The rants are a way to get everyone to stop, and to talk, and to get along better with each other. The women are getting much younger, they haven't a clue, they're fried, they've been fried for a long time.

The part of me that is a teacher, the part I play when I rant is a gangster mama. It's who I've encountered in the jails, a certain kind of language, a certain kind of posture, a certain kind of energy. I think I've mellowed a lot from the early days in my rants. Because the experiences I've had afford a larger distance. I can look at these faces, and recognize trouble.

Jones has rants on body odor and how women need to clean between their legs. She has rants about needing to take responsibility for the show, for memorizing lines, for watching the backs of other women, literally, when they carry someone on stage, not *ever* to let them fall. Reynolds gives the social worker rant, which starts and ends with, "Don't bullshit me. I'm not going to put up with your shit and I'm not going to baby you." Some of the inmates rant. Some of them do it to the group as a whole. Some of them do it internally within the inmate group. The more respected leaders will say: "Come on y'all. We all need to get this together." The rants are often disciplinary based, a kind of laying out of the proper rules for behavior, a grammar of etiquette for these women; it may be the strongest instance of a call that elicits only the strongest of responses—silent acquiescence or withdrawal.

Sometimes during rehearsals there are too many voices, a cacophony of sounds, questions, demands. During one late rehearsal of *Slouching,* Libah Sheppard was practicing her story about being insulted in a Chinese restaurant. She couldn't remember her lines; Jones was giving her directions, to turn a certain way, to speak in two voices, her own and the voice of the waitress. Reynolds told her not to worry about the exact lines, just think about the story, and how it happened, and tell it. Sheppard tried to speak again but couldn't. She stopped. There was silence, and Jones and Reynolds asked her what was the matter. More silence. Jones and Reynolds were getting impatient. Sheppard's chest was heaving and finally she tried again, but broke down and started ranting herself. "Whenever there are so many voices coming at me, it reminds me of all the people in foster homes telling me what to do, where I can go, what I can't do."

Then she's screaming, hysterical, beside herself; the rest of the group is silent, looks down; one girl, Sally, starts to cry. When Sheppard calms down, Reynolds doesn't apologize. She says that there's a difference between the voices Sheppard heard when she was growing up telling her what to do and the directions she and Jones are giving her. Sheppard has a choice to respond or fold. The women begin to talk about what they felt during her fit. They heard those voices too as they were growing up. And then Reynolds begins to talk about the story itself, how if she were insulted by an owner of a restaurant, she would never go back there to eat. Others began to talk about what they could afford and what they couldn't, and from there the conversation drifts to a discussion of anger: Should one hit someone when insulted, or talk back, or never go back? Is anger something you learn because of the way people treated you, or is it genetic, something inborn, bequeathed by one's parent? Is believing in nature a way of escaping responsibility?

The conversation swirled until Jones said that she would hear Sheppard the following night. And someone else came forward to perform. The following night, Sheppard's performance was just about there. She had the voices, the movements, and the sequence down. All the other topics—nature versus nurture, anger, responsibility—were all still waiting to be revisited. Jones commented about this episode:

> In the midst of the struggle to help Libah understand the difference between talking at and talking back, in the midst of that personal struggle, we got to delve into a whole other conversation. That's when it's OK to stop.
>
> This is theater for incarcerated women; we need to find a way to get them to begin the script. I look back ten years now, and as a director, I've learned how to do process, how to process somebody's tears. Libah was unable to be talked at. It's OK, let it go. Rather than people getting antsy, saying "Let's get back to the script," I know the script will happen. It's happening in my own mind already. Some people get frustrated when we talk. But the show is going to live. My job is to string it together, to keep people alive and aware in the moment.

Movement

Jones's background as a dancer and performance artist has given her an arsenal of movement exercises that she incorporates into rehearsals and productions. Certain structures have become standards in the Medea Project's repertory. They are used often as tools of transition in connecting movement in the overall rhythm of production. Jones incorporates exercises and movements she has learned from other performers, but also has adapted them for this particular population. Movement is an essential part of her own work as an artist, and she found it equally vital to get nonperformers to move. Through the practice of coordinating movement, Jones believes the women experience what it is like to be a leader and what it means to be in a community. The difficulty is, as Jones has commented, that this is a population not conditioned, physically, socially, or psychologically to work out together. How do you make them into a community? Many of the techniques grew out of the need to create a system that fostered a different way of interacting.

KICKING DANCE

In every performance of the Medea Project, the women perform what Jones calls a "Kicking Dance." In it, the women stand in line and advance upstage, swaggering, menacing. At a certain point, they all together break out fighting, kicking, arms punching, not each other, but straight ahead, as if at some invisible foe. And then together, they stop, arms to the side, stepping back, en masse, continuing to watch the audience. Forward again, they repeat the Kicking Dance. The version below is from *Reality Is Just Outside the Window*:

"Kicking Dance" (to the music "Do You Really Want Me, Baby" by Salt n' Pepa, performed by the WOMEN)
WOMAN *falls down stairs, then falls all over stage with* RHODESSA JONES *yelling encouragement, latches onto one* WOMAN *and falls to her knees. At every line a* WOMAN *approaches the* WOMAN *on floor, eventually surrounding her.*
WOMAN: I was shot. I want to kill that motherfucker.
WOMAN: I wanted to kill myself.
WOMAN: I wanted to fuck him up!
WOMAN: I wanted to stab that motherfucker.
WOMAN: I wanted to pull his dick out of his socket.
WOMAN: I wanted to get my gun.
WOMAN: I was so hurt.
WOMAN: I wanted to shoot that motherfucker.
WOMAN: I wanted to cut his throat.
WOMAN: I wanted to get him back.
One WOMAN *starts kicking crazily around the stage, other* WOMEN *follow her example, kicking wildly, stop kicking and dance suggestively in cluster which moves around stage.*
ALL: Either you're taking a hit or getting hit; taking a hit or getting hit. (*repeats*)

Jones is always quick to acknowledge artistic influences:

A large part of my education had to do with being in the world and looking at what other artists were doing. The Kicking Dance was something I had thought about because I had seen Bebe Miller, the black choreographer from New York. She choreographed a piece using Hendrix's music and inside this movement she would execute this strange, strange turn. Then, stopping, she

"Kicking Dance," from A Taste of Something Else: A Place at the Table.
Photograph by Keba Konte, 1994

would just rush the audience. The Kicking Dance grew out of that. I wanted
to rush the audience, but I also wanted to find a way for the women to act
out rage.

One day we were talking about the first time we were ever hit. Which had
grown out of Savannah's story of hitting her stepfather over his head with
a frying pan. Her mother sent her back to Juvenile Hall. So Savannah went
on to prison and wasn't in the final performance of *Reality*. But I gave Tanya
Mayo her line, which was, "I wanted to fight back." And the Kicking Dance
grew out of that. The Kicking Dance is mine. I always thought that Salt n'
Pepa song "Do You Really Want Me, Baby" was so amazing. And at the same
time I wondered, what could I juxtapose it to?

Early on, something that greatly influenced the development of the Kicking Dance happened during a performance inside the jails. We were performing inside for the men one day and the women just changed. They had this
line dance that grew out of "Soul Train," where couples come down the
middle and dance with each other. This particular dance was supposed to be
a fighting dance. But in front of this male audience, the women just got so
caught up into all this hip seductive stuff that they stopped dancing with
each other. All of a sudden the dance was in a flat line, and all the women
were competing for the attention of the men, who were screaming and yelling. The women were pushing each other out of the way, and the men were

egging them on. It wasn't what we had made. One of my notes afterwards was, "What happened y'all? That dance was *not* supposed to be 'Look at my ass, but *Kiss my ass!*'" I knew I had to make a different dance.

The Kicking Dance usually comes at some high, incredibly emotional place, where we just experienced some harrowing story and where the audience and the women on stage need a release. The dance was about rage, and so many of the stories that they told in the quiet of rehearsal were about looking for love in all the wrong places. What's going to keep that energy there when we're on stage? When we think of antiquity, we think of something ecstatic, pulsating, moving together, like the Sufis. Now I realize that is where I was going. I wanted to make a dance that dealt with rage but that internally focused it more. The captains will call "Back!" "Stop!" "Don't take your eyes off of them!" I want them to kick ass, to fight back, to find a safe way to fight back.

One of the principal choreographers of the Medea Project, Nancy Johnson, points out the extreme physicality of Jones's work:

Rhodessa's work is very physical, and not everybody who works is that physical. It's important to have people who can support that not only with artists on the outside but with women inside the jail. There's not that much opportunity to be physical inside the jail, and for the most part that population may not be particularly athletic. Although many women may have been involved with athletics at some point when they were growing up, that definitely helps, but they may not be particularly athletic or inclined to move. Or they may be afraid of doing things like forward rolls, or a handstand, or a cartwheel, all the things people need a lot of support with.

I think it's important to be in your body and to think about your body. When you're on stage, especially because the Medea Project is so huge, there are so many people there, you have to be aware of your body. You have to begin to think about where your body is, especially if you're running across the stage along with twenty other people; otherwise you crash, or you can't run, or you stand there and freak out. Even standing there and being comfortable with your body and saying your name is not always something people know how to do.

It's interesting to me doing the Kicking Dance, because every time I do it I tend to time-warp back to a time when I had a fight with a man in the street. And I seem to have that fight over again. I think that showing that side of womanhood and showing that anger and the fact that women *do* fight is really important. I've had really interesting responses from different people who have seen it over the years. I've seen a lot of women saying they didn't like it because it was scary and because they don't like violence. One woman said seeing the anger of it was upsetting for her, and it took her a week of thinking about it, and then she said, "OK, I think it's a good thing." I had some different reactions from men. One man told me he didn't like it. Really, I think it threatened something personal in him, but he said he didn't like to see black women in that light. But I think that part of that had to come with some trippy fantasy that everybody wants to see *Waiting to Exhale* and not real life. Another man was very interesting. He came up afterwards. He was from Haiti. He told me about how his father used to beat his sister up and how when he was a little boy he used to lift weights all the time because he was going to get strong so that he could protect his sister. And it really made him feel good to see women take that power for themselves. People have had really interesting responses to it. And I have fun with that. I always get worried because I think I'm going to hurt somebody because I usually just let it all out when I'm kicking.

I get a little concerned sometimes about women doing it, because I think that sometimes it takes a while for women who are doing it to take it seriously. By that, I mean to be real enough to let themselves go to that place mentally where they're fighting; it's not like they haven't been in a fight before. Again, it's one of those areas where people get goofy. People think of it as boxing. But really getting to that place of being crazy, yelling in that street, where people have been, even if it's physical or not. Couples having arguments in the street. People get really intimidated by being that real. That's one of the recurring themes. That's one of the things that the Medea Project demands: people who look at and get close to that are very scary. Whether that's appreciating your own beauty and actually saying you can caress yourself or facing your anger and saying that you can defend yourself. Or saying sometimes women do get mad enough to get out of control and to really hurt somebody.[11]

HAND DANCING

Accompanying the individual monologues and inset adaptations and songs are the group movements, like Kicking Dance and Hand Dancing, which Jones uses to get everybody to move simultaneously. She is careful to distinguish Hand Dancing from sign language; it is her own personally created set of hand movements that the women perform in tandem with prayers or other chants. She knew she had to make the movements

"Prayer," from Slouching Towards Armageddon, *shows the coordinated gestures of Jones's Hand Dancing technique. At extreme left, Sean Reynolds; second from left,* · *Angela Wilson, in short skirt; behind Wilson, Paulette Jones, with feather boa. Photograph by Stephanie A. Johnson, 1999*

simple, and thought of exercises that would remind the women of things they might have done in school. These are exercises that Jones learned and that build on cooperation, on the idea and practice of community.

Hand Dancing grew out of the time when I worked with my brother Bill, Lois Welk, and Arnie Zane when they were the American Dance Asylum in Binghamton, New York. I went there one summer and did a piece with them entitled *Couple 513*. It was a Lois Welk "spectacle." Lois influenced my ideas about what you can put on stage. Lois did parking lot dances and street parades with retarded boys. She would invite the whole community of Bing-hamton to sit outside and watch. *Couple 513* was also the first time that I had been introduced to sign language as another tool for performance.

Couple 513 was a dance piece about dance marathons. We, the performers, had to learn the rules of the dance marathons from the thirties.

As a performance teacher, when I started to tour with Idris, I kept Hand Dancing as a way to say goodbye in Europe. At the end of the class, the last thing we would do was this: "Dancing is defined as any movement of the feet with the body in a standing position. Dance officials will issue a warning if two persons are not dancing." The thing that's beautiful about it is that I would start to improvise with it, so it became a way for people to move, people who had never moved. I'd say, "Dance with it." So I refer to it as Hand Dancing rather than sign language. Because sign language practitioners' work shouldn't be misappropriated and bastardized.

And then the women in jail built the prayer: "Now I lay me down to sleep." I told them what I knew about Hand Dancing and sign language, and I said, "Let's take this simple prayer. And we're going to build our own language." We made that with the very first group.

It was a way to work with them before I knew we were going to do a performance. It was a way to get everybody together. "We're all doing this. We're all focusing." I got to see the people that were smart and they *remembered* they were smart. I think to learn movement is incredible. I nudged upon someone's memories that they were not always an inmate. One might have been a cheerleader; one might have been the leader in a play in school. But one was a leader! I would find people who were active innovators in their own young lives, and something would awaken in them, and gradually they would start to lead. I have to find ways to enter them so they will expose themselves. So I would see who I was working with. To see what I've got.

At the same time it's a self-esteem builder. "I learned it, I know how to do it. I got it." And then you say, "LaJuana. You lead today. We're going to do it and you're going to be the leader."

Someone would say, "That ain't it. You messed up."

And I would say, "Well then, *you* show us that part." And then everybody is working together. Working together. Community. Vital. Especially with women. We're taught to dislike, distrust each other. Ain't no room for it in the jail when we're all so insignificant. It's political. To find ways to see ourselves as one, as a whole.

With the Hand Dancing it *moved me*. Watching those women work to be together. Women taking other women in hand, saying, "OK, now you don't have this part." *That* is politically correct to me. It's about them being responsible for each other and doing something positive together because everything that we do affects somebody else, and in a theater company you have to be dependent upon other people. So it begins there, looking out at the world, even in jail, as a part of a community.

Sometimes I'd have Tanya help teach people how to clump. "Everybody with a piece of white go over to this group here. How low can you get to the floor?" This is a way to train them to all move together. The other aspect is to make them conscious of other people. If you can't see out in front of you, you've chosen to stand in back of someone taller than you. Or if you're taller and you're out front, then you should be in the back. I want to get people to be sensitized to space and to each other.

If a woman falls down on stage, or if she forgets her lines, I instruct the women that they've got to learn to listen, given that you might be the one near her to whisper, "It's this." And she's got to be willing to hear that. Which is what I have learned watching them on the side, because they would fight so much on stage about who was allowed to support them in performance. They simply don't have a sense of community, and I want to impress upon them the need to work as an ensemble. It's not just about getting it right, but being responsible enough to these people to *want* to get it right.

WOMEN ARE WAITING

"These Are Women Waiting" was the title Edris Cooper used for the Medea adaptation in *Reality Is Just Outside the Window*. She and Jones used the theme again in the third production, *A Taste of Something Else: A Place at the Table*. Waiting, of course, is a good deal of what occupies women in jail. Jones explores the movement of it as well:

I created an exercise called "There Are Women Waiting," and it was all about waiting. It was about jail. There are women in jail, women waiting for bail, women are waiting for mail. How do you give somebody a phrase and what does it mean? "There are women waiting." I needed to see people come up with their own experience.

I ask the women to form a straight line. There are women waiting for what? And how do you wait? Time on stage is very different from time in life. What is waiting on stage? How do you get this feeling of waiting and waiting for hours?

Many years ago, I did a workshop with a wonderful teacher, Jean Cross-man, who was a mime who had studied in Paris. Jean gave us an exercise where we had to create two characters. The exercise had to do with going from one to the other. My character was waiting on the beach for a friend. And then I had to be the friend. And the friend had come to show my character that she was going to fly away, that she had learned to fly.

When I started working with women, I thought, there are women waiting at the jail. These women are waiting. I said to them: "Let's explore waiting.

What kind of a woman are you? An old woman, a young woman, patient, straight, stoned, spaced out, fat, pregnant, skinny, young?" Then they had to tell me why they did what they did. We would *do* it. We'd move across the floor, then we'd move down towards the audience. Work four corners. "Stay in it. Make me see. Make me understand. Don't tell me, you have to *show* me." Which grew out of working with children. "Where are you going? What time is it? Is it cold? Is it hot? Don't tell me, *show* me." Which is the way to introduce nonverbal theater. I use a lot of things I did with kids, things I learned from Viola Spolin. I deal with a lot of people who have had no theater training. And these are some of the ways I make them understand what it's like to experience time on the stage, as opposed to jail, as opposed to reality.

Both Kantor and Spolin are interesting directors for Jones to cite. They both come at theater from nontraditional angles. Kantor believed in the concept of an "autonomous theater," a theater that was not mimetic in nature but which had an independent existence. Even when he postulated in "Theory of a Theatre of Real Space/Theatre Happening" that actors should perform activities imposed upon them by a particular space, the "real" space was always a space that could be corrected, inverted, turned inside out, an alternative to life as it is really organized. In *Theatre of Death,* Kantor wrote: "OPPOSITE those who remained on this side there stood a MAN DECEPTIVELY SIMILAR to them, yet (by some secret and ingenious 'operation') infinitely DISTANT, shockingly FOREIGN, as if DEAD, cut off by an invisible BARRIER—no less horrible and inconceivable, whose real meaning and THREAT appears to us only in DREAMS." Kantor believed acting and theater did not originate in ritual but in activities that were, in his words, "illegal" and, in contradiction to ritual, directed *against* religion, politics, social order, and institutions of coercion.[12] Kantor's theater is oppositional, and in this respect, so is Jones's Medea Project. Her women too appear in the theatrical space as illegal, as criminals, threatening because they have broken out of the space that is supposed to confine them. With the guards sitting down front and standing on the side and women wearing bracelets that identify who is a criminal, Jones cannot help but direct the audience's attention to what constitutes the boundaries of a prison and a theater. The theater too may operate as an institution of coercion, containing the women, disciplining them. The audience can hear Jones barking out during a production, "Darcell! Take out that gum!"

Jones never leaves the stage, and yet she does everything she can to ensure that the women stay there too, experiencing time through performance. She is always in charge and yet creates opportunities for the women to conduct each other. Viola Spolin, one of Jones's theatrical mentors, was herself inspired by Neva L. Boyd, who founded the Recreational Training School at Chicago's Hull-House and was a sociologist on the faculty of Northwestern University between 1927 and 1941. Spolin was trained in the use of games, storytelling, and folk dance as tools to help foster creative expression in children and adults. Working for the Works Progress Administration (WPA) Recreational Project in Chicago during the 1930s and establishing the Young Actors Company in Hollywood in 1945, Spolin is a model for Jones of a director who believes that anyone can act. Spolin also concentrated on physicalizing techniques in the service of communicating. "Show us," they both exhort.[13]

However, when Jones has the women perform the Kicking Dance, what these women "show us" is ambiguous. Watching the Kicking Dance is both thrilling or scary, depending on what one imagines one is watching: women refusing to be bullied, women capable of hurting others. Defense and offense overlap in the performance, such that it becomes impossible to know which is which or whether they can ever be distinguished. Just as Medea, in refusing to be a victim, victimizes others, so here, the women, performing the Kicking Dance, seem to say, "We will kick rather than be kicked." While it is thrilling to see the oppressed rise up against the oppressor, one wonders at what point the oppressed, in adopting the master's weapons, becomes an oppressor, nothing more than the weapon itself—whether that be anger, selfishness, or violence. What is clear, however, is that when women perform the Kicking Dance, we are watching performances that run counter to most cultural expectations. What seems to come naturally to men must be taught to women, or if, as Nancy Johnson argues, women do fight in the streets, they have to be prodded to do it on stage. The Kicking Dance, like the other movement exercises, reorganizes a self with others and against others, forcing the women to watch out for themselves and for the rest of the troupe too.

Movement becomes an oppositional metaphor for the reality of prison. The incarcerated women, all wearing orange T-shirts and orange pants, living in the panopticon round space of a pod, open on all sides to the center post where guards survey them, are trapped. There's not much space to move. They sign up with the Medea Project hoping to escape from one space to another, from the pod to a classroom and, if they make it to the production, eventually to a public stage. Jones hopes that the sorts of movement they practice will invigorate and reorganize their sense of self. The theater allows them to show off their newly disciplined selves, to kick and dance in both rage and cooperation.

Naming

Movement is one way to claim the self as body. Jones also has developed exercises that allow the women to speak their way into old and new selves. These naming exercises include First Memory, Composition, Matrilineage, and Affirmations.

FIRST MEMORY

Autobiography is the primary literary genre for the Medea Project. Jones doesn't worry too much about how true the accounts people give of their lives are. For her, the importance of telling has to do with the exercise of memory itself. What can people remember, or what do they choose to remember? If autobiographies are willful creations, not just faithful renditions of what has happened, they have as much to do with the desires of the present and future as they have to do with the past. Jones explains how the First Memory exercise works:

> The late Nicholas Cinconi, this Italian mime, an acrobat, did a piece, a public performance piece, where he would suspend himself. He'd be dropped out of a window. The first time I saw it was on Sixth Street in San Francisco around 1972 or 1973. Nicholas created this character with two heads. He placed a videographer across the street. Nicholas would find a hotel, usually an abandoned one, and he would suspend himself out the window. He embodied this character with two heads; he had made the mask and he manipulated it. One of the characters talked. And he'd drop down a microphone and he'd say to people on the street, "Give me your first memory. What do you remember first? What do you remember first? First? FIRST? FIRST?" And people would say, "What?" And some people would talk into this microphone and the guy across the street would videotape it, and later it would be put into a stage performance.
>
> First Memory is a way to introduce where we're going now. How far back can you go? What is your first memory of memory? And that, once again, comes from years ago when I started to find ways to do autobiographical the-

ater. As a teacher, I use first memory with everybody, women in particular. Also it's a great party game, a great way to break the ice with people. What's your first memory of your mother?

COMPOSITION

Some of the women are gifted storytellers, but it is not always easy to translate oral stories into written form. They may also have a difficult time making that story theirs, memorizing it, or remembering the ordering of the narrative. Both Reynolds and Jones remind the women that they don't have to stay faithful to every word written, rather they just need to remember the story they're trying to tell, and if they remember it as *theirs,* they will be able to tell it on stage. Jones describes how she helped one woman tell her story:

> Andrea brought me this long rambling piece, and I would say, "Andrea, what are you talking about?"
>
> "Well, I'm talking about how this man abused me and how I felt, why I feel strong now."
>
> "Then this is what you need to write." And I came home. I rewrote Andrea's piece.
>
> I said, "Is this what you're talking about? Now *you* take it and you rewrite this." And that's how that piece came to be.
>
> I remember when I first started to work at 850 Bryant, people were always asking, "Did you see *Oprah?*" *Everybody.* The women who did read, they read Jackie Collins. I'd say, "You know, *you* have a greater story than Jackie Collins. You write your story, you can be on *Oprah.*" I remember people saying, "Girl, you crazy!" I remember those days. And then going to San Bruno, creating the Medea Project and by the time we got to *Food Taboos,* the second production, people really started to write, I mean *really* write.
>
> While in the first year, there was some writing, some rap, there was a lot more movement. I showed the video footage we had made in jail to the local actresses on the outside, and said, "If you're interested in this, I want you to reinterpret it." The second year, the inmates grabbed that pen and paper and started to write. People in jail who had been to school whispered, "I've always wanted to write." Anita Bell had attended college but she had a boyfriend who used to abuse her on holidays and threatened her and made her feel bad about being in school, so gradually she turned into a prostitute and a drug addict. And that's real, that's not television. That happens to people.

At the same time, I loved *Food Taboos,* and it was so wonderful to me because people were just throwing stuff in, there was so much writing.

One of the Medea Project's stage managers, Hallie Iannoli, notes how Jones manages to find the strongest moment in the work and to encourage the women to develop its potential.

> In the class I took with Rhodessa [at New College of California, in San Francisco], there were some people who did not want to perform, and then there were people who thought they were artists and had big egos. One of Rhodessa's greatest abilities is to seek out people's strengths and to say, "This is what you're good at. Keep doing that." She never says, "That's too long." She doesn't say, "That's bad." Ever. You never hear her saying anything really negative. And I've noticed that in the jails. Or when she does, it's a horrible strain on her. To be able to say to an inmate, "It's not working. You cannot be in the group." I'd never heard her say that before. Usually people drop out or they find another way to make it work. So she never said, "This is bad." What she would say to the students at New College is, "Go home. What I want you to do now is go home, investigate this branch or this aspect of this particular item that you've shown us." Because she would say, "That's interesting." And she would point at a particular thing that was interesting. It's more than just positive reinforcement.[14]

Fé Bongolan, a core actress in the troupe, describes the clarity of Jones's direction and her willingness to let each performer develop her own voice:

> We each have strengths. I don't consider myself a dancer, though I do move. I consider myself an actor. *Buried Fire* was much more fun for me because I was doing Aswang, which also came about like a weekend before we opened! I knew I was going to be a half-snake goddess. I didn't know how she was going to look. Rhodessa said, "Let's come up with a pantheon of goddesses. Let us know what she's about and how she reacts to this whole festival." The festival was about: *We're not having it anymore. We're not going to take it anymore: we're not going to take all the bullshit,* the war on women. Rhodessa said, "The only direction I'm going to give you is that the goddess is war weary, she needs a drink, she's stressed out." With that in mind I said, "Do you want her to be ancient or modern?" And she said, "I want her to be ancient *and* stressed out." So we had a lot of fun with that. I went with a

full costume and then used modern urban language to describe what I was going through. Got to hand it to Rhodessa. She knows what she wants. She frames the cartoon and you just build the colors.

MATRILINEAGE

Along with techniques of movement that foster community, some naming techniques reinforce the women's connection to their own experience. Jones wants the women to claim their own past. In each production of the Medea Project, the women perform a Matrilineage, as each woman names their own children, mother, grandmothers, great-grandmothers.

Lineage/Prayer
WOMEN *fall into line across stage*
I am _____. Mother of _____. Daughter of _____. Granddaughter of _____. Great-granddaughter of _____.
ALL—(*with Hand Dancing*) Now I lay me down to sleep, I pray to God my soul to keep. If I should die before I awake, I pray to God my soul to take.[15]

Jones quotes her own mother in explaining how she developed the Matrilineage exercise:

My mother said, and still says, that when you become pregnant and that baby is growing under your heart, you *know* whose baby it is. Now, you can choose to let the man in on it. *But that is your baby.* I heard that my whole life. "This is *my* baby. I'll say you're the father if I want to, *but this is my baby.*" The Haitians say that it is the mother's lineage that is most prominent. It is matrilineage. "I am the daughter of . . . ." So those two things stuck in my mind when I structured this exercise. It is how I introduced myself to these women in jail. I wanted them to think about how they are connected to other people. You are more than a number. You are a name. This is *my* name. Then I had just read a book, *Mama Lola,* about voodoo which stresses that the mother's bloodline is most important. Matrilineage is something that you must hold on to because it comes through her.

There has been some resistance to the Matrilineage. The last thing that we did in *Reality Is Just Outside the Window* was chant: "I am the daughter of . . . ." In that production, one of the inmates, Jeannette Tims, didn't want to name her grandchildren. That was where she drew the line. She wasn't going to pull her family into this, to publicly name them because she was ashamed of herself. But then in the last show, when the family was in the audience, when her whole family is there and everybody's crying and cheering, she was ready to proudly say all this, but because she hadn't practiced in rehearsal, she mispronounced her grandchild's name. From the audience, a little voice interjects, "Grandma, that's not my name. That's not how you say my name." Jeannette was mortified.

Most people are very moved by this exercise. The work, on another level, is about the women reestablishing relationships with themselves, so how do I do that? I use everything. When I was in Florida doing a project at Lowell Prison for Women, it was how I introduced myself, and they all got it immediately. When Susan Sarandon saw the video about the Medea Project, *Open the Gate,* and she came to talk to us, she introduced herself by saying: "I am Susan, daughter of. . . ." And the audience cheered, because we all got it.

I have had people say, "I don't know who my real mother is."

And then I'd respond, "Who raised you? Who impressed upon you? Who got you to this point?"

When people don't know their grandmother, I say, "Next time your mother comes to visit, ask her. It's something else to talk about other than demanding cigarettes. Ask your mother who was your grandmother. Who was your great-grandmother." And for the women who know, they might not have uttered it for years, but to be able to say who your great-grandmother is is a powerful thing. . . .

I met one girl whose name was Bertha while in Florida. Her great-grandmother's name was Aretha. She had never thought about it until everybody responded with a resounding, "No, it *ain't.*"

She said, "Yes, it *is.* That's my great-grandmother's name."

I said, "You have a great-grandmother Aretha? What are you doing in a jail? I can imagine looking at you and imagining what your great-grandmother looks like and, honey, she's not having it. She's not happy wherever she is with what has happened with your life. Drugs, this mayhem, this chaos. You've got to get it together. Do it for Aretha."

The Matrilineage becomes another tool, another psychological exercise. It's also poetically very beautiful. Claim it all, too, I say. Claim everything. *Everything.* Let us begin with our mother's names, every scar that we have, claim it. Every act. Every misappropriate action. Every mistake you made. *Claim* it. If we can claim it, if we can put a pile of it here, we can go through it and find the jewels, the baubles. We got to get rid of the shit, but first of all you got to claim it. It also helps to get you moving on.

James Baldwin said, "If you know from whence you came, there's no limit to where you can go."

AFFIRMATIONS

In *Buried Fire* and *Slouching Towards Armageddon,* the women created Affirmations, in which they each began, "If I live and do not die, I hope _____" and then would fill in the blank. Affirmations change throughout the rehearsal period. Women experiment saying one thing and then another. Even from performance to performance women might change what they hope for or pledge. Jones recites the words to a song:

"There is a man whose greedy hand reaches out across the world / And if we slay this man, we will have peace in the land / That is, if we live and do not die." It's this political song that I heard years ago somewhere. "If I live and do not die." People are so quick to tell you, "You never know, your time could be up. You might not be here tomorrow." Well, if you do not die, what are you doing to do? Because right now, we're all standing here.

I've been working with adolescent girls now in our workshops we hold on Saturday afternoons at the Center for African and African American Art and Culture. So many of the girls I have in my group are so crippled, socially crippled. I've lived long enough that I remember when children were wide open, wholesome and innocent and now there's such a division. I look at Johanna Perez [a young actress who has been a member of the Medea Project since 1993], who is very worldly because of her experience with us. But she still is a child. Whereas I have Latrice, Kisha, and Mona, and they are so sad and so closed. And so inarticulate. At the same time, they're furious. When I rant at them, their eyes slit and their nostrils flare, and tears well up in their eyes. That's the *only* response they can give me. They've gotten better. But there's so much work to be done.

Mona has no dreams. We did Affirmations last night. Mona is almost autistic. At the same time so soft. She's learned the prayer. But all those voices saying, "You're nothing, you're nobody," have made her mute. At the same time, she was so challenged by Johanna. I said, "Johanna, you're going to have to lead them again. You're going to have to show everybody." Mona was actually trembling. Yet she was right on time. I said, "Mona, that's good. Next time you lead it." And she did it. And she slowly calmed down. She still can't speak. She's still not very good at speaking. With her Affirmation, all she said was, "If I live and do not die . . . what my sister said. Be a teacher."

Kisha said, "Have a lot of money." I said, "How you going to get the money? Nobody gives it to you. I don't care what they're doing on your corner. That's not how you get a lot of money." And then she just choked out, "I'm going to be a teacher too." But they've come a long way even so. They're still coming every Saturday afternoon.

Tanya Mayo remembers another woman:

> Chandrika [Newman-Zager], a senior in high school, . . . got up and spoke about this abusive life she had with her father, about how he would beat her and hurt her. During the Affirmation at the end of *Buried Fire,* "If I live and do not die . . ." Chandrika would say, "I would never let another man hit me again." Later on, she said to the group, "I can't say that the night my father comes. He would freak out." But even getting to that point happened because she had the safety and the process, an opportunity to tell her story, to release that, so that she could even go that far with it. So she's gone one more step, in her process, in her life.
>
> Those Affirmations were changed over and over again. Every rehearsal, people would pick different ones until they kind of came to one that felt right to them. We had ten different times during our rehearsal process to say an Affirmation. "If I live and do not die, this is what I'm going to do with my life." What do I want to do with my life? What is important to me? What do I want to say for the theater's purposes? What do I want to say for the group's purposes? What do I want to say as a woman? I started with, "I will help raise children, blah, blah, blah. I would call my mother every day. I will have an orgasm." Everyone would listen to different ones, laugh at different ones, affirm different ones, say it was really good what you said. La Raye [Lynette Lyles], one of the women who was a lot quieter, she played around and then said, "I will learn to speak my mind loudly and boldly and kiss my girlfriend in public places." When we did the show again months later at a fundraiser, she said, "I will confront the men who sexually abused me in my life." I felt that the process she went through from "speak my mind loudly and boldly" to "confront these people in my life," happened because she felt a little more safe, a little more supported.

As with the rant and First Memory, the Matrilineage goes backward in order to go forward. Jones does believe in identity politics, though identity is not necessarily something one is born into and locked down to. Who raised you is as important as the ties of flesh and blood. Though the First Memory game reinforces the importance and the limitations of autobiography as a form of knowledge, Jones isn't necessarily interested in just recalling a primary scene, foundational moment, or true record of the past, though it may be revealing what people can remember and what they cannot remember, what they choose to remember, and what memories seem to re-member them. The aim rather is twofold: to exercise women's memory—how far can they stretch back, with what clarity, with what sense of imagination—and to analyze how memory works. Memory may always be a mixture of the imaginary, the wishful, and the "real," and one may not be sure of the differences or whether the differences matter. Crucially, First Memory allows women to investigate the nature of beginnings. Do they begin with their first memory or before? How far back do they have to go in order to find a direction to their present and then move forward? First Memory may operate in certain ways like the confession of the "dirty little secrets" that Jones alludes to in her rant. Those secrets, she insists, must be acknowledged, told, made public, in order to be properly purged so that the women can move on. Naming an experience becomes the same as claiming it, experiencing it, creating it—as in the root meaning of experience, "passing through."[16] First Memory too, then, is an enabler; it offers the women an opportunity to experience what they do know and what they cannot know, what is accessible to them of their own beginnings and what is inaccessible, to wrestle with what can be changed by imagining differently and with what is irrevocable.

Jones collaborates, though she always, as Bongolan says, knows what she wants. With some of the women, Jones writes a first draft; with others, she can just give a direction, like "ancient and stressed out," and the actor will build from there. A sort of invisible line, which is always moving, marks off what is properly Jones's and what belongs to everyone else. Stories that are shared orally may be written down by others, and spoken by still another. A transfer of ownership may occur in which a story comes to belong to everyone and also at the same time to the author. Many of the stories would never be heard except that in the Medea Project everyone must, at some point, even if it doesn't make it to the stage, tell their story. Most of the incarcerated women don't feel comfortable writing or, even when they're educated and/or gifted that way, they may be reluctant to tell. But once they do commit to paper, either by writing it themselves, or dictating it, or in some combination of dictation and writing and rewriting, the stories are available for dissemination on the public stage to an audience many of whom would never come to know these stories in any other way. These inmates do not show up on *Oprah,* and their stories are tougher and scarier than what is disseminated through print, the movies, or television. To end with the Affirmation is to attest to the ongoing nature of stories and performance. No one knows—not the woman who makes the Affirmation, nor the audience who hears it—what may happen to her next.

Over time, the Medea Project has developed this particular arsenal of techniques, which Jones teaches to the women in each group. The techniques do not in themselves ensure a full-blown theatrical evening; they could be reproduced in workshop settings, a private classroom, a jail. Many of the exercises are aimed at making the women move their bodies, to work out, since most of them are not or have not done so in jail, and to force the women to move in relation to the others in the group. Choral work, clumping, blocking, hand dancing in unison—all concentrate attention communally. The First Memory, Matrilineage, Affirmation, and the ever present Rant are techniques designed to take the women inwards, to their individual histories and hopes for the future. The rehearsal period, whether it is four months or eight months, gives Jones time with the women to build up trust, community, and memory. But it's never enough time, and there are always upsets and intrusions during the course of any workshop, reducing the initial numbers of 150 or so women down to 6 or 12. The combination of the disciplinary system of the jails and the psychological stresses of the women can easily resist the counter techniques of body and soul that Jones teaches. Even if some of the issues Jones addresses—addiction, recidivism, racism, recovery, the criminalization connected to poverty—are highlighted more in one play than another, all are connected to each other, and the tools for talking and moving through these issues are the same. The process, no matter the particular subject and myth, does not change very much. The rants about responsibility and consciousness and discipline are recognizable from year to year. The therapeutic terminology and particular dramatic techniques may be contemporary, but Jones believes that the politics of womanhood has not changed significantly from the time of classical Medea to the modern.

The use of myths, a consistent feminist analysis, and reproducible dramatic techniques may be at odds with a modern aesthetic that privileges originality. Funders from the social work arena know that much of social work is repetitious. They may only be looking for an inspirational leader and hope for the best. But the art world wants to find an original voice.

Some newspaper reviewers of the Medea Project stop coming to shows because to them they seem "all the same." How different is *Reality Is Just Outside the Window* from *Food Taboos,* if Kicking Dance and First Memory occur in both? If the myths don't seem to differentiate the productions for someone in the audience or in the cast, as they did not for Scaggs, are the individual women's stories different enough to generate a sense of an original in the audience? For the women who have participated in the rehearsals, and those who have performed in more than one production, each production registers differently. Each group of women feels different. Some are older, some younger, some wiser, some more "fried." And each woman's personal trajectory will also intersect with the production at a different point. But again, none of that may register for a stranger, a reviewer, a critic. Indeed, what personal changes occur may not appear in either the rehearsals or the final production. Members of the audience will probably not know that someone's Affirmation has changed over the course of the rehearsal, or, unless they come to more than one show, they will not see that an Affirmation can change from night to night. And even if one does see an entire rehearsal period through production, how does one judge the changing Affirmation? The pedagogical effects cannot be assessed entirely within the run of the performance, which is really only just a rehearsal for life.

Acting Real

It's great to go into the wilderness of gender—what is female? A lot of incarcerated women don't have any other identity than their vagina; they don't know how to use it, how not to use it, who to let taste it.
—Rhodessa Jones, quoted in Borris, "Curtain Calls"

Food Taboos was the production that started with the body, exploring desires that the body became addicted to, what women put into the body, what was good for it and what wasn't. When Jones told her brother Bill T. Jones that she was working with the myth of Persephone and Demeter (what did Persephone eat that she couldn't help but eat), he suggested she also read Dante's *Inferno*. Inspired, she decided that in *Food Taboos,* she would dramatize the living hell that many of the women knew well by re-creating scenes of prostitution. In one uncomfortable segment, "Animal Tricks," she had a drag queen and pimps command women to turn over and spread their legs:

VOICE: Now fellas, if you want a little head this evening, let me hear you scream. *(Women turn over and spread legs.)* Uh huh. That's what I'm looking for this evening. Let me hear you: we want some pussy!

WOMEN: We want some pussy. *(gyrate hips)*

JEALOUSY: We want some pussy!

WOMEN: We want some pussy. *(gyrate hips)*

JEALOUSY: We want some pussy!

WOMEN: We want some pussy. *(gyrate hips)*

JEALOUSY: We want some pussy!

Pimps applaud each other, women writhe on stage.

PIMP II: *(sings)* You are here. So am I.

Maybe millions of people go by.

But I only have eyes for you.

VOICE: Come on girls. Let's get this over with. You know how it goes. I want to see more pink. More pink! *(Women have legs spread wide. Two pimps pick up woman from floor and place her in spotlight.)*

Jones realized, however, that "some of the women at first didn't want to admit to the "ho" thing."

I said to them, "We've all agreed when we started to build *Food Taboos* and I talked about the land of the dead, y'all told me you could relate to the land of the dead definitely in the life down in the Tenderloin. Part of it is the Ho Stroll. Let's revisit it, let's create it again. Let's do it with music and lights this time."

I'd gone to Chicago to perform *Big Butt Girls* and saw *West Side Story* then. I was inspired. I wanted to create my own musical fantasy of the "Ho Stroll." I wanted dry ice. I wanted the women to look nine feet tall. I wanted a really big dance number, but that didn't happen. What I discovered is that, first of all, my idea of whores came from TV. The women didn't work the streets in high heels, they didn't know how to *walk* in high heels. They swaggered, they were out there in coats, loping up and down. They emulate men out there; they just didn't *do* the TV sexy thing. What is a real whore? It's just about the money. It's not about acting sexy. One thing I've discovered is that theater for the twenty-first century should explode our ideas of what the subterranean culture looks like.

I brought in Jealousy, this drag queen, because I'd just seen *Paris Is Burning*, and I thought, "What better person to teach these women how to walk in high heels than a drag queen." Jealousy was happy to help out. At first the women didn't accept him as a teacher. But he persisted, and he was fun and so real. He lived in the Tenderloin too. So you saw them having a nice exchange with someone they wouldn't necessarily meet. It was another kind of life lesson for them.

We had them rehearse the number, but for the performance, Sean and I decided not to let the inmates perform the explicit choreography. We had reservations; we didn't think they were ready; we were afraid of what it might trigger in the women, and we didn't want the guards to be put in a position to censor us. Instead Edris Cooper led the number. Everybody's singing, and the women who play the whores are very suggestive, scary, lascivious, and provocative. It freaked a lot of people out. I was accused again: "All the Medea Project does is talk about sex." *You're damn right.* We better explode and explore the sexual lives of women because it ain't all it's cracked up to be.

This is a representative anecdote of the difficulties at the core scene of instruction that runs throughout the project, from rehearsal through performance: confusion over what is "real," what is critique, and what is exploitation when the subject Jones comes back to is women and sex. The notion of "real" is undercut in a straightforward postmodern way, deconstructing the commonsense belief that biological sex equals identity; the man who played women knew how to be more "real" than women. He could walk in high heels, but then we find out that these women, unlike those on television, did *not* wear high heels. Jones's own idea of what a "real" whore looks like, she realized, came from television and *West Side Story.* Jealousy was also performing the television version of women, *not* what *these* real women did on the streets. The women's resistance to playing a whore had to do not only with their resistance to confessing but also reflected the fact that they didn't know *how* to play the whore as Jones first required, because that's not how they played the part on the street.

Jones had to grapple with how the audience might interpret the "Ho Stroll" and also with what feelings the women might arouse in themselves from doing the stroll. Images of lasciviousness may provoke wildly different reactions, from titillation to disgust. Reproducing the walk, either the imaginary one of television or the real one of the streets of Oakland, may not necessarily explode the way women work the business of sex. That the confusion is intensified when the focus is on the prostitute is not surprising. Both the woman who sells her body in order to survive (another possible version of the Medea legend) and the actress who flaunts her sexuality on stage make it difficult to distinguish between the real and

"*Ho Stroll,*" *from* Food Taboos in the Land of the Dead.
Photograph by Keba Konte, 1993

the performed. The whore, as Rebecca Schneider points out, has been of interest to modernists because she exposes the central mystification of capitalism, the cover-up of labor and the randomness of value. In the prostitute's case, she has not been erased as the worker who makes the product to be sold but is quite visible, marketing herself as both labor (worker) and value.

Schneider describes the prostitute as a "mistake, an aberration, a hoax: a show and a sham made of lipstick, mascara, fake beauty marks," but notes that she is also "somehow woman untamed, woman unsocialized, woman unclassed, woman uncultured, woman, that is, 'natural.'" [17] This made-up whore that Schneider describes may be just that: a made-up fiction. The Medea Project actresses taught Jones that there is no such position as the "natural." Rather, these women, doing the work of prostitution, walk like hard-core men gangsters; it is popular culture that makes them up with false mascara. And it is popular culture that also has them walking like male gangsters. The Medea Project has the women inhabit both positions: Jones directs a show—her troupe is made up and decked out with heightened effects, playing whores to music and flashing lights—and yet they are also exhorted to be real, natural, though surely this last category is always in quotation marks.

The women themselves resisted playing the part of the whore in rehearsals, in part because showing the reality of their lives, even to Jones in the relatively private space of the workshop, was too painful. But just as the grandmother at first refused to rehearse saying her grandchildren's names in the Matrilineage because she was too ashamed to have her grandchildren hear her speak their names and then later decided she wanted to after all, so here, the women at first seemed ashamed to represent themselves as whores but later came to embrace the exercise. One could argue with Jones that their initial refusal was more than just a shamed resistance to exposing the truth of their experience and was instead resistance to being once again framed by their bodies, selling their charms.

That Jones made the "Ho Stroll" a focus in this descent into hell guaranteed a dispute about what the subject of women on display means. On the one hand, the Medea Project has been called a male-bashing enterprise, full of lesbians who hate men. On the other hand, it has been criticized as pandering to men, creating sexy displays like the "Ho Stroll" to play exactly to that audience. Jones herself has seen it happen over and over again: women perform differently for men than they do for women. They talk differently. They act differently. That is why she prefers to work only with women. By enforcing sex segregation, jail allows some space to rehearse the performances that take place in a culture in which men lay down the lines and women dance between them. Different audiences have different expectations, and the women know this and may be reasonably cautious. At different moments, for different audiences, different women might take pleasure in acting desirable, creating desire, while others might feel degraded in reenacting the ways their bodies may be bought and sold.

It is impossible to know what is going on in all the women's heads from rehearsal through production, from minute to minute, from evening to evening, much less to expect that the audience will read the depiction of women's sexuality in one way or even agree about what is real and what performed. There aren't live sex acts performed during the "Ho Stroll"; nevertheless, it may be difficult to distinguish between the pleasures and degradation of prostitution on the street and in this reenactment. The special dramatic effects—the repetitions, the exaggerations, the jazzy sounds, the hard-knock rap—can be read in at least two different ways: they can be alienation effects, making the audience read the "Ho Stroll" as a kind of parody and critique of the real thing; or they can be seen as heightening the pleasure of the stroll for the paying audience. Some may listen to the words in the rap, others may just stare at the image of a line of women spreading their legs. The women do not completely escape the normative, even imprisoning, ways of being seen.

Sexual display is not the problem; the problem is the question of how the sexual display is interpreted—as Schneider puts it, "[t]he agency of the body displayed, the author-ity of the agent."[18] Jones insists on featuring the women's work, which in large part has been the work of sex, the business of selling women's bodies. And thus she opens the project to the obvious criticism that the Medea Project is *only* about sex, meaning the display of sexuality, that is, giving (a certain part of) the audience a sex show and thus reinforcing, rather than critiquing, the ways women are seen. Jones believes that people mistake her critique of the ways women are represented (sexually) with a celebration of it. Of course, some people do make that mistake; it would be impossible to expect that some people wouldn't, given the cultural framework in which we are operating. No matter how many signs of parody or exaggeration or how many demeaning words are thrown about, if women open up their legs, someone is bound to be turned on. The eye of every beholder is not disciplined. And this finally is what makes the Medea Project wild, on the edge, not entirely didactic, and never the same.

In taking on the subject of women's bodies—their physical representation, the work they do—the Medea Project puts on center stage for the audience (and for the women) the different ways we engage and pay for desire. The women are working their bodies and memories privately in rehearsal and then performing them publicly on stage. None of us, we come to realize, knows the fullness of the entire process from rehearsal through performance and beyond—not Rhodessa Jones, not any of the women. Watching the women perform in public, witnessing the extraordinary courage it must take to perform painful stories or to kick dance in a chorus, I do not find they look like victims. Even when they do play one stereotyped victim, the prostitute, I find that the point is obvious, which is to make us think critically about our preconceptions of what constitutes reality.

Jones's genius is expressed in the way she is both "a theorist who remains 'on the ground' and a passionate activist who gets us 'off the ground,'" terms Cornel West has used to describe Paulo Freire, in the way she has developed a process of embodied artistic community.[19] The pedagogical process is centered around conversation and critical thinking, the sharing of information, of what is real, what seems real, and what are the myths we live by. Those who become visible remind us that there are so many we do not see; when the women are told to "Be real," we wonder whose reality they are inhabiting. The public productions are really only a rehearsal, a practice, opportunities to play around with rigid and oppressive notions of reality. The trajectory of this project refuses any of us a passing grade. Our education should just be beginning. If the project is successful, we leave the public performance needing to know more about the particular people and about the kinds of institutions and institutionalization that construct our reality.

CHAPTER 3

Prison Discourse

Surveying Lives

This might sound crass. But to me, the Medea Project would be worth it if nothing else happened but the effect on people out there, even if it didn't do anything for the prisoners. Because the hysteria in this country and the need to want to pretend that our criminal justice system is doing something to improve the quality of our life—it's a joke. People in the business know that they're really not doing anything except temporarily separating a finite group of people, with no impact whatsoever on crime, not to mention poverty or anything else. And when we have a performance like Rhodessa's, it exposes that. Jail really isn't the solution. Not only that, it exposes the universality that these are people struggling. They might be black, they might be poor, they might have ended up using drugs or become hookers, but the issues they're struggling with are the issues that everybody struggles with. They were unable— because of themselves, their families, and society—to overcome them. It just redefines the issues of crime and justice and incarceration for that moment while people are seeing it. There's nobody running for office, there's nobody in this business speaking to the public in slow, sober ways, saying, "Hey. This is much more complicated than we've led you to believe. And it's going to be very expensive. And it's not going to happen with the criminal justice system. We're going to have to start way before that."

—Michael Marcum, Assistant Sheriff, San Francisco

After each performance of the Medea Project, the incarcerated women return to jail, but jail, we are told by a jailer, is not a solution.[1] But what is
the problem? Is it personal? (What is *her* problem?) Is it structural? (What
is *the* problem?) Is *she* the problem? Is *jail* the problem? Are they both
problems, and are they both responsible for a solution? The discourse of
problem and solution permeates discussions of prison, and obviously, the

ways in which the problems are characterized determine the kinds of solutions offered. If the problem is an increasing crime rate and the public's fear of crime, then jail might be a sensible solution; if the problem is the acts of violence done to innocent victims, retribution might be in order; if the problem is poverty, injustice, racism, modernism, liberalism, and/or global capitalism, the solutions might have to be found outside jail walls; if the problem is moral laxity, degenerate hearts, cultural bankruptcy, and a breakdown of community structures, we might be in real trouble.

In this chapter on the Medea Project and incarceration, I do not presume to propose solutions or even to identify the problem, but rather, as a confessed nonprofessional, a non–prison expert, I attempt to survey the ways in which the present discussions of prison are framed. I am aware of Rhodessa Jones's admonition to the incarcerated women: "Be real. This is not *The Wiz*." I don't offer a way out.[2] I aim only to interrupt and create some space for reflection, though even in this I am aware that my act of surveying is itself part of the technique and discipline of the modern world. A survey is necessarily selective, overlooking other data, ignoring alternative ways of organizing material. As Michel Foucault points out,

> Our society is one not of spectacle, but of surveillance; under the surface of images, one invests bodies in depth; behind the great abstraction of exchange, there continues the meticulous, concrete training of useful forces; the circuits of communication are the supports of an accumulation and a centralization of knowledge; the play of signs defines the anchorages of power; it is not that the beautiful totality of the individual is amputated, repressed, altered by our social order, it is rather that the individual is carefully fabricated in it, according to a whole technique of forces and bodies. We are much less Greeks than we believe. We are neither in the amphitheatre, nor on the stage, but in the panoptic machine, invested by its effects of power, which we bring to ourselves since we are part of its mechanism.[3]

As I chart the prison terrain, I take part in that panopticon gaze that Foucault describes, which means to centralize knowledge and power, but I recognize I cannot possibly see everywhere—into the hearts and minds of people, into prison cells, into the streets, and into private homes. No matter the rhetorical gesture of confidence and objectivity, a survey—whether through the prism of theory, statistics, autobiography, or politics—confines and obscures as much as it illuminates.

In the past few years, the prison has become a contested space, not only within the walls, where fights and riots occur, but outside too, where some people see them as the solution (and thus advocate building more) while others see them as the problem (as places that breed more crime). Prisons used to be a place for people to be rendered invisible, but the money we now spend to make people invisible, the political usefulness of hard-line positions on crime, and the big business of managing crime perversely have made criminals more visible or at least more of a problem to be discussed. The various professionals who have taken on the management and interpretation of prison—the criminologists, sociologists, social workers, lawyers, cultural activists, business people, police, sheriffs, guards, and politicians—as well as the artists and teachers who work in the prison and the incarcerated people themselves have drawn on and created an abundance of metaphors to describe the purpose of prison: rehabilitation, reform, punishment, a vacation; warehousing the deviant, the gangster, the delinquent, the victim, the victimizer; managing the rabble through the revolving door of recidivism; refusing or making a place at the table. All of this talk has made the invisible prisoner become visible, if only for a moment, as a statistic or part of a crime story in a newspaper, surveyed in the service of some particular cultural agenda.

There is no doubt that the prison may be one of the most revealing sites for describing our national desires and fears. Just as it is impossible to understand the national passion for equality without reflecting on the United States' long-term legitimation of slavery, so the pursuit of liberty may not be fully appreciated without an understanding of the usefulness of the American prison in maintaining an American collective notion of itself as a land of the free. Alexis de Tocqueville came to America initially not to write a comprehensive guide to democracy in America but quite specifically to investigate its prison system; he recognized the originality of the New World's penal institution. It is unimaginable to think of the United States as a place that does not guarantee liberty as a right, and it is also unimaginable to think of it as a nation without prisons.

Since 1992, when the Medea Project began, statistics regarding incarceration have skyrocketed upward, and narratives chronicling the history, justification, theory, and funding of prisons in the United States have proliferated. The statistics are astonishing. Everyone who has written about prisons in the last twenty years of the twentieth century quotes statistics first precisely because they are so mind-boggling (see Figure 1). Though contested as to meaning and even, in some cases, as to reliability, the fact that the United States imprisons more people than any other country in

FIGURE I. *Selected Statistics on Women and Crime*

· Incarceration rates per 100,000 in 1992 (prisons and jails combined):

Holland	36
Sweden	61
England/Wales	98
Canada	109
South Africa	332
United States	445

—Morris, "The Contemporary Prison," 237

· From 1970 to 1980 the population of the prisons of the United States doubled; from 1981 to 1995 it more than doubled again.
—Morris, "The Contemporary Prison," 236

· California has the third-largest penal system in the world, following China and the United States as a whole: 125,842 prisoners at last official count.
—M. Davis, "Prison-Industrial Complex" (1995), 229

· California prisons house the largest number of incarcerated women in the United States: "From 1970 to 1990, the number of women felons [in California] increased from 588 to 5,858 (an increase of 896 percent). For the same time period the number of men felons increased from 20,460 to 88,264 (an increase of 331 percent). The most frequently cited offenses committed by women felons in California were drug law violations. In calendar year 1990, 38.4 percent of all women felons were incarcerated due to drug offenses. 34 percent of the women were incarcerated due to property offenses, 24.3 percent incarcerated due to violent crimes, and 3.4 percent incarcerated due to other offenses."
—Come into the Sun Coalition (Delinquency Prevention Commission), "Come into the Sun: Findings and Recommendations on the Needs of Women and Girls in the Justice System," 28

· In the United States, the rate of growth for female inmates has exceeded that for male inmates each year since 1981.
—Singer, Bussey, Song, and Lunghofer, "The Psychosocial Issues of Women Serving Time" (1995), 103

· At the end of 1994, almost 95,000 women were incarcerated in state prisons and federal institutions and jails nationwide.
—Barry, "Women Prisoners and Health Care: Locked Up and Locked Out," 250

FIGURE I. *Continued*

• African American women are eight times more likely than white women to go to prison.

— Kurshan, "Behind the Walls: The History and Current Reality of Women's Imprisonment" (1996), 151

• Although black women are only 7 percent of California's population, they are 34 percent of women who are convicted and incarcerated. Of those,

    34.1 percent are African American

    22.7 percent are Hispanic

    36.7 percent are Caucasian

    6.4 percent are other races.

— Legal Services for Prisoners with Children, "Statistics on Women and Girls in State Prison and Juvenile Facilities," February 1996

the world is disputed by no one.[4] Writing in 1998, Eric Schlosser reported that the American inmate population was perhaps half a million more than Communist China—"imagine the combined populations of Atlanta, St. Louis, Pittsburgh, Des Moines, and Miami behind bars"—and noted that California has the biggest prison system in the Western industrialized world, holding more inmates than France, Great Britain, Germany, Japan, Singapore, and the Netherlands combined.[5]

The stratospheric rise in the numbers of Americans who intersect at some point with the penal system—short of incarceration, including incarceration, and beyond—has happened very recently. For the first seventy-five years of the twentieth century the incarceration rate in the United States remained fairly stable, at about 110 prison inmates for every 100,000 people. In the mid-1970s, the rate began to climb, doubling in the 1980s and then again in the 1990s. The rate is now 445 per 100,000. During the last two decades of the century about a thousand new prisons and jails were built in the United States, and the inmate population was increasing by 50,000 to 80,000 people a year. At the turn of the century, 1.8 million people in the United States were behind bars (about 100,000 in federal custody, 1.1 million in state custody, and 600,000 in local jails).[6] In addition, there were approximately 600,000 on parole, 3 million on probation, 60,000 in juvenile institutions. Altogether, about 5.1 million people are now incarcerated, on parole, or on probation.[7]

The statistics for African American males in the penal system and for women are equally noteworthy. One out of every fourteen black men is now in prison or in jail. The numbers projected are that one out of every four black men is likely to be imprisoned at some point in his life.[8] Blacks make up 12 percent of the population of the United States but 50 percent of the population in prisons and jails. In the District of Columbia in 1997, almost 50 percent of black men between the ages of eighteen and thirty-five were under criminal justice supervision. There are more young black men under correctional supervision than are enrolled in college, and it costs more to imprison a person than to send him or her to Harvard.[9]

The number of women sentenced to a year or more of prison has grown *twelve times* since 1970.[10] Three out of every four female prisoners are mothers. On any given day approximately 125,000 American children under the age of eighteen have mothers in prison.[11] Two-thirds of women in prison are members of minority groups.[12] From 1930 to 1950, five women's prisons were built in the United States; during the 1980s, thirty-four were built.[13] Though women are still a relatively small proportion of the overall United States prison population (roughly 7.4 percent in 1996),[14] they are also the fastest growing subset. At the end of 1994, almost 95,000 women were incarcerated in state prisons and federal institutions and jails nationwide.[15] In California, 76 percent of women inmates were incarcerated for nonviolent crimes (37.8 percent for drug possession and 34.1 percent for burglary, petty theft, and property crimes; of the 24 percent serving time for violent charges, 10 percent were in defense of battering).[16]

The statistics are so striking in part because they are such a recent phenomenon. The role of the prison has changed from the early model that de Tocqueville toured, in which prisoners (mostly men) were incarcerated as punishment and retrained to become workers in a capitalistic system, to prisons today, which house, still, mostly male prisoners who are no longer being trained or educated for life after prison but rather in many states face "three strikes and you're out" laws, laws that promise precisely that: to lock them up for the rest of their lives if convicted of three felonies. Incarcerated women have always been treated differently from men. During the nineteenth century in Britain, while male prison reform "emphasized uniform treatment, formal direction, and rigid adherence to rules," women were to be treated "with gentleness and sympathy so that they would submit cheerfully to the rules and cooperate willingly in their own reform." In this approach, "men were rewarded for diligence and productivity, but significantly, women earned their marks for good conduct, honesty, propriety, and 'moral improvement.'" Increasingly, women in the United States in the late part of the nineteenth century were sentenced to reformatories for longer periods of time for treatment, because they were believed to need counseling rather than rules to restore them to their "natural" and best selves.[17] Because at present many corporations have moved operations from the United States to countries in which they can spend far less on wages, there's no longer the incentive to retrain incarcerated men (or free ones either) to become industrial workers. Clearly, with the greatest increase of new prisoners being women in the past twenty years in the United States, the view of women as different from men and needing to be reformed differently has changed as well. For incarcerated men or women, reform rarely seems to be the emphasis any longer, perhaps because of these quite specific historical and cultural changes.[18]

The statistics of the racial breakdown in United States prisons also has changed over the last 150 years. As Angela Davis points out, the dominant models of imprisonment developed at the beginning of the nineteenth century were "based on a construction of the individual that did not apply to people excluded from citizenship by virtue of their race and thus from a recognition of their communities as composed of individuals possessing rights and liberties." "These prisons," she explains, "were thus largely designed to punish and reform white wage-earning individuals. . . . [W]omen's prisons reveal a quite different penal function: that of restoring white women to their place as wives and mothers, rather than as rights-bearing public individuals."[19] African American slaves were disciplined and punished by masters, not by prison; they did not need to be rehabilitated as wage earners. Following the abolition of slavery, a series of laws were designed to ensure that blacks would continue to be an ongoing workforce; for instance, vagrants—defined as "anyone who was guilty of theft, had run away, was drunk, was wanton in conduct or speech, had neglected job or family, handled money carelessly, and . . . all other idle and disorderly persons"—could be imprisoned. But more often, ex-slaves worked out their penal sentences through convict leasing.[20]

From the mid-nineteenth century to the present, the population of incarcerated people has remained the same in certain ways: inmates are still poor, and many have been imprisoned because of drug-related crimes. What has changed is the preponderance of people of color and the increasing numbers of black women. According to Karl Rassmussen, executive director of the Women's Prison Association of New York, "150 years ago it was poor whites, their names often Irish—and alcohol abuse. Today, it's poor minorities and drug abuse."[21] Statistics may thus yield a representative profile. If the small proportion of off-the-chart psychopaths and otherwise mentally ill are ruled out, most of the people in prison are poor and uneducated, and the populations are racially skewed. In the United States as a whole, the differential rate of imprisonment of African Americans to Caucasians, proportional to population, is in excess of 7.5 to 1. The poverty most incarcerated people come from would seem to allow us to make an obvious connection: the well-off don't need to break the law; or they do so quietly, without risk of jail time; or, with money and influence and connections, they are able to escape the penalty of the law.

Statistics also suggest that in the United States a sizable majority of men and women in prison are *not* there because they committed a violent crime. As Schlosser reports, "About two thirds of the people sent to prison in California last year (1997) were parole violators. Of the roughly 80,000 parole violators returned to prison, about 60,000 had committed a technical violation, such as failing a drug test; about 15,000 had committed a property or a drug crime; and about 3,000 had committed a violent crime, frequently a robbery to buy drugs."[22] Steven Donziger notes that one in ten arrests in the United States is for a violent crime. Only three in 100 arrests in the United States are for a violent crime resulting in injury. However, he also states the obvious: that violent crime is a major problem in many inner cities. During the 1980s, teenage boys in all racial and ethnic groups became "more likely to die from a bullet than from all natural causes combined." Though the incarceration rate is far higher in the United States than other industrialized countries, our overall crime rate is not, *except* in two categories—homicide and attempted burglary.[23] The federal Centers for Disease Control reports that domestic violence is more likely to cause women to end up in hospitals than are all muggings, car accidents, and rapes *combined*.[24] That is, certain sorts of violence (domestic violence and drug-related violence in inner cities) are statistically very high, historically and relative to other countries. But what we seem to have done is respond to the *fear* of violent crime by incarcerating a majority of people who have not committed violent crimes. And we have not been effective at stopping domestic violence through incarceration or any other means. While other Western industrialized countries have very strong gun control laws and do not incarcerate as many people for nonviolent crimes, the United States has chosen instead to veto strong gun control laws and, no matter the severity or nonviolent nature of the crime, to incarcerate increasingly large numbers of people.

The rebel/criminal has always been an object of fascination in modern times—from Moll Flanders to Jack the Ripper to Mack the Knife to ghetto gangsters—but alongside fascination, and even glorification, is a heightened fear of the criminal and a political manipulation of that fear.[25] No day goes by without news media filling our ears with rhetoric and statistics about crime, victims, victim's rights, lawlessness, gangs, drugs. Local and national elections have been fought and won by manipulating people's fear of crime, from Governor Rockefeller in the 70s through President Bush's use of the rape and murder committed by Willie Horton while on weekend furlough. Demonization of the criminal seems sometimes to be the only appropriate response for some of the horrific crimes committed. But the statistics also show that the demons (and the rebels), although they may be culturally very significant as reflections of cultural attitudes, are very small in number.

Although no amount of explanation seems to match the pathology of a Jeffrey Dahmer who killed and ate his victims, for the run-of-the-mill, representative nonviolent criminal, biography, history, and economics all may give some clues. Jerome Miller believes that much of the research coming out of U.S. Justice Department grants in the past twenty years has focused on statistical evidence to support more efficient techniques of managing crime and has ignored narrative, biography, and critical thinking. This focus on how to better "identify and catch the criminal, widen police authority, improve prosecutorial efficiency, develop more intrusive and lethal anticrime armamentaria, justify harsher sanctions, and build and manage more jails, prisons, and camps," he concludes, "was not simply a matter of political partisanship." Instead, he argues, "one came away with the impression that should we enter a more progressive political era, these positivists would just as eagerly provide the prerequisite statistical validation for whomever their new funders might be."[26] The preferred method for management is statistics, since biography is too messy and impossible to quantify. The statistics, however, as Miller points out, could support the construction of very different kinds of management: prisons for "tough on crime" politicians or, alternatively, halfway houses and treatment programs for some progressive politician who has yet to be elected.

I myself find most persuasive the argument that prisons, while necessary for locking up the most violent, pathological persons, are not the solution for the vast numbers of people we now relegate there and that a whole range of alternative programs—including gun control, treatment programs, and community payback—might be far more effective and far less expensive than incarceration. However, this is a minority position and has not been implemented as solution. At least three broad explanations account for the current particular formulation of crime as personal problem and incarceration as solution: (1) prisons are a profitable business; (2) they reflect a racist culture; and (3) they create and reinforce modern ways of organizing life. All three explanations are mutually compatible and together provide formidable incentives for continuing what may seem to some like an irrational social choice.

That prisons have become profitable is easily documented. Many prisons are now built and managed by private companies. Since communism is no longer a threat, the argument goes, business has moved from sponsoring a military-industrial complex to a prison-industrial one. Private businesses that have moved aggressively into the prison world, building and sometimes managing them, need to maintain their profitability by making sure there is a constant (if not increasing) supply of prisoners to fill their prisons.[27] Others believe that racism explains the disparity of incarcerated peoples and "legitimates" the construction of more prisons. Angela Davis points out that some form of incarceration has been used by the U.S. government against every major minority group in this country: slavery for African Americans, the reservation system for Native Americans, the internment camps for Japanese Americans in World War II.[28] Along with Davis, David Cole, Jerome Miller, and Katheryn Russell all argue that the disparity in numbers between races (and class) prove that the criminal justice system is racist and classist. (If it were projected that one out of every four middle-class white men would end up in jail during their lifetime, would the arguments for building more prisons be as fervent?) Moreover, the disparity in sentences, especially relating to the death penalty and the different penalties now attending cocaine or crack convictions, disproportionally punish blacks and, even more specifically, black women.[29]

Still others emphasize, as did Foucault, that the modern prison's main purpose has never been rehabilitation, or even punishment, but rather the exercise of discipline, in this case, management of the undisciplined. What Michael Marcum refers to as "the business" of incarceration may not only *not* be the solution; it may create, sustain, or exacerbate the problem. The most persuasive part of Foucault's argument occurs just here. Prisons have never seemed to cure delinquency, and, in fact, people have recognized this failure from the very beginning. While advocates of prisons claim that prisons simply have not been rigorous enough in employing techniques of punishment, Foucault argues that prisons have never *curtailed* criminality, but they have quite successfully *produced* delinquency:

— prisons do not diminish the crime rate, rather, it remains stable or, worse, increases;
— prisons cannot fail to produce delinquents by the very type of existence that they impose: useless work, no employment;
— prisons encourage the organization of a milieu of delinquents, loyal to one another;
— families of prisoners often become destitute (generating more opportunity for delinquency to thrive) [30]

The real production of prisons, Foucault writes, is the distinguishing of delinquents from other citizens, tracking, containing, and distributing delinquents between a prison and the streets and back again: "punishment in general, is not intended to eliminate offences, but rather to distinguish them, to distribute them, to use them." [31]

In *Discipline and Punish: The Birth of the Prison,* Foucault's larger project has less to do with investigating the individual site of prisons (much less individuals inside prison) than with critiquing the ways in which "mechanisms of normalization" have infiltrated all arenas of modern life. He writes at length about the many forms of professionalization that attend the birth and development of the prison, the different sorts of professionals necessary to scrutinize and watch over the prisoner. From the older forms of punishment, which were always conducted in public—the criminal beheaded, hanged and quartered, put in stocks, guillotined in a market square—to the modern forms, conducted in private—the criminal sequestered from society—the features of the modern world become apparent. Modern culture is marked less by appetite for spectacle, Foucault believes, than by the belief and desire for surveillance and interrogation. Prison is a symptomatic modern institution precisely because it employs all the techniques that we, who are not officially imprisoned, are also subjected to: we all have files compiled on us—by schools, by doctors, by the government. We are all being judged in relation to the "norm," which we never quite meet: "The judges of normality are present everywhere. We are in the society of the teacher-judge, the doctor-judge, the educator-judge, the 'social worker' judge; it is on them that the universal reign of the normative is based; and each individual, wherever he may find himself, subjects to it his body, his gestures, his behaviour, his aptitudes, his achievements."[32] We learn to analyze ourselves, to question our motives, to confess, and thus to discipline ourselves. The prison simply concentrates disciplinary techniques and becomes, in Foucault's words, "a coercive theater in which [the prisoner's] life will be examined from top to bottom." He explains the broader significance of this role:

> The legal punishment bears upon an act; the punitive technique on a life; it falls to this punitive technique, therefore, to reconstitute all the sordid detail of a life in the form of knowledge, to fill in the gaps of that knowledge and to act upon it by a practice of compulsion. *It is a biographical knowledge and a technique for correcting individual lives.* . . . Behind the offender, to whom the investigation of the facts may attribute responsibility for an offence, stands the delinquent whose slow formation is shown in a biographical investigation. The introduction of the "biographical" is important in the history of penality. Because it establishes the "criminal" as existing before the crime and even outside it. And, for this reason, a psychological causality, duplicating the juridical attribution of responsibility, confuses its effects. At this point one enters the "criminological" labyrinth from which we have certainly not yet emerged: any determining cause, because it reduces responsibility, marks the author of the offence with a criminality all the more formidable and demands penitentiary measures that are all the more strict.[33]

Obviously, we still operate in this "criminological labyrinth," a matrix of beliefs supported by techniques of various disciplines. Even when the beliefs are different, the techniques bolstering their credibility remain the same. Statistical techniques, as Miller has argued, can be used to justify very different projects, reflecting very different beliefs. The social workers, sheriff, guards, halfway house directors, and artists at work in prison whom I have interviewed and who speak in this chapter do not stand outside the coercive technique of examination. In fact, they all can be said to conform to Foucault's definition of workers in the coercive theater that is the modern world. Like psychiatrists, judges, and teachers, all of the people at work in the Medea Project attempt to reconstitute lives through forms of their disciplinary knowledge. They ask the incarcerated and formerly incarcerated women to discipline themselves in different ways, to reconstitute themselves as something other than incarcerated, to stop coming back to jail. But none of them believe that jail by itself will achieve this end. Most believe in the power of biography and eschew statistics. Whether they also advocate "normalization" is not entirely clear. Foucault argues that the means Jones uses (observation, self-examination) are still techniques of surveillance and serve only those who already have disciplinary power. Jones believes she can use the master's tools to empower the delinquent to become something else. Theoretically it does not seem to be practically possible. Can she prove the theorist wrong? *How* can she prove it? As many have noted, it is very difficult to prove a qualitative change by quantitative methods, even though people cite statistics to prove almost anything. How to calibrate the difference between recidivism reduced, or time outside jail lengthened, or the differences between the causes for returning to jail? What methodology or questionnaire would enable the evaluator to distinguish among personal internal changes? It seems crucial, at least for funding purposes, to be able to prove the usefulness of the Medea Project, to demonstrate a clear connection between art and personal transformation that will benefit society. Otherwise how can it justify its existence?

Can the charting of the human heart lead to liberation? All the people involved in the Medea Project believe it can. But this belief cannot be corroborated either by statistics or by biographies of lives still in medias res. Though anecdotes will never satisfy statistical measurements, they are, in the end, even though they are *not* at the end, the best, most satisfying evidence there will be.[34]

Recovering Selves

Jones's third Medea Project production, entitled *A Taste of Something Else: A Place at the Table,* is anchored by the seating-arrangement metaphor: who gets to eat good, satisfying food; who gets to sit next to whom; who is banished altogether. Our national seating arrangement has always been, to put it mildly, tricky, fluid at best. Surveying the individuals who have been deemed unworthy and the reasons why may make us see the shape of the table differently, may make us imagine the taste of something else, may make us survey not only what is but what may be. Jones says this third production was about recovery and helping women find their way home:

> Change the things she may desire, yearn for: that's a taste of something else. A place at the table was a return home, a place that's rightfully yours. Home being oneself, actually. So much of the incarcerated woman is splintered, disassociated. True disconnection. Organic and mental. It's like, to

have done so many horrendous things when you're out there in the light that you can't return to that physical place that you knew. On the cover of the *New York Times Sunday Magazine* there was a picture of Matuschka, the photographer, a woman who lost her breast to cancer. Accompanying the photograph was an article about the responsibility of the government. This issue of having "a place at the table." When is there going to be enough scientific and medical research around breast cancer and all the lives it has claimed for women? It should have a place at the table.[35] And "A Taste of Something Else" came from the food section, and it's about pasta and Italy. [*Laughs*] That's Rhodessa Jones gathering information.

By the third Medea production, Jones and Reynolds were seeing the same women leave jail and return just in time to be included in another Medea show. Jones made the myth of Sisyphus anchor this show: Sisyphus cheated death, so death punished him by forcing him to repeat the meaningless task of pushing the rock up the hill only to have it roll back down again. She wanted to investigate what it might take to recover (or to develop) a sense of self that would keep women out of prison, liberate them in their lives outside. The life of fruitless labor may aptly characterize those women Jones saw coming back to prison: the tricks, cons, theft, and addictions kept them pushing uphill for a while only to end up back at the bottom in prison. Jones also had to begin to question her own labor: what good was the theater doing if the same women were back to perform from inside? She recognized how splintered, fragmented, and dissociated the women were. The odds for recovery of a "wholeness of self" and liberation were low.

Indeed, everyone who works around prisons has very low expectations regarding rehabilitation; the hurdles that formerly incarcerated people have to face seem close to insurmountable. Sheriff Hennessey in San Francisco believes in the value of small victories: "You're never going to get 100 percent. No program can do that. The question is: does it work for some people? And by my standards, then it is worthwhile. And secondly, does it work better than nothing? In which case, then it's really worthwhile."[36] Michael Marcum also believes in supporting programs that seem to have small statistical success:

This is a real frustrating business, and there's no coherent national leadership on corrections and what should be happening and shouldn't be happening. Some of the more academic people here will really criticize Rhodessa's work . . . saying, "What good does this do? This doesn't get people jobs. This doesn't get people decent housing." [This is exactly the sentiment of Karen Levine, program coordinator of the San Francisco Jails, who says of the Medea Project: "I would see her program as more effective with people who are already in treatment. Because I think it's premature. I think they get a lot into this whole glamorous thing of performing on the outside and being in a play and it's grandiose for where they're at."[37]] And part of the reason they're saying that is that we see some of the stars, some of Rhodessa's stars . . . come back in. That doesn't mean a *thing* to me. I mean, as far as *I'm* concerned, we've got people whose lives have been horrendous for ten, twenty years. Thirty years, forty years sometimes. And Rhodessa has them for three, four, five, six months. Each time people go through that, even if I think that they fall every time, I see them, they look sheepish. They look kind of ashamed. They know. I say, "Hey, it didn't work this time. You're stronger than you were last time. You're going to get more this time." It's two, three times—the chances of them staying out are going to be much stronger.

It's ridiculous to expect somebody to turn their entire life around on one profound or even ecstatic experience, but it's a step toward that. And Rhodessa doesn't deal with the lightweights. The people she's dealing with are your extremes. They're not first-timers. They're not people who never had any problems in life and just made a little mistake. They're people whose total lives are out of control. Who have been institutionalized and have a long way to go. But that's also why their stories are so rich and powerful. Because they hit something in all of our lives when they're doing their performances.

Though the sheriff and assistant sheriff, the arts coordinator, and Rhodessa Jones must justify the efficacy of the Medea Project in relation to other programs when arguing for grant money, and so make use of statistics to show how a program impacts the rates of recidivism, they know their best "proof" exists in what cannot in the end be fully measured: the degree of consciousness shifted—their own, that of the audience that sees the performance, and the hearts and minds of the women in and out of prison.

The women Jones works with are not "lightweights," as Marcum reminds us. Their lives didn't just take one small wrong turn. Most of them have suffered abuse for long periods of time. In the end, the Medea Project focuses on only a very few women, and in this chapter, even fewer women are heard from. I can't claim that they are a representative sampling or that my survey of them is in any way comprehensive. Instead, my gaze is extremely narrow: when I talked with them I was interested in how they believed the Medea Project helped or hindered them in creating a new self or recovering an old one. I was interested in their techniques for managing and presenting their selves, their sense of themselves, the sorts of self-surveillance and self-discipline they labored to present. I quickly realized that I would not be able to argue, on the basis of these stories, for quantifiable Medea Project success. Some of the women stay out of prison, some don't. Some of the women will say they are free because of the Medea Project; some will say it, and then return. But it's too small a sample either way to determine cause and effect, and in the end, their participation in the Medea Project is just one element in the complex labor of living their lives. Further, if there's anything the Medea Project teaches, recovery, and a more complex and realistic narrative about recovery, depends in part on ongoing, sustained dialogue—relationships that go "belly to belly"—and a transformed social structure. Recovery is an ongoing process.

Of the five women who speak here, all of their narratives share a basic characteristic, which one of the women, Barbara Bailey, calls "Before and After." In varying degrees of certainty, all assert a recovery that entails both looking back and seeing what they were like before and recognizing the difference they feel in themselves now. As they speak, they manufacture a past self, a present one, and, one supposes, a self they may inhabit in the future. They all are aware of the power of consciousness, but none is so naïve (I think) that she believes simply speaking constructs a different self. An interview is another sort of performance, a sort of rehearsal of what a different self sounds like. It may only be my own suspicious nature, but the more assertively a woman spoke of the break between "before" and "after," the more dubious I was about her odds for recovery. That may just be a personal prejudice, or it could be that my training in literary analysis causes me always to be suspicious of emphatic assertions. I know many religious conversions carry the same antipathy between selves; and, by his own account, it certainly worked for St. Augustine. Still, I wonder about the kind of dissociation and fragmentation that Jones notices in the women. Perhaps the break between then and now is necessary because the then was so horrendous that rejecting it entirely is the only road to hope of being able to carry on differently now. Or it could be that claiming their past selves may be another method of composing a new whole. Or it may be that no generalizations are possible about how individuals plot their lives.

I've chosen long excerpts from interviews with five formerly incarcerated women, all of whom participated in the Medea Project. The interviews took place when the women were out of jail, living either in Milestones Human Services, Inc., a residential and outpatient drug and alcohol treatment program, or in other halfway houses in San Francisco, Walden House or Safehouse; or on their own. The five—Paulette Jones, Angela Wilson, Felicia Scaggs, Barbara Bailey, and Andrea Justin—have performed in different shows, but among them they cover the first five productions. In their interviews they talk about why they chose to become involved with the Medea Project. They each speak about how much they enjoyed working in a group of women, their appreciation of Rhodessa Jones and the other women from the outside, and how different this group was from other therapeutic groups, because the project was composed solely of women and because the women seemed to care more deeply about what happened to them.

I never asked what their specific crimes were, but most of the women involved in the Medea Project are in jail for stealing, prostitution, forgery, drugs. Most have children who have had to live apart from their mothers. Their individual stories share some features: the influence of men and drugs, the struggle to become independent, the absolute precariousness of life after jail. In these interviews, the women reveal the ways in which they seek to be in control and to fight being controlled by drugs, men, desires. All five have given powerful performances on stage. Paulette Jones, Bailey, Justin, and Wilson have presented personal testimonies on stage, each ending with a recovered sense of self, insightful, hopeful. Both Bailey and Justin, who are friends, are shy, not natural performers; Jones, Wilson, and Scaggs, in contrast, appear at home on stage. The interviews were much more tenuously staged renditions of the self than their performances on stage. The interview format catches these women in the thick of life. There is no doubt that the Medea Project has given them some new language to talk about their lives: therapy for recovering addicts (for Paulette Jones); feminism (for Justin); writing (for Bailey); performance (for Scaggs and Wilson). But it is also clear that they, like most of the rest of us, are not "cured" or entirely in control.

PAULETTE JONES
(*Food Taboos, A Place at the Table, Slouching Towards Armageddon*)
Paulette Jones is a powerful performer, a professional singer long before she wound up in prison working with the Medea Project. She struck

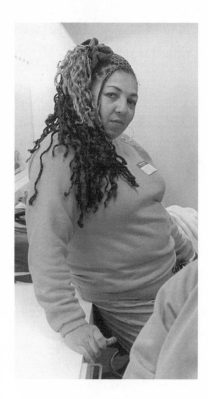

Paulette Jones.
Photograph by Ruth Morgan, 1993

me as self-aware and the most restrained of all the women I spoke with. Older than the other women, she has a longer and more varied history to tell. She was the most guarded about her chances, the most sober and realistic about the difficulties of change. When I talked with her just before *Slouching* opened in 1999, she had been out of jail for a few weeks. I went along with the two Joneses, Rhodessa and Paulette, to listen to them record an interview at a local radio station, and I also spoke with Paulette in between rehearsals. The songs she has written for the Medea Project— "Ladies of the Long Hall," "A Place at the Table," "She'll Never Make the News," and "Revolving Door"—don't offer a vision of liberation. Instead, they reinforce images of anonymity, repetition, and hopelessness; of getting a hustle on, of a baby in the trash, of being tired of the revolving door. The cycle of recidivism is almost guaranteed in these songs. In them, escaping a sense of misery means doing the same old thing, which lands the ladies right back on their bunks, counting time, with no light to see by. Discarded as trash, not important enough to make the news, there's no hope to sing of. Jones writes the songs of recidivism because she knows it so well.

It didn't bother me that every time it would roll around for the Medea Project to come into the jail, there I would be. I almost looked at it like, "Wow! Isn't this great, Rhodessa, that I'm always here when you come in?" There's nothing great about that. But I used to think, "Wow! Timing is perfect. I'll be able to participate." I had so much fear. I couldn't see beyond that. I couldn't see that there's nothing wrong with doing it from outside. You don't have to be in. It's OK to do it from the outside. But I was almost afraid. There is a fear to hope. It's risky. It's easier to say, I'm always going to be here and at least I have this to look forward to. That even though I'm in jail I know the Medea Project is going to be coming around and I'll be able to be in it.

I've spent so much time off track and very temporary times that I'm on track. When I got strung out on heroin in New York when I was performing on Broadway, really since then. In the 70s, I was in *Hair* here in San Francisco, in 1969, 1970, 1971. I stayed in the show for the entire run, for a year and a half. I moved to San Francisco and then went on the road, and all of that to me, that was just a part of the life of a hippie. I was a hippie; I was so glad to be away from Sacramento. I had three children, I was seventeen years old, I had a one-, two-, and a three-year-old. I was a basket case. I couldn't wait to get away. I was like, "Mom! I'm off to be a star." And she was, "Oh, I know you're going to make it." Little did we know I was going to come back from New York strung out on heroin.

It was in the mid-70s. When I left here, I was a flower child, and I was all into love, peace, and happiness. And my little experimentation with drugs was dropping acid every now and then, and that's it, smoking weed. I went back to New York and everybody back there was snorting heroin. It was the chic thing to do. Everybody in the theater was doing it. I was the youngest person in the cast of *No Place to Be Somebody,* that was Charles Gordone's Pulitzer Prize winner. And I did what everybody else did. I kind of stuck out like a sore thumb because I was so young. Then once I got into *Superstar,* basically we were a bunch of different people from different *Hair* casts. Ben Vereen was playing Judas, and he had been playing *Hair* with me. We already knew each other. The cast members were actually living the way that they looked on stage. We weren't putting on costumes; that's the way we lived. And at that time, it was totally controversial. But once I got strung out on heroin, I came back to Sacramento.

They had done this big thing in Sacramento, small-town girl makes big, you know. It was on all the TV newscasts, and my mother was so totally disgraced. She just really battered me emotionally about that. "God, I thought you were going to make our family proud, and you go to New York and get yourself addicted to heroin and you come back here and you're a flop." So it's like, "Oh well." So I just spent the next, I don't know, fifteen years trying to make up to her for that embarrassment that I caused her and try to be a normal person, get a job, a straight job, but it didn't work, because by then I was an addict and didn't know anything about it. I wasn't educated about addiction. I went to a psychiatrist, and he told my mother he could get me off the heroin addiction. But back then, heroin addiction was a very taboo thing. Nowadays you hear more about it, but in the 60s, 70s, honey, god, you might as well have had leprosy if a person actually found out you were what they call a junkie. So he said I'll get her off the drug, and all he did was get me Valium and Quaaludes, so now I had another addiction. Now I was a pill popper.

I still worked in Sacramento. I did the music circuit, all kinds of piano bars. I could always get a job in a piano bar because I play the piano. I don't need a band, I can play myself. And a bar is a bar is a bar. Basically people come there to drink. I don't care what anybody says. It's OK if you sing, but people really aren't listening. And people were buying me drinks, and so all I did was drink. I was a very heavy alcoholic. There were times when I would just keel over off the piano bench. That's an addiction too, but it's acceptable in this society. People made excuses for me, people covered up for me. I was always late wherever I worked at because I had a serious problem. I was drinking and taking pills. Pretty soon I started getting into trouble with the law.

And I got married, I had two more children, and I kind of lived that housewifey life, but I was very miserable. I drank all day long, from first thing in the morning, so my marriage went kaput. And I started engaging in criminal activities because I was back on all kinds of drugs. Then I came up here for a weekend and I found a place up here and then ended up in jail in San Francisco in 1992. I had been to prison and everything by then, shoplifting. I would always be drunk. I would go into a store and always be shoplifting. It would always be in the police reports, "This lady was falling down drunk," but in Sacramento no one ever intervened all those years I was going to prison. No one ever offered treatment. No one ever said, "She's drunk. She doesn't even try to conceal anything." I was totally out of my mind. I got sent to prison.

Now sometimes people say, "Oh we're going to make a tape." That just does not move me. I performed on Broadway. I made it already. Now I have to deal with who I am and how I can live a semblance of a normal life because going in and out of jail is not—I know that's not what I was put on this earth to do. But basically that's what my life has become due to my addiction. The fact that I can sing and write songs and play the piano is totally irrelevant at this point. Because that don't mean shit when you're locked up. Except that you start singing in jail, that's what happens. And everybody there just gets a free show. That's all, you know what I'm saying? You don't get shit out of it except some validation, and if you need it that bad, I figure you're a sorry soul, you got to go to jail or prison to get some validation in your life. And I've been doing that in my life for a lot of years. Going to jail, singing for the ladies there, not that there's not some gratification in it. I'm sure many people's lives have been touched by the singing, but in the meantime, what about Paulette?

[When I sing with the Medea Project,] it gives me a sense of I haven't lost it all. It gives me a sense of that. I struggle with that issue, very, very much so. It's one of the reasons that I use. It's because I say to myself, "I have wasted so many years." I have wasted so much of my talent. I have done fifteen years in prison on the installment plan. You know what I'm saying? Going back and forth. All of that time is gone forever. I'll never be able to get it back. And I have a real issue. I have a real issue with my watch. It's like, Oh my god. I woke up one day and it was 1999. I'll be fifty years old this year. I didn't think that this much time was going to go by. I was just pissing my life away. In and out of institutions and jails and all the horrific places that drug use takes one. And what surprises me always is that I can still sing. That I can still write songs. I mean literally that my brain still functions in that manner. I'm totally shocked. Because of the situation that I've placed myself in. Where my life has been on the line. And what if something bad had happened to me out there or even in prison—the stabbings, the rapes that I have seen first-hand with my own two eyes—and that I was spared that. It didn't happen to me. But nobody got me into prison but myself. So when I started doing the Medea Project, it encouraged me and it motivated me that maybe it's not too late. There was a while there, number one, where I was suffering with deep depression, on Prozac, seeing my therapist. In '94, so many issues were going on with me. I'd gone to jail again, and during that stretch of time of being sober I'd gotten some clarity about my life. And being clean and sober in jail and prison is a choice, believe me, because there's more drugs in there than I'd ever seen on the streets, but I just started thinking—it's over for you. You know what I'm saying? You're all washed up. You're a has-been. These are things that my husband used to say to me. He was very verbally abusive, and when we were together, I'd try to get a job singing, and he'd say, "Why are you even trying?" So for many years I was of that mind-set. That you might as well be on the road you're on, you're probably going to die an addict, you're going to die in somebody's prison or jail. I was very, very deeply depressed, and the Medea Project is what really motivated me to say to myself, "Honey, you have still got it. You can still write songs. You can still sing. You can still play the piano and as long as you're still breathing, there is a chance for you. To make it better, to do it right, to still do something meaningful, versus it's too late to do anything."

I have a very negative way of thinking. I've been in therapy for it for years because I think the worst. And it's a learned behavior. I'm trying to unlearn because even now, in the good things that are happening, I have to struggle with thoughts of, "Oh, everything is really going well—*for now*." I have an issue with that. I struggle with it every single day. "Well, we're just waiting to see how long Paulette. . . ." It's terrible. I don't want to think like that. But I do. It's very difficult for me to be positive. That is what the Medea Project helps me to do. It reminds me that I performed professionally thirty years ago and, instead of depressing me, it encourages me and it actually lifts me up. Honey, baby, I still got it. I still got it from—as good as I was when I was nineteen years old. On Broadway. If anything, I'm better. Because then I didn't even know what my talent was about and how much I could do with it. And I think life experience has enriched my expression through my music. If I had never been a lady in the long hall I could never have written "Ladies in the Long Hall." I was one. That was how I wrote it.

There is no doubt about it that the Medea Project was extremely instrumental because when you're just sitting around doing time, you kind of get locked into going back and forth. There's a way that you do your time— it's called jailing it—that's what the old-timers call it. When I step off the bus into the prison yard, there's a jacket I put on. That jacket is a way that I know I'm going to have to be for however much time I'm going to have to be down. To be able to do something like this in the midst of that is like stepping out of that old—"I'm a prisoner, I'm a convict."

My dreams are being in the studio and recording my songs and having my songs out in the world. Sharing my songs with the world. I'm not one of those people that if I can't sing my songs it ain't going to be heard. I'm not one of those people. Whoever wants to sing my songs, if they can sing it, I don't have an issue with that. I entered "A Place at the Table" in the National Songwriters Association, and it's in the semifinals. I know that I've written some very good songs. I think maybe because of my age and because of the struggles that I go through in my own life I'm not so hyped up on putting me out there.

Now I'm in Safehouse. I'm not going to be undertaking any projects real soon. Because, number one, in the program I'm on, they allowed me to do the Medea Project because they figured I was already involved with it in jail. They would not stop something that I had already started. But first of all, you can't work for the first six months in that program. You can't work or go to school. You have to focus primarily on yourself. It's only women, only eight women. It's not a program really, it's transitional housing. You're not being pressured with a job or overwhelmed with commitments. They ask that you make that kind of commitment to your own self and you will be working on *you*. The basic needs are being met and you are to work on you. You are not to try to undertake other things. They know that this is over Sunday, and then I'll have to really buckle down to my program. And that's the only way I've been allowed to remain in my program, because I have an understanding with my director that when this show is over, I will demonstrate to them that I am working on recovery, not working on a show, not performing anywhere, not singing anywhere. And if I choose to do that, I will have to leave, because that's not conducive to what they have going on.

But I'm very tempted. At the gala the other night I had three people approach me and ask me did I have an agent or a manager. I had a couple that own a jazz club in New York City and in Washington, D.C. They offered me a job in either place. They gave the club in Washington to their children. They told me that I could stay with their children while I test out the jazz club and see if I'd like to work there. I had to say, I can't do that at this time. That's a wonderful opportunity.

Maybe I'll do it in six months. I would like to do it right now had I not done something like that before and it blew up. I just flaked out. I was a flop, because situations like that are triggers for me to use. The expectations that they put on me, and I don't do well under it. The hope is that behavior modification—and I am drastically and tenaciously trying to do that—because my best ideas have landed me in the penitentiary. Those are the ideas that I came up with. So I've got to trust that the process I've involved myself with that I can get some help.

Art does not save me. I really wish that it did, but it does not. And that's been the hardest thing to accept. I remember when I got out of jail in '94 and I went to Milestones and left Milestones and Rhodessa offered me a job working with them at Cultural Odyssey and I worked with them there for a while and I taught a music class on Saturday. After *A Place at the Table*. It lasted for a while, because I was clean and sober, then I relapsed and I stopped going. Then I went back to prison. The Medea Project came around again, and during that time that I'd been working for Rhodessa they had agreed to write up a proposal for me to receive a grant from the California Arts Council. I am the first person ever to receive that grant while still in jail. I got the letter, "Congratulations, you've been awarded the California Arts Council grant. You've been chosen to be an artist in residence." Something that I would have died for. And I blew that—I know—I didn't last thirty days. Because I got out of jail and this is the way that it works: you're able to do your own work, and I was collaborating with Cultural Odyssey to teach music classes to children on Saturdays. All you have to do is go once a week to class. I could have done it in the jail or anywhere but we opted to do it there. And I think my first paycheck I went out. You know what I'm saying? They never seen me again, they never heard from me again.

Nothing would help me. If I haven't grasped—there has to be a shift in consciousness—and this is a wonderful thing—I believe it is happening—but it had not happened then. I remember Rhodessa saying to me at one point, "You know, you're like a drowning woman. And all I have to do is throw you a lifeline. But I can't make you take it." I saw that look on her face and she was baffled. She could not . . . she just said, "How could you still want to use drugs and you have an opportunity?" Because at that time, Idris Ackamoor was also working with me on a one-woman show for me to take back to New York City, and part of that show was going to say, "I was here twenty-five years ago performing on Broadway, and I am back." And it was a dream. They were beginning to work on it, they were beginning to build a show for me. And she was, "How could you?" And you know what? I beat myself up for a lot of years on that because I thought, she's right, how could I? But you know what? If you're not educated about addiction, then you *will* be baffled. No one can understand. That has nothing to do with being an addict—you throwing me a lifeline, you giving me an opportunity. If anything, that's a reason to use—because I got a job. I lost a job—that's a reason to use too. I'm celebrating, I'm devastated. They are all reasons to use for an addict. So until you get that under control . . . . People that are not addicts don't look at it in the same way. They go, "Well, if somebody gave me an opportunity like that, I would never want to use drugs again." You crazy? Yes, you would.

My songs—all "Ladies in the Long Hall" says is "Go out and give it one more try." What else can you do? Go out there and give it one more try. You might make it and you might not. That's all that it says. That's the end of the song. It doesn't say, "And all the ladies that leave the long hall never go back to the long hall." Because most of the ladies in the long hall have been there before. "Revolving Door?" It just says that I want to get out of the revolving door—and how about some education to understand my situation. It's just about—can we educate women about what's going on with them that causes them to do what they do? "A Change Is Going to Come," by Sam Cooke [sung in *Slouching Towards Armageddon*], says, "There were times that I didn't think I could last so long, but now I think I'm able to carry on." That's encouraging for me. I do feel like that. Like I said, I believe that something is happening that did not happen all the other times that I got out of jail, went to programs, had jobs, had opportunities, it never worked. I don't know how it happened. It's some kind of miracle. I just know that it's happening. There's a long, long pattern of a way of thinking and looking at the world, at my life, and what is possible for me that is changing. It is shifting into something that is absolutely glorious, that just might be the beginning of something totally totally wonderful. I dare not even speak it out loud for fear that it is going to disappear.[38]

I was most struck during this interview by the realization that Paulette Jones's "best ideas" were not her songs or an "art career." Though she is ironic, of course, about her "best ideas" having had more to do with breaking and entering than thinking of ways to break the cycle of addiction and depression, that which I would have thought "best" about her could not, does not, save her. But the language at the end, which speaks to the "change" in her sense of her self and therefore perhaps her life, is tentative and vague. A miracle seems perhaps apt to explain shifts of consciousness. Why would more therapeutic talk be successful now when it so clearly wasn't before? In the end, it may be a mystery, totally wonderful, but mysterious all the same as to how, as Sam Cooke sings, a change comes.

In August 2000, Sean Reynolds and Rhodessa Jones mused about Paulette's journey:

SEAN REYNOLDS: I loved performing with Paulette Jones. We have kind of
    the same sense of humor, and I love being on stage with her. Whenever
    we were doing "Down, Down Baby," a childhood game, I would wait
    for Paulette to come because I knew it was going to rock. Paulette made
    me more comfortable. There were times Paulette would wink at me and
    I would know it would be OK. Paulette could just throw little things in

that would just crack me up. They were just marvelous. The night Paulette forgot her lines—in her story about the river [in *A Place at the Table*]—she forgot to say the line about the man with the knife. She got it together though. We were so funny together. Those little internal jokes.

RHODESSA JONES: Yes, she got it together. "Honey, you out there alone. What you going to do?" Paulette found her thread.

REYNOLDS: You can't tell me that that doesn't mean something if you're standing there in front of 700 people and you know that they know— and still you can pull back and get it together. I know how it feels. Ad libbing. *Now what do I do?* I might be a little quicker, because I'm not as drug impacted and broken down. But I know how it feels: I got to get something together here because all these people are watching. They're some moments! Paulette's fabulous on stage. I love working with her.

JONES: Paulette has a history as a performer. That's the most heart-breaking thing about Paulette. My fantasy for her has been to get her a CD, get her a show, get her a cabaret-type show. But at the same time have her talk about jail, her life. She and I used to laugh. I'd say, "Paulette, I dreamed I saw you in an off-the-shoulder red dress with gold jewelry and a beautiful white piano. And you're telling this room where you've been as you're on your way somewhere else." Craig Harris, a musician from New York, a trombone player, came out two summers for the African American Performance Art Festival. When he heard Paulette Jones, he said, "This woman has a future. When she's ready, I'd love for her to send me some of her sheet music. I would like to get some of the people I know to play it." That is the heartbreak. That is the heartbreak when you cannot retrieve a person like that. And you have to let them go. It's like somebody jumps out the window, you grab their hands, but you can't hold on.

On a certain level, what we knew about Paulette was that she was an alcoholic, dabbled a little bit in drugs. Paulette did have a drinking problem. Paulette also had a drug problem. Paulette also was addicted to men. And that combination took her down again. She was our California Arts Council [CAC] artist. She and Nancy [Johnson] both were CAC artists with me in the beginning of 1995. Paulette was at Milestones. She left Milestones with this man after one of the groups. They were called before the group, and they were told, "You can't do that here. How can you have a relationship when you're supposed to be working on yourself?"

They chose to leave, agreeing that they were going to go in a day program. They didn't do any of that. They broke into our office, stole our equipment. Paulette ratted on him, so she got less time. It was really tawdry. Got the CAC grant while she was in jail. We applied for it when she was doing *A Place at the Table*. She was already back in jail. We told them [at the CAC] what happened. They said, "You told us she was getting out." A judge got her released early. Another social worker stepped in to help her. This woman is talented, she's funny, she's smart. The minute she started getting money she started messing up. She had a place to live at Odyssey House, a halfway house. But she was doing drugs. And she had these people so manipulated at Odyssey House that they didn't tell *me*. They said, "She begged us *not* to tell you." But then I guess the third time she came in loaded, they said, "You're going to have to leave. So we got to tell Miss Jones what's happening." That's how I found out.

Paulette was in a great place of trust. She was a leader when we weren't there. When we got the CAC grant, I went downtown and found her. I said, "What you going to do? We got this grant. You're getting out?" She said, "Oh, I'm so happy." Paulette has these big brown eyes. I mean she's an adorable woman. But she's also a con artist. You know what I'm saying? But I think she was genuinely happy. And I said, "Now, what I want you to do is to start talking to the women inside about this. I want you to start working on this and this and this." "Child of Mine" was her song that we used in *Buried Fire*. Other songs we couldn't use, they were just too raw. She was very excited and happy. But the minute she got out and had some money, she dropped out.

She's talented, she's beautiful. But on another level it doesn't surprise me that much, because it's taken me nearly fifty years to realize that I'm talented, that I have a right to my successes. There's such a mixture of jealousy and suspicion even within those communities that praise you. My brother, Bill, says it isn't what people say, it's watch how people say it. Yeah, I have a right to this. I'm not a charlatan. This really happened. This happens to me: not being able to take praise. Yes, I can understand all of it. So when it's Paulette falls off the wagon, it breaks my heart, but on some level, she's had it a lot harder than I had. And I have not had it easy. It's just a shame there isn't a magic potion that we can inject people with and they'd be all right. She'd wake up and not remember any of that and be able to move on. . . .

Five months after she talked to you, Paulette is back in jail, for the one, two, three, four, five, sixth time. I grapple with not talking to her if I go back inside. "I can't help you. I did what I could, but obviously my interactions did not in any way enhance you. You didn't talk to me when you were in trouble." Paulette Jones may die alone because she may never get it together to value this community. Maybe it's too late for Paulette. And I don't know if that would have been different anyway any time.

ANGELA WILSON
(*Slouching Towards Armageddon*)
Angela Wilson was, as she recounts, the only white person left in the workshop leading up to *Slouching Towards Armageddon,* the fifth Medea Project production and one funded by the Rockefeller Foundation to discuss race and racism. She seems not to have been intimidated by this role, instead eager to learn what difference might mean. She recalls:

I remember when this really powerful woman came in. Her and Sean Reynolds came in together. I can remember exactly what they were wearing and how they stood. The deputies got everybody together. Every inmate in the pod had to stand there; it was mandatory. The deputies said, "You stand here and listen to this woman." I don't know how it happened before, but that's how it was when I was there. And Paulette was actually in jail. Afterwards she was in the bathroom and told me "You gotta do this, Angie, this is the greatest thing to happen." Paulette and I had this whole thing. . . . When you're in jail, everything is pretty ugly and negative and everyone is really rude to each other. It's like a bunch of bitches and "hos"; there's no respect for each other and no respect for life, for womanhood, boundaries, space. But Paulette and I would talk a lot. We would counsel each other in the bathroom about how wonderful each of us were. She telling me how wonderful I was, me telling her how wonderful she was. And so that was happening before Rhodessa actually came in. So this is just another night, we were in the bathroom, I was in the shower, she was doing whatever she was doing, her hair, she always had a lot of visitors, that's how that went. And she said, "You've got to be a part of this." And I said, "Really? Well, I write a little bit. When I'm sad. When I'm happy, I can't write."

So Rhodessa came in and she was really powerful. You have to have a way to go in there to jail, to a bunch of hardheads, a bunch of untrustworthy women that can't stand the sight of anything that gets to leave at night. You know, "*Fuck you.*" But Rhodessa has this way, it's amazing, she came in with confidence. With the attitude of: "You're a jerk, that's OK, you can do shit to me, I don't care, I get to go home. Or we can do it *my* way which is really the way it works." That's what attracted me in the first place to her. Because most people who go in for the first time are scared.

It started out to be thirty women, gung ho, but it dwindled down. I was the only white girl left, which was interesting, and this performance was supposed to be about race. I'm from Idaho, born and raised on a farm. And I never saw a black person until I was twelve years old. My father was pretty racist, so I had a lot to talk about. Concerning that and the learning experiences that I had in jail. Jail was not always a negative thing for me in my quest to be a more liberal person about race or culture. Some people were like, "I'm black, you're white, I don't like you. And the only reason why I'm next to you is that we're in jail." But my feeling was, you learn a lot from people and about people through being in jail because you're on top of each other. I had never been around so many races before, and it was really really interesting. Some people were like, "Fuck. I'm in jail." And I felt like that too, but a lot of it was a great learning experience about people. I often think if I hadn't gotten to jail I would never have met Rhodessa and done the Medea Project.

When those of us in Medea went back to the pod, we started eating dinner together, we started talking to each other, we started finding out about each other. That was one of the main ingredients of the project: that you have to be honest. It didn't matter whether you were black, white, yellow. No one would mess with the other one when we were there. It was really amazing. We would hug each other when we went to bed at night. And a lot of the women were really hard. Nikki—she was the hardest little girl I've ever seen in my life. Nineteen. We got her hugging! White people are really more huggy feely than black people. I don't know why, that's what I've come to think, that's my own trip, maybe. Anyway, it was just so weird, and I noticed that when I was there. . . .

The Medea Project gives me a sense of belonging. It's not a substitute for a rush, it's not a substitute for anything. I never completed anything my whole life. But I completed Walden House [a halfway house], and that amazed me. And if I complete these next three performances [benefit performances for the Medea Project], that will be amazing too.

I don't owe Rho anything. I don't feel like that. But I'll tell you I'm really thankful and really grateful to her. She's not like an idol, but I want to say that I owe her a debt of gratitude, for lack of a better word. It's the way I feel after a performance, an ultimate high. I don't get a rush off of dope like I do out of performing. With the Medea Project you get to connect with people and you get to tell them exactly what happened to you. And they pay you! It's amazing to me. It's so in your face. People eat it up, it's really bizarre. I would like to be a professional performer.

Now that I'm out, I believe in everything a little more. When you're locked up, people can come and tell you anything. Sure, the people are dedicated who are coming in. But you don't *really* know how real people are and how influential they are and how much their heart is in their work until you get out. The Medea people are a part of my life now. They weren't there just to make money. Rhodessa really truly has her heart in her work, and she really cares about what happens to women, to me, to women like me, and so does Fé, Edris. They all really care about what happens.

When I was in Walden House, it was my motivation. It was like: I don't have to be a junkie anymore; I can be a mother to my child; I don't have to do the things that drugs led me to; I can talk to my mom; I can look you in the eye; I can work an everyday job; I can do whatever I want in the whole wide world, and Rho told me that. She just believed in me when I wouldn't believe in myself, and she continues to believe in me. Now I believe in myself a lot more, but even when I don't, she's ready to believe in me until I'm ready to believe in myself. I've never in my whole life had someone like that, a woman influence. My mother was a wonderful mother, but I never had that—"I'm going to believe in you until you believe in yourself." It taught me to trust in people. She's an amazing person. She's really helped me change my life. I just knew that I wanted to be clean. If I'm sober, I can do anything. So I called her when I was at Walden House. I said I really want to be a part of the Medea Project. I didn't know what her response would be. I knew in my heart. But I'm from the streets. We don't trust, we don't trust *at all*. Even normal people don't trust, but I *really* don't trust. I have a lot of trust issues. So intuitively I knew. But I needed to hear it. And she said, "Come." I'm totally down for this.

I have an ingredient that worked for me, but you have to work hard. It's not osmosis. I went through Walden House. I've been thinking a lot about Paulette [back in jail]. Her first intro to drugs, or so she says, is through performing. And perhaps there are people, places, and things she needs to avoid. Perhaps she needs to lead a normal life. I mean *not* be involved in performance. I don't know if that's true. I think you also have to stay grateful. But I'm not in her mind. I feel sad, I write about her a lot, but I don't send her letters. I loved to look at her in rehearsals, because we had spent time together in jail, in the bathrooms telling each other how wonderful we were so we wouldn't forget. You know what I mean? Because you get to start thinking like you're a piece of shit, you're a junkie. We both abandoned our children, we did all sorts of crazy shit, and then, she was free when we were doing *Slouching*. Now it makes me feel sad; it feels not the same without her. I don't know what I can do—but if I could do something for her to make it OK, I would.

By the grace of god, I don't think there's any certain way to recover. I don't promise that tomorrow I will be here. I could be in orange two days from now. I'm off probation now. That's really weird. When I first got off probation I was kind of nervous. Because I love crime, I'm addicted to crime, to the rush. I said, "Oh, my god! I'm not on probation. I can go commit a crime and not be sent to a federal penitentiary." That was my first thought! So you fight battles and sometimes they win. A lot of your battles go on in your head, with addiction, crime, drugs, men, people. What can I get from you? All these old behaviors can come up. Perhaps that's what happened to Paulette.[39]

Rhodessa Jones speculates:

Paulette who should be the obvious gem. If any of this is supposed to be a miraculous, transformational machine, she should have been top dog, but instead it's this white girl, Angie Wilson, who has taken this information and is making it work for her. This also politically puts the nation on notice that this is no longer just women of color in jail. More and more women are going to jail. But through exploring incarceration, the women who get it move to another place. Women like Angie. She is growing into an organizer; she is really the producer of this fundraiser. My ego sometimes wants to be remembered for having created the Medea Project in its initial form. But in the end that's not important. That's just my own conceit. It's more moving to have these women here to help. They have their own ideas, and watch out for me, think of me, are supportive of me and this project.

I never set out to say I was going to transform everybody's lives. I wish I could have done more so that they owned their lives, themselves, and were clear about the future. But then, God has a real sense of humor. That's OK, I don't feel I failed. Here's the other side. I look around me and see that little girl in my office today. I can be her sister, teacher, artist, friend—that just takes humanity.

Felicia ("Fefe") Scaggs. Photograph by Lorraine Capparell, 1996

Everyone acknowledges how "amazing" Rhodessa Jones is. Her "mother influence" makes Angela Wilson believe in herself. But Wilson is careful to say also that Jones is not her "idol." She knows she could be back in orange tomorrow just like Paulette Jones. There is no certain formula, and Wilson doesn't speculate for very long about what works and what doesn't. And neither does Rhodessa Jones.

FELICIA ("FEFE") SCAGGS
(Reality Is Just Outside the Window, A Place at the Table, Buried Fire)
On stage, Felicia Scaggs commands attention with her presence; she is big and assertive, she has a sense of fun, a great singing voice, and a wagging finger she uses to great effect. She is also young and breezy. She doesn't seem bothered, but she doesn't seem all that deep or engaged either, which may also be the reason she has performed in the plays within the plays but has not written or performed a confessional monologue:

It's like this. I used to like steal clothes, living the fast life or whatever. So I went to jail. They sentenced me to forty-five days, which I only did fourteen days. Within those fourteen days, I first got to San Bruno. I knew some people who already were in jail. And that evening they were like, "We're going to go practice for a play." And I was like, "Oh, I want to go," you know? Rhodessa and Sean came in to the dorms to get the girls and I was like, "I want to come, I want to come." And she was, "Are you going to be there? Are you going to stick with it?" I said "Yes, please." It was like, anything, *please,* to get me off the dorms. So I went in. It was pretty far along. The show was on the next month. Rhodessa said I came at the thirteenth hour to save it.

It was a wonderful experience. Rhodessa was wonderful. I came a long way with them. She is a hard woman; she is hard. I used to think, "Oh god. She just so mean." But she does it for a reason. To make us strong and focus on just one thing, doing what we have to do. If this is what we want to do. If we want to act, you know what I'm saying? "It's going to be hard," she always tells me. She stays on me. And I love her for that. Beautiful woman. I love her.

I always wanted to be an actress. I always wanted to be on a stage doing something. You know what I'm saying? That was just a way—all those people going to be seeing me. This is what I want. I want these people to see me. I want to get that applause. I just clicked right with the show. It was lovely.

Sometimes I miss a lot of rehearsals. Things just happen. But I think if I just stick it a little more and just give it my all in all. I haven't been giving it my 100 percent like I did before, and acting, theater work, is really what I want to do. I've also been to school, art classes at Laney College, and this is something that I want to do and I'm very interested in it. But it's something else is kind of like badgering me, kind of pulling me away. But then I won't let it just get me. But I got to be strong. I've kind of been praying on that because theater work is really what I want to do.

I've never done a monologue. And the reason was the women who wrote monologues were able to do that because things had happened in their life. They wanted to express it. My life has not been perfect, but it's been OK, enough for me to live in. The major thing in my life was boosting, just taking something that wasn't mine, not from people, but from stores. I would go to Neiman Marcus, I. Magnin, and steal their stuff and sell it and make a lot of money. It was an addiction too because it was easy money for me. But I never did a monologue about that, because after I left the jail, I knew that I didn't want to go back there. So I just stopped doing what I was doing. It didn't get that serious for me. It was like a blessing from God to have that removed away from me, you know, straight removed away. So I was never able to do a monologue. But you know you can do a monologue like if somebody writes it, you can act it out. But Rhodessa always had something else for me to do.

As far as the rehearsals went. We're a bunch of women. We have a lot of mood swings. The type of person I am, I'm a pretty happy person. I don't get mad a lot. Know what I'm saying? I don't be having—now sometime you will catch me with that attitude. But it's not nothing mega serious. I'll crack a smile sooner or later. I don't let too much stuff get to me. So I was able to deal with anyone, anybody. I'm a people's person. I haven't met anyone yet that I was like . . . "Oh, I can't handle it."

We're on vacation now. But when we go back, I'll be there. I'm really into the art part. This is very serious. This is one day be a part of my life. This will put food on my table. But the Medea Project just helped me. Like a rehearsal within itself to build me up when I get bigger and better.

Unlike Paulette Jones, Felicia Scaggs is young and professionally untried. Her idea that "art is going to put food on the table" seems naïve at best, a fantasy or dream. Halfway through this short interview, which took place in 1996, Scaggs began to speak about her difficulties in staying on task, focused, serious. Though she does not name that "something else" that badgers her, it is clear she has at least two different tastes. Like Paulette, she prays to stay strong, but I'm not sure whether that is just a figure of speech. Many of the women in these interviews seem to turn to such a figure, God, to save them, to watch over them. "God is the other drug," Rhodessa Jones says. But they also know that they have to do more than be willing to be saved. Jones approves of some of the attitudes the women have:

The thing that I've always loved about Felicia is that Felicia has real attitude about being a big woman. She's not apologizing. And she learned very early that her tongue had to become the double-edged sword.

We're not going to romanticize anything. That's what I say to the public, "Do you care? Can you look at Fefe?" I have a couple friends, they're visual artists and I know they can't look at Fefe. That is not beauty. In the street, they'd look at her and do this [looks away]. Can we really begin to look at rehabilitation for everybody—I'm just not talking about women—until we, as a culture, really look at each other? And appreciate each other? And appreciation will take a while because people have been burnt, people have been maimed.

Fefe's back in jail. Last week they told me she's in jail. I talked to her family last week. Her cousin said she's in jail in Hayward. That is like a knife in my heart. I called her house to return a phone call. And her cousin said, "Don't you know?" And I thought the worst. No one has called me. If I were the social worker of old, I'd get in my car, and drive to her house and talk to her mom, but I know her mother probably feels very bad. Fefe went back to school. But her mother said, "I felt like she's going to get into trouble. Because she's not working, staying out all times of night." Fefe is really symbolic of one of the challenges, and that is that to become an actor or a performer is more than a notion. People get very lofty after being on stage and playing to full houses all the time. That: "Oh, I'm going to be an actor." And also she was feeling like, "Well you know, I'm in school. What do you all want from me? I did go back to school."

Sean and I were saying it probably has to do with a Fourth of July outfit. She's a booster you know. She's a booster, which is like, you go in the shop and you steal things for people and they give you money. That's what she's been doing since she was very young. That's all I can imagine, but I still haven't heard from her family, so I don't know the particulars. *I* felt so bad, I had a headache. I had to lie down. And I don't know what her mother is going through. Fefe had just finished probation in San Francisco County. Again this speaks to poverty, a lack of direction. What criminal justice does to people is that they become addicted to someone telling them what to do, and the minute they have no probation officer to visit, they don't have a jail program, they don't have a drug program, they are on their own, what do they do? How many people can move on from here?

BARBARA BAILEY
(*Buried Fire*)
Barbara Bailey was a friend of Andrea Justin's when they were in jail, and they both joined the Medea Project when they were living at Milestones, the residential drug treatment program. Bailey and Justin sat by themselves against the wall for many of the rehearsals, and both of them surprised themselves when they came forward to tell their personal stories. Bailey's performance, "Alone in the Woods," was particularly impressive because she took on so many voices in telling it: screaming at a rapist, pleading with a judge, desperate for a hit, and then ending with the "after" voice of the saved.

I'm a recovering addict. There's so many womens, mainly womens, that I'm mostly concerned about women, because I'm a woman. There are so many women out there who are still in the system. And I'm out of the system. And I would like to pull them out of the system, like I'm out of the system. Because it's such a great recovery to be yourself all over again. It's

Barbara Bailey (second from right, in leather vest).
Photograph by Lorraine Capparell, 1996

like a comeback to be in a reality of your own. To say: this was you then, but this is me now. The way I was then was pitiful, but the way I am now—I'm a woman, I feel good about myself, I got my child back from a foster home. It's like a creation. You create it to come into the world, and you can also create to change your life to a better person that you really are. You can be a real person.

This had been in my mind ever since I woke up. I was loaded. I was sitting in this laundromat. Something just hit me and said, "Isn't you tired of being tired? Isn't you tired of looking so bad? Don't you realize that your child has been taken from you? Don't you know that your mom and dad passed away now and you're all alone? Don't you want to, like, show them, although they're gone, that they can still look over you and watch the things you do now? Don't you want to make them proud and let them rest in peace that you can actually change your life around?" So I just got up and walked to the program. I knocked on the door, Milestones, and I asked them, "Could you please help me? It's time for me to change my life. It's time for me to get off dope and be the woman that my mother raised me to be. To get my child back, to be a mother like I supposed to be a mother." I wants to be this way.

From the day I knocked on the door, which was March 1991, I have not relapped. I don't urge for it anymore. I see it every day. I walk past it. I live in the Tenderloin, right in the heart of the dope area. And I smells it as I walk by. I see people loaded. But that's them. That's why I wish that this was some kind of society where people like us, a recovering addict, could share with the public the things that I have learned. Because I've been smoking dope, drinking alcohol, ever since I was twenty-one, and there's been thirty or forty years that I've been under the influence of drugs and alcohol. By being clean the way I am, I feel like a queen that it can happen. Anything is possible if you put your mind to it. I stopped.

I feel so proud of myself. I want to be a foster parent. I want to be a foster parent of mothers that are addicts that have gotten their babies taken from them. So they can see that I am a recovering addict. "I have your child. I am a foster parent to your child. I was an addict. But now I'm a recovering addict. Why don't you be me? Come and get your child. Come and get it. But you know what you have to do to get it. It's not as hard as you think it is. It's all in the mind." So that's one of the reasons I want to be a foster parent and a counselor to a lot of women that's still under the influence of drugs and alcohol. To let them just get the big picture. They can just think a little bit. And once they start thinking, that thinking can lead into a big recovery.

A lot of women don't listen because a lot of people be talking to them who haven't been through the experience that they're going through or never even got high in their life. But they say, "I understand. Just because I never got high don't mean I don't know." But I think a person who experiences can get more to the addicts than the people who have never experienced it before. . . .

I came to the idea for my performance when Rhodessa asked us to walk down a line, walk straight down a line. "Go straight being who you are," she said, "and come back to me as somebody else." It just hit me. When I walked towards her I was me. But when I was coming back, just out of the blue, I just started acting out as being an addict, as being raped, as being really fucked up. It just came out naturally. She said, "Oh my God. I didn't know you had that in you." It just came out. Then Rhodessa said, "Please do this on stage." I said, "OK, I'll try."

I appreciate that she let me be involved with the girls because there's so many fabulous, exciting people. I was just honored being around them. I looked at them and would say, "Those are professionals." Nancy Johnson [dancer] moves just like a snake. It's like working around movie stars. It was a creation for me. And I loved that.

My first performance, I think I did great. I just did it. First the lights caught me a little bit. And then I realized there were people there, and then

I just visioned that they wasn't there. And I just did it. Each performance, each night it was great. My story was so real, it took the stage fright completely away. It made me just come out and do it, like I was in this room, alone. And it was like a full house, but I didn't care, because my mind was telling the truth. It wasn't something to be jumping up for joy, because it was a sad story, but it was a true story, and that's what makes me proud to do it all the time.

Each night made me more stronger, made me more willing to do this. Because I wanted to get my word through to the right person. And I feel like one day, the right person is going to hear me, and they going to realize what I'm saying and maybe I can save a lot of lives out there. That's my main concern. I'm telling you, I was like dead. I was dead brain. All that dope, that drinking, in my system. I was dead brain. And so I feel like actually they are dead brain right now. So if I can wake them up to say, "You're not dead yet. You might think you're dead, but you're not." If I can just shake them. I mean my words to shake them.

From the end of my story, it seemed like they all were touched. But I want to know, by you hearing it, did it work, did it mean something to you? Because sometimes you can hear a person but . . . so that it's actually going *in*, sinking *in*. But my main concern is that I want people to feel what I'm feeling and react as well to what I'm going through. That it's not just a story, it's not just an act. Like, in other words, if you can just put yourself in me at this particular time and see what I went through then come back out, then you'll see exactly what I'm saying.

I'm a writer. Writing is hard, but I have a typewriter. I'm a patient person. I just do a little bit. Set it down. I'm not going to give up. Someone have to hear me. Someone have to read it. Can it go somewhere? I know in my heart, I know it can. The lifestyle I've been through and the lifestyle I'm in now. And the creation of what I've built since I've been clean. It's an incredible thing to even see what a human being can actually do. Because it can be done. People have to see. People look at a movie. They'll see it's a true story or a regular rerun. People are into real stories. This actually happened. This person is talking about something that really really happened. Not only that, but it happened to her. She's telling it like it is. There's a reality to everything that you do.

My daughter, Myrna, she always come when I'm typing. She says, "Mom, what are you doing?" I say, "Well, I got to put in a couple more lines with it." She says, "What you discover so far?" "Well, I turned around and I was looking at you when you were asleep, and I thank God that I have you in my life. I thank God that you can accept me." Because she knew what I was doing. She was old enough to see that. She seen that I was taking myself down. She seen when she was taken away from me. She was thirteen. She was heartbroken. Because we was like this: peas in a pod. It was like even when I was on drugs. I could never do nothing without her. Because as long as I made sure she had food in her system, made sure she was asleep, then I did my little sneaking out to go get high. But then I never would neglect her, but I *was* neglecting her. Because I was leaving her alone, which was dangerous. I left her because I'd rather get high than spend time with her. She needed any help with homework, I wouldn't do that. I'd say, "Oh, come on now, you know how to do that." Every excuse in the book just to get to the dope. She's seen a lot of neglection. She's seen that.

But as I speak, she is so proud of me to know that I have not relapsed. She is so proud to know that we can pick up the pieces. And just say, "OK. We know what we did then, but look what we're doing now. We know what we can do now and continue to do as we speak." She loves going to AA meetings with me. She just gets a kick out of that. She won't miss it. She wants to raise her hand. "Mom! Mom! Can I get my chip?" I send her to get it. "This is for my mom. My mom did this." She just loves it. I'm teaching her to type. I want her to know what it's like to feel free to write even her feelings about me. Of what happened to me and how she really felt when I was using. When she was taken away. . . . I want her deeply in my book. She writes now, she writes a page a day. Because she's shy. She's a very shy girl. I want to get all into it. She wants to give me a little bit of her at a time. But I accept her too. I know there's a lot that she wants to actually say that—I want to know her feelings. I know she was hurt. I know that off the top. Because I was even hurt that she had to leave me. But I know she was hurt, because when I had to visit her, when I was fighting to get her back—I had to go through visitation rights and all that—when I was visiting her, just the separation of saying goodbye to her after the visit was over, I seen all this hurt in her. So I want her to just let it out. Now that we are together and you can't be harmed. Nobody can take you away from me again. Let me know exactly how you're feeling, what you were feeling then, what you're feeling now. So I told her it would be of great interest to me to know this.

She looks over me. She wants to be sure. She knows how long I've been on drugs. Ever since she's been born, I've been smoking dope. So she knows that anything is possible, but she knows that I'm so strong because I've never relapsed, and she knows that I'm really fighting for my life to stay this way. So she's a big, big part of my life to help me stay strong as well. So when

I did the performance, she made it her business to be there. She brought a couple of friends. "My mom, she's acting, she's in this play."

I wouldn't tell her what part I was playing. I wanted to surprise her. And when I did it, [she] was like stunned. I seen her where she was sitting. I focused on her. And when I focused on her, the day she was there, that was a really strong performance. I was even more willing to speak out, because I was speaking directly to her. It just blew her away.

My story is very long. It's long enough that it could make a whole show. If I could start my act or my play from the beginning to the end, it would be super long. It's a long piece because of the lifestyle I went through. I like to describe it, because it means a lot to me it that I actually did this to myself. I felt it, I seen it. It was scary.

When I was on drugs it was like being possessed. That's another thing I write about in my book. I look on myself as an exorcist. The name of my book is *Before and After*. The main thing with drugs is I can say a lot of words about drugs. It's like being possessed, like being controlled, like some kind of demon came from the sky; it's like Captain Kirk from Star Trek came down and just beamed you up. It's so many creative things that you can say about drugs. Just being on it, as soon as you hit the pipe, you're just like, *Eyes Boom! Wide Open.* You can tweak in. You want to pick things up. You're like a mummy. "Now you're under my command. Go kill that person. Go rob to get some more dope. When I say, 'Stop. You stop.'" It's like a control thing. It's like someone else is controlling your mind. And the main thing that's controlling is that rock, the dope is controlling. It's so incredible that a piece of rock, dope, whatever you want to call it, crack can actually. . . . You hit it with a pipe, you inhale it, you blow it out, like—wow! you're in a whole space world.

Like, "How did I get in this planet?"

"Well, hit some more of this dope and you'll get more into it."

"Wow. Yeah. I don't want to stop. I want to go on. I want some more."

It's like once you hit it, your mind is taken away from the reality of life, and it says to you, "Now that you took my command, took this pipe, hit this dope, you are actually mine, to keep." It just takes you away. Everything. You talk to someone, first thing you want to say is, "Who are you? What do you want? I don't know you." You're in a whole new world. It's just so incredible.

It's like what the cops do. Tuesday and Thursday, they call it Vice Night. They'll come and clean the youngsters off the street for like a couple hours. Then they're like birds. They'll fly away, then two seconds later when someone puts out some crumbs, they're back in their same place. It's sort of strange. And I just look. I just look at them. And then when I look at them, I look at my baby. And I say to myself, "If I knew what I knew now, I would never in life have took, never have picked up a glass pipe, never have buy dope." For what reason?

It's not even worth you to take your life that you was cherished and brought here with the grace of your mother and father with their help to bring you here. When they brought you here, they wasn't zombies, they wasn't on drugs or alcohol. They wanted kids. They wanted to bring their kids up to be respectable adults. To take their lives somewhere. To go to college. To make a career out of themselves. Be doctors, nurses, all of that. They didn't turn them out to be saying, "I bet you when you grow up, you're going to be the biggest dope dealer there is. When you grow up you're going to be the biggest addict that I've ever known. And guess what, you're my baby daughter, guess what, you smoke more dope, I am *so* proud of you." That was the last thing on their mind for you to grow up to be.

It's a lot of things I done for myself. I honor it to my mom and dad. Because when they was living, I was still smoking dope. When they died, I smoked dope also. Because I said, "Oh good, they're gone. Oh, now I can really smoke dope. Shit. Now they ain't going to get on my case. They're not going to say, 'Oh look at you. You look so damn bad. Jesus. Is that really you? You're not my baby.'" And I won't have to hear all that. At the time, I thought it was nagging. But all they were doing was being concerned. Then that's why I said I woke up. I seen what I knew in the laundromat. I seen all the things that everyone in my family had been telling me. Which I have twelve in my family; I'm the baby. And just the only one on drugs. Everybody, all my brothers and sisters tried to pull me out of the madness. And I turned out to be homeless, and I didn't have to. I had eight brothers and four sisters. The majority of them had homes. I coulda went to stayed with them. I didn't want to stay with them. I wanted to be out there on the streets. I made myself homeless, because that's what I wanted to do. I knew if I go and live with them, first thing they're going to do, "You know you don't smoke no dope in here. We don't allow that here." And then you'd have to go to church on Sundays. It was a hurting situation.

But as I speak, being clean the way I am, my family, they are so proud of me. And I feel that my mother is too, because I see her ghost at her gravesite. I sit down and take my paper and pencil and I writes to her too. I don't want to feel like I'm crazy. But I do ask her, "OK, mom. How would you answer this question?" And I actually think she answers it, because I answer it for her. I know she's dead, but I just got a habit of going to her gravesite. Because I feel like there's so much that I have to make up to my mother. I hurt my mother so badly when I was on drugs. My sister told me her last words was for to tell me to please at least try to get some help so I can be a mother to my child. My mother was very old-fashioned. She come from Louisiana. She believed in just trying to do the right thing for her kids, and she tried to do everything in her power to make us happy and wanted us to be somebody in life. And she told us, that "the day that the damn dope came to this world is the day that I ever regret that I even brought you to this world if I knew you'd have to be involved in it."

So I have a lot to make up to my mom and dad. My father I can't find yet, but I will find him. Because they buried him somewhere and I don't know where. Because I was under the influence of drugs. I couldn't even make it to the funeral because I had to get my hit. Only funeral I made it to was my mom's. I made it to my mom's funeral because I was out of money. And it was the day of the funeral. But if I was loaded, I wouldn't have made it. So I made it to her funeral, but as soon as the funeral was over, I wanted a hit. Saying, "OK. My mom gone. Can I have a hit now?" It's like, wow, she just went on vacation or something. She's actually six feet under.

But that dope was so damn incredible. It's one of the most powerful things that ever came to this lifestyle today. And it's the biggest killer. It's like a virus. Like a virus of AIDS. 'Cause once you got AIDS, you got it. It's definitely a deadly disease. That's what dope is. Dope is a deadly disease. Once you get it, if you don't get out of it, and the only cure for dope is your mind. There's no medication for it. Only thing that can cure dope is you. You are the best medication there is. The only difference is, if you don't take care of yourself and you continue to deal with drugs and all, then you just want to take the virus and kill yourself with it.

It was very, very dangerous on the streets out there. I think it was that God gave me a chance, to see that He wasn't ready for me. He seen there was something better to me than what I was doing. And He knew that I was going to wake up one day. Because I was actually there on death's road, because I'd seen death a lot of times. One house I was into was raided and a gun was pointed up in my face. I'd been around it all. I actually got little youngsters punching me all up in my face because I wouldn't buy dope just from them. I been through it all. You're taking a chance in a million just to get a hit. It's danger out there. You can be here today and gone tomorrow, which is true. But also if you watch your ass, you don't have to be here today and gone tomorrow. If you're doing the positive things, then that's cool, because then if you go, you're going in the right direction, you're just not actually falling, saying, "Fuck it," and boom, it's over. I feel like a champ. I really do.

I got married. My marriage is not . . . It's . . . OK. I'm in love with my husband, but he relaps all the time and it really pisses me off. It pisses me off because I'm like his counselor. And the first thing he's saying is, "Oh, I don't know what I'd do without you. Oh, you're always there for me." And I say, "No, I'm not. Because if I was there for you, you wouldn't go get that dope. So now the word is if I'm there for you then you will fight that urge. That's the meaning of 'I'm there for you.' Because if I'm saying anything that's meaningful to you, you wouldn't go get the dope after I've finished lecturing you. You think you're saying that I'm there for you, but I'm not. Because you don't want me there for you, because right now Mr. Demon out there is a little bit more powerful than . . . whatever I say. Only *you* can say: 'I'm married. This is my stepdaughter. She don't need to see me like this, because I know what she went through with her past with her mother. She don't need to see her stepfather coming into her life seeing this.'"

Myrna gets kind of nervous. She's seen him a couple of times under the influence of dope, and I hate that because that gives her a little doubt in me. "Damn, Mom, your husband on it. Don't you think he's going to try to get you back on it too?" Of course it's only natural for a child to think like that. So that's the only thing that kind of messes me up with my husband.

But I'm working on it. I hate to just throw him out and say, "Boom. Get out of here." I don't need this. We met in the same program. Milestones. I met him there. When he's not under the influence of drugs, he's a very hard-working person. A very beautiful person. Gorgeous understanding and personality, he have it. But then what he do? The area we live in is the area that he came from. That definitely ain't good. Because everybody in the neighborhood knows him. He walks out the door, and he done seen somebody, "Hey Alvin! What's happening?" Giving him no kind of encouragement. The area we're in is an addiction area. But right now when you're on a fixed income, you have to be where you have to be. You have to deal with the reality of survival at that particular time. Like I say, it's not easy.

I told him like this: "Well, it's just not my area, but it's dope. The dope is here. The dope have no relation to no one. It just one color: white. It don't say, 'You're my sister.' So you can't always say, 'This is the area I came from.' Don't please use that for an excuse. Dope is dope. If you move to the Sunset and you saw some youngsters selling dope, you wouldn't drive all the way back here." I'm trying to deal with him, but it's not easy. It's not easy at all.

He'll stop for a couple of weeks. But that's nothing. "If you can't give me six months, three months, then you're not giving me nothing." I tell him I'm not being greedy, but that's what I prefer. Two weeks is like, please. You know. That's not nothing at all to me. Like I told him, "I'll take so much, but I don't think I'll continue it." Because the rehearsals that we've been doing . . . I've sort of not been coming because I've been afraid to leave him alone at the apartment. I know push come to shove, he will take something out of the house to go get high with. So I've been kind of been more of like a housesitter.

Since I've been clean, I've created a lot of stuff, stuff that's valuable to me, and I know you can get a few dollars for. Which he has done it. He took money out of my purse. Every day I go home I hides my purse. My valuable things like my rings, the stuff that I have on my finger, I take this and put it in my purse and hide my purse so it will be with my purse. I don't lay my purse on the table. Oh no. So I can't be comfortable. Anything that's valuable I have to keep it more closer to my possession so I know it'll be there the next day. 'Cause that's what he does. He makes his moves at night. I just bought a camcorder. If he confiscates that, then he would have to go with that. I think I would have to let him go.

I love him dearly. This is my first marriage. I'm his third wife. I don't believe in divorces. My mom and dad got married when they were thirteen. Now that I'm married, I think my husband is mine. I can't get rid of him. He have to be there. Because I don't believe in separation, I don't believe in divorces. So now what am I going to do? I can't tie him up when he has the urge. So I have to stick with him. Regardless of what. But then again, if it gets a little too serious, I think he have to do something really, really big for me to say, "OK, I'm just going to have to take an exception to one of those religions I have. You're going to have to get the hell out of here." But life goes on. I still stay strong.[40]

Of all the people I've interviewed who appear in this chapter, Bailey was the only one who insistently engaged me in a discussion of what this book would look like, who was getting paid for it, about royalties, copyright, who is given credit for the production. She claimed ownership over the piece she performed for the Medea Project and worried if anyone else would ever "play her." She identifies herself as a writer, and this may be why. Telling her story, or writing it, is most emphatically about control. Who is possessed by whom or what? As storyteller, Bailey insists that writing and performing her life can be a way of saving others. She wants to know if her performance on stage "worked." She trusts that if we follow her words, "see what I went through," our response will be what she wants it to be, that we will see her experience as transparently obvious: "You'll see exactly what I'm saying." For Bailey, talking the language of "before and after" seems to be a way of keeping herself safe. If performed enough times, one habit is superseded or controlled and firmly recedes to the "before." The new habit, the life of the writer, comes to the fore, and a different habit of the heart and mind may be in place.

Part of the great power of the modern Medea Project for the audience is the presence of these women, unmoored from their usual routine. Sprung from jail for the evening, off the streets of Turk and Jones, displaced, they burst out onto the stage. Like Medea, Bailey steps out of her neighborhood and insists on performing her own self, as a warning and a cry to rethink boundaries of sympathy inside the walls of the theater. I'm not sure Bailey is as dependent as Euripides's Medea was on associating herself with cunning, wit, disguise. In fact, Bailey seems to reject the notion of herself as an actor *acting*. She believes that what the audience craves is the experience of a "reality" that she and the other women bring up on stage, a reality that she does not envision existing within quotation marks. So much of contemporary performance theory highlights the ways in which identity is constructed; however, Bailey's performance (and her recounting of her life), the "Before and After" that she has constructed, in which she is now clean and yet *not* clean, suggests how fragile the construction of her self is, how vigilant she must be in regulating what touches her, how helpless she is at Turk and Jones, and how much she yearns for a better regulatory system.[41] She also keeps returning to us—the audience, the interviewer—to ask what *we* think, whether *we* were moved, where *we* are in her story.

I was unsettled by the same conjunction of absence and presence expressed by Bailey, so similar to what I heard in Paulette Jones's and Felicia Scaggs's self-presentations: the notion that "something" just "hit" Bailey one day while she was in a laundromat, and she said to herself, "No more." She was going to change. God gave her a chance, she says, "He knew I was going to wake up one day." But why? What hit her exactly, what mysterious force grabbed her *then*? There is the same juxtaposition of clear, vivid descriptions about the powerful attraction of drugs with vague justifications about why she chooses to stay with her addicted husband, imprisoning herself to keep him under watch. Being able to describe reality and being able to assign motivations to actions one takes are two different kinds of writing. Bailey's performance on stage was riveting because she was able to show all the different voices operating when she was high and afterwards. This interview too conveys both her passion and her vulnerability.

Rhodessa Jones believes that to reach Barbara—"to connect with her, to have her really get it"—would take at least two or three years. "She's timid. She's really timid actually." Jones recalls:

> She told me she was a writer, but even her story, she didn't write that story down. She told me when she came to the group, "I'm a writer, you know. That's what I do. I'm a writer. I write." And so at first she said she didn't want to perform because she was a writer. She never wrote anything. Maybe she is. Maybe she was ashamed or scared to show it to us. Maybe I just haven't seen it. I'm not saying she didn't do it, but in relationship to us. . . . Sean might rant and rave about it. But that's what we went through. She would not do this work. I read her interview. She sounded so passionate about it. And I swear she would not write anything *down*. OK? You talk about fried. That's what I mean about being fried. You know?
>
> Barbara's story is a powerful story. She got something there. The first time she did it in the jail she blew my mind. She had never said much of anything. You know? Walking and speaking. Oh, she was just amazing. She did it much better then than she ever did again. And the combination of being terrified and also being possessed and also for that moment in time she was free in a supported environment to relive it.

ANDREA JUSTIN
(*Food Taboos, Buried Fire*)
Andrea Justin performed in *Food Taboos*, and then gave a testimonial in *Buried Fire*, which was the story of her abusive marriage. It was one of the most rousing testimonies in the production. Just as she finishes, the troupe breaks into the Kicking Dance, Rhodessa Jones shouts out encouragement, and the audience cheers. Although Justin kicks free of her ex-husband in the production, in this interview, conducted a few months later, the "before" and "after" are much less clearly divided. I met her at Milestones, the halfway house, where she was living. She spoke slowly, animated when she told the story of becoming addicted, then subdued when she revealed her precarious health and her ambivalence about returning to her husband:

Andrea Justin (standing). Photograph by Lorraine Capparell, 1996

The Medea Project used to come to 850 Bryant Street in San Francisco. I was in jail, but I didn't get into the Medea Project there. I came to Milestones in '93 and somebody was in Medea already. I told them I wanted to be in it. Martha Stein, the director of Milestones, let me go. I was late, but I caught up. People would talk about what they would do and then everybody was all excited and stuff, and that's what made me want to do it. I was curious. I've always been curious. But this time, for the right reasons, so it was OK. It's hard work with Rhodessa. Rhodessa is very demanding, because she's serious about the Medea Project, about you getting on the stage and doing your best and working hard. We did a lot of work. We was real tired, but we didn't give up.

We work on different things, different pieces, and in some kind of way they come together. That's the good part, the amazing part that makes you feel really good. Because you're doing all these different things, you're working, you're practicing with Nancy, Rhodessa, Fé, and all of them, and then all of a sudden, all of it comes together. It's true. It's cool. I never thought I could do it. I just never thought I could do it. Because with some of the abuse that I did suffer, it made me think I couldn't do nothing. That I wasn't worth anything. So with the Medea Project, it was the very first thing I accomplished.

Maybe it was because it was all women who could relate to what I was saying, and they was there for me and they sympathized with me, and some of them had even been through some of the stuff that I had been through. Maybe it was the bond, because I felt closer to them. In other workshops, they were all strangers I didn't even know. The first time I tried to get a lady's number to call her, she acted funny, so I didn't call her. I didn't feel close to her or anything like that. It's the women in the Medea Project and the bond, and they're strong. Especially Rhodessa. She bring out stuff you didn't even know you had. She'll get on your case too, she will. But you will appreciate her later, because she will push you to the limit.

Barbara [Bailey] and I had a real bond. We was in jail together, and at the Medea Project we used to sit on the side and shy away. I was kind of like shy. From me being put down in my marriage, I even thought some things I had to say wasn't worth saying. I didn't think nobody would be interested. Nobody would get anything out of it. Even like now in a program and doing your share, telling your story, your life story like how you—what happened in your life—talking about your dysfunctional family. . . . I don't think I had a dysfunctional family. I just had a dysfunctional marriage and that's *it*. It's the people in the Medea Project. It's the women who are real, real strong and they always there for you. Whatever you need to talk about, and you're crying, they'll be with you to get you through it.

They kept saying I never said anything. And then they asked me did I have a testimonial, and I said, "Yeah," and then I did the one about my marriage.[42] It was pretty cool because it helped me to talk about it. I was going through this incest survival class, and they talk about all kinds of different things and I would talk about that, but, I don't know, I don't think it really helped me. Not there. But I think the Medea Project did, because, I don't know, it was just a lot of women. You got a lot of support.

I wasn't raised as a dope fiend. I wasn't raised as a thief, you know. We was raised in church. We had to go to church. We had to go to school. We did everything together as a family. We came to San Francisco, we still had to go to catechism, we still had to go to school, to church; we still did everything together as a family. And when somebody did something, somebody was always there—and then I met my husband and then that was it. Not right away. But pretty much. He taught me how to pickpocket; somebody taught me how to pick up purses, he made sure of that. He made sure somebody was teaching me how to boost, which is stealing, and everybody around me was nodding and I wasn't, and this was all I saw. And then we started selling dope, and that was the only thing around me, and I wanted to be a part of him, and so eventually I went into the bathroom with him whenever he shot cocaine. I had to be in there with a towel because I was scared he was going to die or something. I was there with him, and so eventually I wind up snorting and then wind up with a needle in my arm. It was a lot of verbal abuse with him and then a lot of women, because he had to go have sex here and sex there. So mentally I went through a lot. I went in and out of psychiatric hospitals, because he would even call me from prison. "Bitch this and bitch that." It was really a trip. I talked about that. In *Buried Fire*. Some days, I didn't say it. But some days I said everything that happened. I spoke about the sex that he had with people in my family, the sex he wanted me to do with him that I wouldn't want to do. At one point, all he would call me was "bitch" or "female"—that was it. I talked about that. And I think I felt embarrassed about it at first, but I got to the point where I didn't feel embarrassed. I would just say it. I would get real, real mad. One time I got so mad, I was so excited, when we went backstage (we do the Kicking Dance right after), I was hyperventilating. I couldn't breath.

Yeah, it was a trip. People from here came. Well, I thought, shit, well, if people talk about me. . . . But they didn't. Some of the men would come up to me and say, "Well, Andrea, I didn't know you went through all that." And when my husband got into recovery and started coming around, I told him I had talked about him. "You used my name?" I said, "Yeah. When I'm doing a share, yeah, they all know you." Shit. There's a lot of men who have done it. And they sit downstairs and share about it and how sorry they are about it. And now they think that women are queens, and I don't give a damn what color they are, it's like, he needs to get to that stage. Because now he has this outlook about women that they are less than, lower than the man instead of equal. We know we can't do everything a man can do and get away with it, but you know, *damn*. He didn't know I was performing. He was in prison. I think he would have killed me [laughs] if he had come. After we did my testimony, during the performance, Rhodessa would say, "This is for you, Aaron. *Kick his ass.*"

When I talk to him, because he's in a program now and he wants to get back together, and it's like . . . because I was really, really faithful to him. A lot of people said that about me. They was trying to figure: how come I didn't even look at a man? He went to jail for a year and a half. And I was very young. And he would come home and have sex with different women. He never once said he was sorry. He listens to me now, though. When I told him about the bitches, and if you want me to have oral sex and I didn't want to and you made me do it, about you having sex with this person and that person, about all the things that I didn't appreciate and you did to me. He listens to me, but he never told me he was sorry. At first I couldn't see myself ever getting back with him and never thought that would never happen, like they said in recovery, but it did, and he wanted to see if we could get things together. When I was with him, I was like a puppet, whatever he wanted, I was willing to abide by whatever he wanted. Everything was for him and not for me. Now everything is totally different.

I stopped messing with him eight years ago, but we were still married. Since he's gotten into recovery he wants to get back together, and I was willing to give it a shot, but it was like we had to talk about everything, not just like nothing ever happened, like everything was wonderful. I still shied away from him, even like him touching me, I couldn't come to him instantly like everything was OK. I just didn't want him to touch me. Still the put-downs, even that was still there. He'd say, "Andrea you're not all *that*." And one time my daughter told him, "Don't tell her that. She *is* all *that*." Because it's another form of putdown. I guess I feel I am different. I'm not the person he knew before. I'm *not* stupid. I'm *not* naïve. I never was stupid. I just thought I was because he called me stupid. I know more about relationships and how relationships are supposed to be. And the things you're supposed to have in a relationship to make a healthy relationship, to make a good relationship. So now I don't have relationships because I'm not willing to get hurt no more, and right now I'm just working on myself and spend my time with my family and with my daughter and we talk a lot. I would like to get her in the Medea Project. Strong women there. I think she would like it. I think she'd get a lot out of it because I do.

I talk to my daughter about a lot of stuff that I went through, especially with men. I don't down her daddy, and I don't talk bad about him, but I tell her about how men can be. Men think that we are men bashers. That's what they say. Maybe we do a little bit. That's what my husband can't stand. He says, "Women's lib. Oh, *well*." We're going to be independent and be OK with myself and not having to have a man. I love men, but I can live without one now. I heard someone say about me: "I want to know you as *you*, not as Aaron's wife." The Medea Project has built my self-esteem up. It has made me stronger. It really has.

My daughter wants us to be together. I tell my daughter we would sit down and have a long talk: "I'm trying to talk to your daddy. If we do, we do; if we don't, we don't." Fuck it. It's not that important to me. But I would love to be able to forgive and make amends. But it's hard for me to forgive. Because that marriage really messed me up. And I didn't know any better, because it's like he raised me. I met him when I was fourteen years old. At a point in my life, my mother stopped raising me, and he started. He showed me a lot of messed up things, and no matter how faithful I was to him he treated me like a dog, and I just can't act like everything is OK and shit. He didn't want to talk about a lot of things. He acted like, shit, nothing ever happened. But we have to talk about it. I can't take a chance.

I just think that God put these different things in my pathway so I won't make the same mistake, because I don't think it could ever be. Rhodessa said if I ever need to talk about it or stay in her house to get away, I could. But they don't have to worry, because his ego isn't going to let him hide behind me. So that's cool too. It's kind of like messing with me. I just wish he wouldn't have ever come back in my life. He couldn't take rejection from me. Because my daughter, Angelique, thought that something was fixing to happen, and it didn't and it's not. I know it's not. I'm not going to let it happen, I don't think.

I don't be going around no more. It's not because I don't want to. It's my feet are killing me. Then I have this cancer thing. Sometimes it's worse than others. I'm depressed or crying, you know, and sometimes when I talk about it, I need to cry. I don't want to cry and stuff is bundled up, and then I can't help but cry.[43]

There's such an emotional rawness in Justin's story, especially toward the end. All the feelings of depression, fears about her health that were "bundled up" spill out, and tears well up in her eyes. She says she "can't help but cry," and that sense of helplessness seems stronger than any or all other realizations. Within a couple of years, Rhodessa Jones hears that Justin is back with her husband, taking a chance. Jones believes the women are addicted to the wrong men, not just the wrong drugs: "In the Medea Project, all the failed stories that have come out of people with great potential—the stories have been about men—that's Andrea, Paulette, Barbara. I'm sure that even Fefe being back in jail—it's got something to do with trying to look good for a man. Back with Boo, her boyfriend." But any diagnosis of what goes wrong for these women seems short of the mark, too simple, because even if one could be sure of correctly identifying the problem, that knowledge doesn't necessarily lead to a solution. How much more would someone have to know about these women before one could successfully intervene? How much more insightful would any analysis have to be? And even if one did survey their families, their friends, their community, how far back and how continuously, and how far forward, and what kinds of power would one have to wield to make a difference? As Rhodessa Jones said, if someone jumps out a window, you can stretch out your hands to try to catch them, but at some point you're going to have to let go.

In my interactions with these women, I almost studiously avoided asking about their lives before or after their involvement in the Medea Project. Except for what they chose to tell me, I don't know anything about their families, their friends. My project wasn't to find out in order to correct—but then neither, exactly, is that the aim of the Medea Project. In one of Jones's rants, she specifically tells them that it's not about getting into their business. Other parts of the prison apparatus make it their business to know something of their lives for the record. It has been somewhat surprising for me to find out that Jones and Reynolds are as much in the dark about a particular woman's addictions as I am. They too avoid asking, because they believe that's not their business. Their business is to redirect the women's attention to their own business, their own lives. My project in interviewing the women was to find out what they thought about the Medea Project. What they all said was how much they enjoyed working with other women, with Jones and Reynolds especially. They all said it gave them great satisfaction to perform, to say something about their lives to an audience, and they all testified that their ideas about themselves and others changed because of what they learned in the Medea Project, that they became more confident, more assertive about what they needed, more able to see the need for boundaries between themselves and the people who abused them, between themselves and the things to which they had become addicted. But it is also clear from subsequent history that the project alone cannot ensure a place at the table nor can it ensure that a taste of something else will suppress the appetite for more familiar fare.

The sounds of the women are imprisoned by the moment at which their interviews were tape-recorded. At this moment that I write I do not think they are back in jail. I have heard snatches from Rhodessa Jones of choices some of the women have made, but all that too is old news by the time it gets to me, much less by the time this book is published or a reader reads it. And I assume most readers, like myself, will want to know what they will not find out here. What's happening to these women now, as you sit and read? This record is as useless as statistics, welfare reports, criminal records, and individual testimonies in not divulging what we most need to know: the crucial knowledge, the whole contour of another's life.

Making Room at the Table

More women are going to jail, and I think the feminist movement has a lot to do with it. I think on some level women realize they can go out and make some money. You know, maybe they can go out and commit some crimes that men usually commit, not women. I think that women have been thrown into the pool. I think that the law is much harsher against women than men. Because women are under this dual kind of system here. We are supposed to be at home, having babies, cleaning up, taking care of the kids, or we're supposed to be career women. You know, we're supposed to be trying to break through the glass ceiling, which is another crock of shit notion that they feed us. We are not supposed to be out on the corner—raising hell and gaping our legs and talking back, talking back to men. Being bad girls. We're supposed to be at home.

I think women are judged differently. If a man commits a crime, especially an economic crime, the judge, perhaps because he's a man will think: "Really, this wasn't right. But he was trying to make a way for his family." But a woman, she's just a whore, she's incorrigible. She's a girl in juvenile; she's incorrigible. Nobody bothers to think about why she's incorrigible. What's her history like? Everybody thinks they know what the man been through. Even with the races, there's a common ground. Well, man, you do it, you do what you have to do.
—Sean Reynolds

Michael Marcum had said these women tell powerful stories; they are surely at least as striking as the statistics that open this chapter. But like statistics, the stories are subject to interpretation. And analysis, ventured solely on the basis of these short stories, feels extremely unscientific, to say the least. Like the social scientists employed by the government, we might find ourselves making interpretations about these women's lives based on preconceived notions: these women are incorrigible; they're bad, so lock them up; or they're in need of more therapy, they've got to be separated from those bad men. From the individual stories, we "naturally" move to generalizations, and much of these have to do with the cultural myths we believe about women and men.

It is hard to know how to (or whether we can) distinguish among myths, personal observations, and documentable behavioral surveys, but almost everyone who comes in touch with this project speaks generally about women's "complicated" nature. What makes for the complications (or the perception of complication) is not exactly clear: is it simply that women have not been adequately surveyed, and therefore remain mystifyingly complex; or are they too complicated to be satisfyingly surveyed? All of the people who work in the San Francisco jails and who are sympathetic to the Medea Project believe that women's problems are different from men's, that therefore the solutions might have to be different and might be harder to come by. Ironically, as many people testify, jail may provide more ample space than the streets to experiment with different solutions for the complexity of women's problems.

While there has been much debate in general about the usefulness of incarceration and much attention paid to male delinquents, there has been relatively little research paid to women in prison. That is changing now, because of the huge upswing in numbers of women being incarcerated and because of feminists who insist on paying attention. Organizations like Amnesty International are now focusing their attention on abuses that are particular to incarcerated women.[44] But perhaps because their numbers are still small in comparison to the numbers of incarcerated men, or perhaps because our culture favors men, the number of programs for and the amount of research on incarcerated women are still small. Anyone working with incarcerated women has to justify spending resources on them because they are few in number relative to incarcerated men. Jones says, "I tell people all the time I have eight brothers, and we're constantly being told the statistics about African American men. I understand that. But the lives of women and girls from time immemorial have been shoved under the rug. And it is time that we stand up and everybody faces everybody else. Everybody's life is important." Jones argues both on general principles: historically, women haven't been seen as important as men, and this isn't fair; and individually, everybody is important, no matter who they are. Sheriff Hennessey argues that it is worth spending a little bit more money on women than their proportion in jail would merit (8 to 12 percent of the prisoners in San Francisco jails) because they are not only valuable as individuals but they represent their children as well:

> Women play a very dual role in our society and in this community. They
> are not only individuals who we are concerned about, but they are the care-
> takers of children. The vast majority of women in our jails are mothers. And
> they are oftentimes mothers without husbands. They're going to continue to
> be the mother of that child some place. So I think we owe a little bit extra
> concern as a society and as a criminal justice system to women custodies be-

cause they are not only the individual we are concerned about but they help create and form the lives of the next generation—more so, unfortunately, than our men prisoners.

It is a somewhat disquieting logic (what would be the fractional break-down—a childless woman is worth three-fifths a man, but four-fifths or more if she has a child or two or three?), but it is a familiar argument and one that appeals to a society that *believes* it values motherhood. The burdens of a woman are different from those of a man because we still expect women to have children and to take care of them. Men, unfortunately, as the sheriff points out, are not expected to take care of their children in the same ways or at all. Motherhood is one of the foremost complicating differences for women inmates. Jones says: "We get pregnant. Some man has to participate. But then we spend these nine months growing this thing and then it all leaves us. I think women are far more complicated than men. With violence, drug addiction, we're far more dangerous. And when a woman learns she has nothing more to lose, she's *really* dangerous. And she might even choose to die." The stakes seem to be higher for women with children, and more dangerous for everyone. Medea's rage against her husband is expressed by killing her children. It is her transgressions against her children—not those against Jason or his new bride, and certainly not Jason's betrayal of his wife or his children—that terrifies. A bad mother is far more dangerous than a bad father, so the myth goes, perhaps supported by our observation and statistics, or by our fears.

We hear a lot too about how women, when they're in trouble, have to rely on other women in their lives to take care of them and their family. Sean Reynolds speaks of her experience with this point:

> For the most part, incarcerated women don't trust each other, nor do they trust women in general. They'll tell you point blank, "Oh no! I don't hang with women in the free world!" Or they'll tell you something like, "The only person I can depend on is my man."
>
> The irony is that with a little self-scrutiny, they will admit to having been sold down the river by most of the men in their lives, and they will admit to being emotionally supported by mothers, aunts, sisters, etc.
>
> They are not unlike many other women in this culture who believe, uphold, and support the lies of men . . . from the wives of presidents to the incarcerated woman.

And yet, women don't trust each other. Competing over men, they are able to shove other women aside, to take their place at his table. One of the guards who has worked with the Medea Project from the beginning, Marcia Colhour, said it was easier to work with men in prison than women: "It was easier because women tend to be a bit catty, nails are always out. They tend to be aggressive. Men say, 'Excuse me.' Women don't say 'Excuse me' to other women. Women were always in competition with other women. Women are very, very complicated. And emotionally they'll do things and hurt themselves and not know it. Cut off your nose to spite your face."[45]

Martha Stein, the director of Milestones, where Paulette Jones, Barbara Bailey, and Andrea Justin went once they had been released from jail, concurs:

> I think of teenage girls, to some extent, when they start getting interested in boys, they maybe don't trust each other. They sort of see each other in more competitive kinds of situations, and I'm not sure they ever get past that. Our clients, in terms of social development, are kind of stuck. They haven't really matured into well-rounded people. They're kind of like fighting for their own little turf. People say it goes back to boys being on teams, and women aren't, and sports, and all of that, and I don't know if it's all that. But there's probably some difference in socialization too.
>
> In many ways, women's experiences have probably been more psychologically and emotionally damaging. Both men and women have certainly had abuse as children, sexual abuse as children, but probably more women have experienced those kinds of things than men. And also many of our women have prostituted [themselves]. And have neglected their responsibilities as a mother. I don't think that men have had those same kind of psychological issues.[46]

Culture at large and culture of the jails are not differentiated here: girls are taught that boys are the most important thing they can catch; they learn they have to compete with each other for the prize; their worth is measured not by their own accomplishments but by the men they can attach themselves to, perhaps by the children they produce. Prostitution and neglectful mothering can be seen as the fallout from this particular way of organizing relationships. Expectations for women may be complex or at cross purposes because they must direct themselves to pleasing men and pleasing their children, to need protection and be able to protect.

Partly, what surveyors of crime feel they need to do is to discriminate between the people who deserve to be punished and put in jail and those who deserve to be punished and helped, so they can be helped to not repeat the same hopeless way of living, pushing a rock, pushing people over. No one I interviewed, not Jones or Reynolds, believes that prisons can disappear or that all people are salvageable. They are acutely aware of the complex interweaving of biography, history, economics, and morality:

RHODESSA JONES: I think there are sins in the culture. There's something to be said of the old Arabic system that we've heard about. If a man's a thief, you cut off his hand. If a man is a rapist, what do you do? These are the questions I lay at the foot of inmates. What do we do in the name of taking a life?

Some people should be in jail. I'll be the first person to say it. But if we are a humane society, on the morning of the twenty-first century there should be a consciousness that includes humanity as well as the environment, because it's all the same thing. Are we ready to really look at each other and think of all men and women as family, as a human family? We're not ready. We don't know how to look.

SEAN REYNOLDS: I am not saying that we should not have jails. Some of the people in there *should* be in jail. They shouldn't be living here. *I* shouldn't be looking at them. Because some of them *are* crazy. You might not start out being crazy when you're homeless, but in a while you will be if you go back and forth, back and forth because you can't never get a toehold. That's what it's really all about, isn't it? It's really about economics.

I heard on the radio the other day a discussion concerning the death penalty for the guy who killed Polly Klaas. Someone said because of his background he *should not* receive the death penalty. What about the Menendez brothers? The jurors said, "We don't want to give them the death penalty because *they're such nice boys.*" You cannot have it both ways. If you cannot give the nice boys the death penalty, how you going to give the man who was beaten the death penalty? I don't get it. I don't get it. The Menendez brothers killed their parents, went out and bought a Rolex. Something is wrong here. *Scum* can get the death penalty. But these are nice boys. And we won't even talk about the Kennedy boy. He's scot-free in medical school in New Mexico. Another nice boy.

There's something wrong here with this system of justice. Again, some of the people I've met are far, too far gone for whatever reason. They're just too far gone. They're *not* going to recover. They *can't* turn around. It's over, it's too late. But that's a very small percentage, especially among women, because women are just *beginning* to enter the system. Ninety-nine percent of the women I see are salvageable. They really are. I firmly believe that some of the men should be dead. I've never felt that way about women.

I hope that there's not a person on the face of this earth who has not committed a crime. I don't want to know them because they probably couldn't be that interesting. It's not about the crimes we commit, it's about our *morality*. There's a difference to me between law and God's law. I would tell women, "You ain't knocked an old lady down? You ain't murdered nobody? OK, what have you done? We can deal with it. *It's how you feel about what you've done.*"

I find all of these voices so compelling because they are alive to the complexity of life and no one offers easy answers. The five women talk about their situation in mostly personal terms. They do not talk about poverty or lack of education, and they rarely refer to history, just to their families. They blame bad husbands, loving bad husbands, addiction to drugs; but in some way, they are honestly a mystery to themselves. The others who speak about the incarcerated women speak more generally about the social conditions that surround them. None of them offers a solution that would guarantee the end to Sisyphean labors, an end to the cycle of recidivism. They know that experimentation is necessary; trials will lead to errors and perhaps to some success. They fight for resources for their experiments, because they know that different people will respond to different approaches—some to art, others to religion, or formal education. Jones says that prisons are not the solution. Even the Medea Project, she says, is not a solution: "The Medea Project isn't about biography, and it's not an attempt to find solutions. It is an attempt to look at the process. It's about finding a voice. It may not be what we want to hear. Maybe what we learn is that we don't ask the right questions."

Or, perhaps, we don't sufficiently describe. Wittgenstein has written: "The difficulty—I might say—is not that of finding a solution but rather of recognizing as the solution something that looks as if it were only a preliminary to it. . . . This is connected, I believe, with wrongly expecting an explanation, whereas the solution of the difficulty is description, if we give it the right place in our considerations."[47] How to fully, rightfully describe? Fundamentally, no matter what the statistics may be in 100 years about the individuals who came through the Medea Project, any hope of widespread individual liberation must address the social and economic configuration of the table at which we all sit.

CHAPTER 4

Community Work
Imagining Other Spaces

For me, "Who should speak" is less crucial
than "Who will listen?"
—*Gayatri Spivak, quoted in Mercer,* Welcome to the Jungle

It has been argued that the principle of participation is foundational to modernity, even a prerequisite.[1] In his seminal work published in the early 60s, *The Structural Transformation of the Public Sphere,* Habermas recognized that "the communicative network of a public made up of rationally debating private citizens has collapsed; the public opinion once emergent from it has partly decomposed into the informal opinions of private citizens without a public and partly become concentrated into formal opinions of publicistically effective institutions."[2] Instead of rational debates, we have talk shows, or "conversations" after a theater performance, or town hall meetings—all of which seem staged for consumption (how stupid people sound or perhaps, once in a while, how smart), but none of them provide ways to move from a speech, even an exchange, to action. Lauren Berlant has argued that there is no such thing as a public sphere in the contemporary United States, "no context of communication and debate that makes ordinary citizens feel that they have a common public culture, or influence on a state that holds itself accountable to their opinions, critical or otherwise."[3] Habermas has given up on the possibility of any sort of publicly influential organization to develop or express a rational collective will. Instead he looks to voluntary organizations that organize themselves outside the range of public institutions already in place.[4] Our postmodern disappointment with the possibilities of serious public discourse in the public sphere is profound and, almost paradoxically, shared by almost every citizen. The Medea Project presents an opportunity for many organizations and individuals to merge voluntarily in an effort to work out more flexible ways for people to participate with each other in public. It seeks to reanimate a public sphere or, if that is too nostalgic and historically inaccurate (since we know that past publics have always excluded exactly the population the Medea Project is *for*), then to create a more inclusive, animated, public sphere.

When I try to find a way to describe just what this public sphere of the Medea Project looks like, I am torn between writing prose about the everyday space of contingencies, accidents, who works where, who has money, and writing the most metaphorical poetry of dreams and utopian hopes. Of course, it is the absolute conjoining of the real and the imaginative that marks the Medea Project's most profoundly transformative nature. The "human geographers" I am thinking of—Soja, Rose, Bhabha, West, hooks—all mix metaphorical abstractions with the material ones. In Soja's words, human geographies "are made more 'real' by being simultaneously 'imagined.'"[5] It is this particular sort of hybridity— not just racial, not just cultural, but at the level of description—that distinguishes the work of the Medea Project. Soja tells us that when the French philosopher Henri Lefebvre was confronted with the "Big Dichotomies" (subject-object; man-woman; black-white; center-periphery, etc.), he would say, "[T]wo terms are never enough to deal with the real and imagined world. *Il y a toujours l'Autre*. There is always an-Other term, a third possibility that works to break down the categorically closed logic of the 'either-or' in favour of a different, more flexible and expansive logic of the 'both-and-also'."[6] I think of the Medea Project as an embodiment of this third possibility, what Soja has called a "Thirdspace" or "lived space," a place in which "making practical and theoretical sense of the world requires a continuous expansion of knowledge formation, a radical openness that enables us to see beyond what is presently known, to explore 'other spaces.'"[7] The Medea Project makes a space for a different sort of politics, one that, though still progressive, does not slavishly follow any one master narrative, Marxist or race/class/gendered, but rather acknowledges the power of contingency, a sense, as Doreen Massey writes, that the future is "genuinely open" and that life may yet produce "the genuinely novel." It is a political space that depends upon "an acknowledgement of difference and a multiplicity of voices."[8] And it mostly refuses "the politics of polarity."[9] The Medea Project provides the space for people to reflect on *relations*. It is not so simple (as Massey reminds us) as to argue that if only we recognize our interrelatedness we will become happy and equal; rather, it argues that if we can recognize that we *are* related, then we may begin to examine just *how*. And in that space, the politics of resistance, opposition, and solidarity does, indeed, emerge.

As Benedict Anderson has pointed out, most communities made up of large groups of unrelated people "will never know most of their fellow-members, meet them, or even hear of them, yet in the minds of each lives the image of their communion." "Communities are to be distinguished," he notes, "not by their falsity/genuineness, *but by the style in which they are imagined*." [10] As in a nation where no one person knows every other, so in the theater an individual might not know who she is sitting next to. But the audience that comes together to support the Medea process forms a community all the same, knit together in a collective imaginative act of identity, known by the style in which they imagine each other. For more than most theatrical ventures, the Medea Project depends upon its audience not only to listen but to speak back, and not only to speak about what they believe is the real project, but more importantly, to speak of what may be only imagined. The Medea Project's audience constitutes a community that is more than just the people who come one night to a public performance; it also includes the audience who will not come, the missing fathers, guards on duty or not interested, people who believe this has nothing to do with them. Being able to imagine a different audience, not only in the sorts of people who would have to be persuaded to come but in the kind of work the community might do to make it in their interest to come, becomes part of the project of the future.

The Medea Project has always imagined itself as more than the sum of its parts because the parts do not yet make up a necessary, sufficient community, either in numbers or function. The community needs to be not only bigger but transformed, changed from a passive audience that listens into a community that can perform by speaking back, creating different places for citizens to live and work. In this final chapter, I concentrate on describing the communities that surround the Medea Project, how they exist and how they imagine a new style of social art work in the new millennium. Though much of the Medea Project centers on work with individual women and though even a discussion of community cannot avoid describing key people, nevertheless, aggregate social forces, what one might think of as contingencies—history, geographical location, politics—are critical in determining the future of individuals in the Medea Project. In this chapter, I briefly sketch San Francisco history, the conjunction of the self-esteem movement and the development of the Arts in Corrections organization in California, and some of the local foundations that have supported the Medea Project, ending with imaginative projections of its future.

Fortuitous Alchemy

I think there's a kind of alchemy at work . . .
—*Kary Schulman*

The Medea Project manages to bring together some of the very different worlds that make up the city of San Francisco: incarcerated and formerly incarcerated women, artists, political activists, and the wealthy elite. In the first group are mostly uneducated, unskilled women who have not managed or have not been willing to work at low-paid jobs in the service sector; the illegal services of prostitution and drug dealing or drug using have landed many of them in jail. Artists and political activists expect to be able to transform these beaten-down women—some looking much older than their years, with missing teeth, bad skin—into kick-ass, moving, wild, proud women. A third part of the Medea Project's community are elite local families who have made money by selling products (for example, the Haas family, who have been responsible for selling Levi jeans to the world) and who, if they themselves don't come to the theater, are funding the theater through their foundations. The Medea Project has generated as much local enthusiasm as it has at least in part because it employs ideals that are prized by each of these very different groups: the rhetoric of individual responsibility, the importance of self-esteem, and aspirations to make bridges among communities. Kary Schulman, the director of Grants for the Arts in San Francisco, which has funded Cultural Odyssey over the years, tries to explain the chemistry that makes the Medea Project possible:

First of all, you know, I think Rhodessa Jones is really good. And that's a big plus. Because sometimes you have people who are terribly energetic and not that good. She's both really good and really energetic. She's also absolutely fearless. To just sail into the jails and do that.

And I think that there's this ethic in San Francisco that's really interested in social change issues, issues of social justice, a very strong feminist center. I think there's a kind of alchemy at work that you could kind of tease out. Things that went into it. There's an extremely progressive sheriff in San Francisco, who was there before 1989 [when The Medea Project began] but co-incides exactly. In another city, or in this city with a different sheriff, [Jones] might not have gotten in the door. I mean, you know, that's a gatekeeper position. And the fact that he was willing to take a chance on this and really support it and be interested and bend the odd rule here and there. . . . You could have a different personality who could have said, "I don't think so. I don't think this is for us." And it would have died aborning really.[11]

Alchemy, social ethics, gatekeepers: the metaphors are as mixed as the tangled influences that make up what is peculiar to a particular place. Without the progressive ethic of San Francisco, the history of the arts in corrections movement, and the city's tourist-driven economy, which thrives on cultural productions; without the support of "gatekeepers," *this* particular sheriff, and *this* particular Rhodessa Jones, the Medea Project would indeed have "died aborning." The oft caricatured portrait of California, and San Francisco in particular, as a place tolerant of, even supportive of, wacky, experimental projects of all sorts has real consequences. Rhodessa Jones always says in her opening remarks to a Medea production that she is grateful to the city of San Francisco, "full of fruits and nuts," for supporting her work. (The audience always laughs, I think, with approval and self-congratulation.) There is synergy, for the Medea Project reflects exactly the cultural and economic and political mix that is San Francisco, bringing together those who have been left behind by the particular configuration of the late twentieth-century economy with those who have profited from it. The public performance of the Medea Project, for all of its grittiness, and maybe even because of it, celebrates a recognizable San Franciscan way of life: progressive, activist, risky, utopian, energetic, optimistic.

Modern California history, beginning in 1848, has been particularly volatile, fueled by extraordinary events—the discovery of gold, cataclysmic earthquakes, manmade diversions of water to fertilize the southern desert—and by waves of immigration. California tantalizes the world's imagination as a place that is always warm, where fruit can be plucked off trees; its most famous exports entertain the world with moving pictures of love and violence and views of the future. At the turn of the twenty-first century, California has replaced New York as the gateway to the United States and to the United States' future, as immigrants from all parts west and south arrive now on its coast. For a hundred years, San Francisco was the most powerful city of the territory and then state. Its population exploded in the space of a few years following the 1848 discovery of gold in the California hills to make the city the most important center in California, a place where people came to live off the transfer of gold: "gold—and later silver, cattle, and grain—made the city into an entrepôt, a middleman in the nation's economy. Its people did not make goods; instead they transferred them."[12] The economy of the city has largely remained the same; never an industrial center but always in need of laborers (first, construction workers, especially as the city burned more than once, even before the 1906 earthquake; and then longshoremen for the port). One hundred fifty years later the kind of laborers needed are for quite different occupations. The Port of San Francisco has long been superseded by the Port of Oakland, across the bay; and the geography of San Francisco, tightly hemmed in by water on three sides, has been built up to saturation.[13] Los Angeles has long since outgrown San Francisco in numbers, political influence, cultural eminence, and capital. But San Francisco still enjoys a reputation, now almost a quaint one, as a tourist destination as well as a financial center: "San Francisco has been reduced to the role of serving as the region's 'symbolic' center and as a convenient source of cultural amenities, fine restaurants, and venture capital to fuel the region's real economic engines in San Jose and Silicon Valley. . . . Approximately one in eleven city jobs is generated by nonprofit or for-profit arts organizations. One in nine city jobs is in the tourism and hospitality industries."[14] White-collar workers—lawyers, financial workers, computer technicians—now power its economy. With a reputation from its earliest Gold Rush days for being a hospitable place for outlaws and more recently for bohemians, beats, hippies, gays and lesbians, and New Age cultists, San Francisco has always been seen to be amenable to cultural experimentation and liberal attitudes.

Today, San Francisco advertises, even capitalizes on its nonconformist status: "Symbolic gestures intended for national consumption are a staple of local politics. Hardly a week goes by without the announcement of some type of organized protest, boycott, rally, demonstration, declaration, or resolution that is almost certain to offend mainstream American public opinion."[15] To market itself as a first-class tourist destination as well as a financial center, San Francisco can rely on its natural beauty and its geographical position perched on the Pacific Rim; it cultivates its tolerance for nonmainstream cultural positions, benefiting both from its immigrant populations—many of whose members work in service industries and who bring with them their foods, language, and cultural habits—and from the highly educated workforce with cosmopolitan tastes whose members appreciate the mix of people and cultures and can afford its high cost of living.

In 1995, San Francisco was selected by *Fortune* magazine as the best city for business in the country, and it is regularly cited as the most livable, though this does not exempt it from problems that plague other cities, including persistent crime, a deteriorating municipal transit system, overcrowded schools, homelessness, and environmental woes.[16] There exists a huge disparity between those who live on top of its most famous hills with a view and those who live on the flats. In 1980, San Francisco was ranked as the nation's most ethnically diverse large city, above New York and Los Angeles; its diversity has only increased since then. Over the last thirty years, huge shifts in the distribution of ethnicity have occurred. In 1960, 18 percent of the city was classified as nonwhite; by 1990, that number was 53 percent. In 1974, Frederick Wirt described African Americans, Asians, and Spanish-speaking immigrants as "arriving ethnic groups," but by 1990, Asians and Pacific Islanders were the largest single ethnic minority group (28 percent), followed by Latinos (14 percent) and African Americans (11 percent).[17] Tension exists among the city's minority groups, who compete for goods and services and representation. San Francisco's economy, skewed in two directions—on the one hand, to the most highly educated workers, employed in banks or software companies or arts organizations; on the other, to uneducated workers who are relegated to restaurant and hotel work—reveals the starkly different opportunities the city offers.

San Franciscans, relying on the city's progressive reputation, try at times to find ways to bring the disparate communities together. The juxtaposition of the art world and prisons is but one intersection. William Cleveland, former administrator for the Arts in Corrections Program in California, recounts that history at the statewide level in his book *Art in Other Places*. In 1978, the former chair of the California Arts Council, Eloise Smith, met with state senator Henry Mello, California Department of Corrections director Jerry Enomoto and deputy director George Warner, and California Arts Council (CAC) chairman Peter Coyote. She wanted their support for expanding a program she had been running at the California Medical Center at Vacaville. The CAC had already been distributing grants through their Artists in Social Institutions program, and by 1980–81 they had received enough support that out of a $500 million Department of Corrections appropriation, $400,000 was earmarked to pay for an arts program, a program manager, and six full-time civil service artist/facilitators. Influenced by M. C. Richard's book *Centering in Pottery, Poetry, and the Person,* Eloise Smith believed that "an inmate could improve his self-esteem, and thus his behavior, by replacing his lost physical freedom with an inner freedom gained through the discipline and rewards of art."[18] The self-esteem movement and the art in prison movement merged; people on the opposite ends of freedom's scale, the incarcerated and the artist, collaborated to redefine freedom as disciplined, internal, personal.

There is no question that the Medea Project is influenced by the self-esteem movement. Jones, Reynolds, and just about everybody else who works with the project are imbued with the language of the movement, because the rhetoric of self-esteem and its disciplinary expectations are strongly associated with this historical moment and place. During the late 1960s and early 1970s, when nationwide a full-scale attack was made on the "rehabilitative ideal," and in the 1980s, when serious crime fluctuated, declining and then increasing but not to the former highest rates, many educational and rehabilitative programs were cut.[19] At the same time, there was a countermove in California, focusing on self-esteem as a cure to all sorts of social problems, including crime. In 1983, California Assembly Bill 3659 established the Task Force to Promote Self-Esteem and Social and Personal Responsibility, and its key finding in 1990 upheld the belief that self-esteem was an effective solution to all kinds of social failures: "Self-esteem is the likeliest candidate for a *social vaccine,* something that empowers us to live responsibly and that inoculates us against the lures of crime, violence, substance abuse, teen pregnancy, child abuse, chronic welfare dependency, and educational failure. The lack of self-esteem is central to most personal and social ills plaguing our state and nation as we approach the end of the twentieth century."[20] Barbara Cruikshank believes that the task force meant the doctrine of self-esteem to work as a "technology of subjectivity," one that "promise[d] to . . . solve social problems from crime and poverty to gender inequality by waging a social revolution, not against capitalism, racism and inequality, but against the order of the self and the way we govern ourselves." Such a position diverts attention away from governmental responsibility for social inequality toward the personal realm: "Self-esteem is a technology of citizenship and self-government for evaluating and acting upon our selves so that the police, the guards and the doctors do not have to."[21] The corrective arts could become either an escape from a coercive and repressive disappointing social system or a way of making the warehousing of inmates more manageable. Of course, most of the artists and inmates working within these programs do not believe this to be the case. They see the arts sometimes as a literal life preserver in prisons, a way to pass time without hurting someone else, a way to construct a better sense of self there and beyond.

Whichever way one argues, while California was building more prisons and cutting back on other rehabilitation programs, Arts in Corrections grew to become one of the largest institutional programs in corrections in the world. Building more prisons and building arts programs for prisoners to enhance their self-esteem seemed not to be a contradiction in terms. Jones and others involved in the Medea Project are not untouched by the discourse of self-esteem. Most Americans have been influenced by Ralph Waldo Emersonian and Booker T. Washingtonian beliefs in self-reliance, both cast in a tougher idiom perhaps but not altogether different from contemporary sentiments of self-esteem. But the Medea Project community understands, as popularizers like Gloria Steinem do not (or do not care to admit), that the personal is infected by power, by the relations between communities that have power and those that do not, and that social ills that plague us cannot be cured with a miracle one-shot vaccine of any sort. No one involved in the Medea Project believes that individuals are going to be able to live differently than they have in the past without a whole array of different sorts of institutional supports that at present do not exist.

Sheriff Hennessey, Assistant Sheriff Marcum, and Ruth Morgan, the director of Multi-Residencies for Artists in the San Francisco jails all describe the highly provisional nature of their treatment programs. Even in this most progressive of cities, such programs are tentatively funded, and they largely depend on advocacy from individuals. Marcum laments the lack of budget for these sorts of programs:

> Treatment programs are funded by private grants, government grants. There is State Department of Education money. We get funding through community agencies that we bring in, and they have their own budgets. But there is very little city money, so it's a yearly struggle to maintain things. So Sunny Schwartz and her fund raisers are constantly going to private foundations, to the state, to the feds, trying to get other money. There's very little security with people on this end of the business, unlike people who are running the jails and managing the jails. So there tends to be an awful lot of that

jealousy. I'm generalizing. I'm not saying that's how everybody feels, but it's an issue.

One of the stresses I have and that Hennessey has before it became clear that he was going to be reelected over and over again was that all of the stuff we've built, we've always felt, that if Hennessey was gone, if I was gone, then this stuff would disappear. Because unlike the walls, unlike the culture of captivity, these things *don't* get institutionalized. They require constant reawakening and reinspiring. And these places tend to just keep wanting to go back to "us and them."[22]

Morgan feels somewhat blessed for being exempt from the state Arts in Corrections program because of its bureaucratic demands. She has a partnership with the California Arts Council and the sheriff and also applies for money from the San Francisco Art Commission. But she too is aware of the fragility of her programs: "If there are new people who come in, they may not be quite as gung ho. But I've also been doing it for so many years, so there's some way in which it is institutionalized."[23] If a sympathetic person continues to be reappointed or, as in the case with Sheriff Hennessey, reelected, then to that extent a program may be institutionalized. But there are limits. Sheriff Hennessey knows he can experiment only within the boundaries of what the voters will approve:

> Arts programs in prisons are an ongoing experiment. If you removed me and Michael Marcum and Ruth Morgan, and you brought in the sheriff from Los Angeles or Contra Costa County, these programs wouldn't exist. They would fail to exist for a couple of reasons. One of which is some administrators philosophically don't believe in this type of thing. You only have to look at this crazy sheriff in Phoenix, Arizona, who makes them watch Newt Gingrich movies to know that there are people who believe in making things as uncomfortable as possible, and that's the philosophy that runs their jails. Secondly, programs of this nature require some department resources, and ultimately an administrator has to make an evaluation of "Do I want to spend money on this, or would I rather be able to say I've saved the city $10,000 in overtime by eliminating all these programs? Now we don't have to go out to these performances and guard the inmates and transport them back and forth. We'll be able to save this money and we've converted that into buying more bulletproof vests." For some administrators that would be their priority. And you might get a Ruth Morgan inside an organization fighting to keep the program alive, but it's harder for her. Then if she leaves, the question

Michael Marcum (holding water bottle). Photograph by Yuko Kurahashi, 1996

is, who picks up the mantle and runs with it. So these programs can exist, but they really require supportive administrations. And they also require a public willing to support it.

There is no question that San Francisco citizens, San Francisco voters, are a very compassionate group of people, a very intelligent group of people, and highly educated. Obviously, they elected me; they're very intelligent! But they like nontraditional things. So you can definitely try things here that you couldn't try elsewhere. Because elsewhere it becomes philosophically politicized or it's just not supported by the public, which wants to be more punishment oriented.[24]

Perhaps because of their interest in the arts, these three are equally open to experimentation with arts and correction, appealing to various ideals to bolster the connection in prisons.

Hennessey appreciates the arts as a form of communication, and the Medea Project in particular as a vehicle for confession: "I see the arts, and particularly the Medea Project–type of art as a way to communicate and for people to maybe say something about themselves that they weren't able to say before. They really need to seek forgiveness for their transgressions and express their desire to change and hope that expression will be accepted. And we respond by saying, 'OK, now that we hear that you want to change, we'll help you change.' So I see arts as a way of communicating." He believes the way "we'll help" is in part by creating a space for the most unsuccessful (by society's standards) to enjoy some taste of success—by completing the project, by hearing the audience's applause: "I feel that for them to get back into the mainstream, or to feel that they can get back into the mainstream, their mind has to be changed to where they believe in themselves that they can be successful. And it's got to start someplace. Jails and prisons are an odd place for it to start, but through the arts they can experience and enjoy success. They can paint a picture and receive praise. They can see that it's completed. They can be part of a play that receives public adulation." This is self-esteem rhetoric in a nutshell; if the mind changes to believe one can enter the mainstream, then maybe one can. But he knows as well as Morgan and Marcum that prison is just a "start."

Many of the professionals who work with inmates believe that prison's segregated halls may be a good place to start to enable men and women to redirect their thoughts. As far as Sean Reynolds is concerned, her job as a social worker and educator in the prisons is "to practice sedition." She continues, "I hope that is what I do. To help people to think, to believe in themselves, to behave in ways which will serve the greater community. Even to attempt to help incarcerated women empower themselves is seditious. When people learn to read, they can learn to change. Consequently when they change for the better, they can have power. That is what Paulo Freire wrote about in *The Pedagogy of the Oppressed*."

Medea Project actress Tanya Mayo sees some advantages in the isolated world of prison: "There's a certain amount of isolation, or certain amount of comfort, or a certain amount of openness that is allowed in this really weird world with no windows." The enclosed, protected environment in prison sets up the possibility for different relationships, a place to become sober, if one chooses, to learn something else, but as soon as prisoners are released, they are once again up against powerful expectations, desires, and habits. One of the senior deputy sheriffs who has worked closely with the Medea Project, Marcia Colhour, says:

Unfortunately, some women have to come here in order to get cleaned up, to see who they are, and then you're almost afraid to let them go back out. Some of them don't want to go out. They're really afraid. They don't have any place to go. They can't even figure out how to spend five dollars correctly. How are they going to be able to figure out how to get from here to there, to go fill out papers, to get any type of help? You try to give them some tools, some survivor skills, so maybe they don't have to come back as soon.

It's hard for people to start over. You have to learn to make new friends, find a job that you don't want because it's minimum wage and you don't like the clothes that you have to wear because they're not new, you have to buy them used. You can't go every night to eat. Can't get your hair done. Can't get your nails done. You don't have any money. It's very difficult for them to not have anything. I can understand that. I'm lucky. I've never had to do that. But I can understand. The odds are tremendous that they'll come back.

Hopefully this kind of jail, with different programs, with managing their anger and directing it can keep them from acting out and becoming violent and coming back for assault charges. The women are getting more violent. They're fighting back, and they don't know how to fight back, unless they use weapons and resort to violence. Because they have no skills. They have none.

Marcia Colhour.
Photograph by Ruth Morgan, 1993

Ruth Morgan found it easier to "make a dent," as she put it, in jail than in the public high school where she also worked, explaining, "In the jails there's more time for them to reflect." But the pride people may feel because of what they accomplish in jail is hard to hold on to outside. Marcum speaks of that:

> Some people find a sense of esteem for the first time in their lives in jail—as crazy as that sounds. But they've come out of horrendous backgrounds. They've given up on themselves. Maybe at age seven, eight, nine, they already knew there was no piece of the pie for them. They began to act in destructive ways toward others, toward their families, toward themselves. They come into jail and all these resources are sort of force-fed to them, and people start thinking. There's pride over a paper somebody writes, or getting a GED, or taking a risk, or saying "I'm sorry" for the first time. And then unfortunately, unrealistically, people start thinking, "Wow! I can make it out there. I can get a piece of the pie." And it's stress for the staff, because we know the world hasn't changed and we know that between six and eight of every ten people that we work with are going to be back.

Finally, when talk about statistics and recidivism and self-esteem is done, Hennessey, Marcum, and Morgan support arts programming because they find it fundamentally more *interesting* than any other sort going. Says Marcum: "It's still a jail. I've been thirty years in the business. I know what works and what doesn't work. I don't mean that arrogantly. I've

192 : COMMUNITY WORK

sort of seen it all, and I know from my own personal experience, before I worked here, what art has done. What it did for me. What it did for other people. And without it this would be a very boring business. Let me tell you. You just have a bunch of numbers, stats, and data, and these endless debates about does the GED reduce recidivism, and you get one survey that says it does and one that says it doesn't." Without a doubt, these three people—Hennessey, Marcum, and Morgan—form a unique and catalytic group of gatekeepers. They believe in the potential power of art as a vehicle for self-exploration. From their point of view the Medea Project, in its public manifestation, becomes a conduit of information, a way to make a larger part of the San Francisco community more sympathetic about its most down-and-out members and a warning that the jails, while sympathetic enough to sponsor this public project, can't be expected to provide a cure for the stories of woe heard.

Once Sheriff Hennessey gave permission for the Medea Project to perform outside the gates of the jail, Jones had to find other sources of money to support the public performance. The specific alchemies of particular foundations shape the possibilities of the production. One of the most consistent local funders of Cultural Odyssey, Jones and Ackamoor's producing organization, is, in fact, the city of San Francisco. Kary Schulman, director of Grants for the Arts, dispenses monies collected from San Francisco's hotel tax; in 1995 she had a budget of about $9 million. The Grants for the Arts program, started in 1961, predates the National Endowment for the Arts (NEA). As early as 1956, Mayor George Christopher had been lobbying for a hotel tax to be used to boost the city's "publicity and advertising" budget. Between 1956 and 1961, he met with serious resistance from business representatives and hotel owners but was finally able to push the measure to a vote by the board of supervisors—and even then it barely passed, 6–5. San Francisco could point with pride to its cultural history: between the 1848 discovery of gold and the 1906 earthquake, more than 5,000 performances of opera were presented by more than twenty companies in twenty-six different theaters; in 1932, the city opened its War Memorial Opera House, which was the first municipally owned and operated opera house in the United States. But by the early 1960s, the city was also in step with a sea change in public opinion about funding the arts. It seemed clear that private individuals could not be expected to pay for major cultural institutions, and either private foundations would have to begin to support the arts or the federal government would. The National Endowment for the Arts (NEA) was created in 1965, and by 1967 all fifty states had also created state arts councils with grant-making powers. San Francisco took the lead in funding the arts.[25] Schulman explains:

> The basic idea was that this is a tourist-derived tax, and tourism is San Francisco's major industry. . . . Even in the early 60s, it was, if not the major industry, at least very substantial, and so the idea was that this money was an economic investment. It's an investment in the city's ability to attract visitors, in the city's national and international reputation as a cultural mecca, and a way to assure that once a visitor is here there's a huge palette of activities to take advantage of. So having said that, we are able to fund a huge range of activities. We fund almost two hundred organizations from the very, very largest to very small activities. And the criteria: basically activities have to be high quality, well managed. They also have to add to the mix of the activities a tourist can take advantage of, and they have to be available to the visitor to the city. So, in fact, our funding is most probably different from some [other foundations]. . . . It has to go to activities that are publicly advertised and publicly available.

Money from this fund cannot be given to private social service sort of work. With money from the city's Grants to the Arts, Jones can pay technical people for their work during performances, she can pay her own salary or rent a hall, but she cannot pay people to go work in the jails, because that isn't defined as a public service, and a tourist would not be able to see that work. But what is most useful is that Jones can expect to receive the support of Grants for the Arts every year as long as her organization is still performing and well managed. She does not have to prove each year that she is doing something different, new, original.

What Schulman likes about Cultural Odyssey as an organization is that its different productions attract different crowds, or niche audiences—black and community-oriented for some of Idris Ackamoor's jazz works; a younger, hipper, feminist, and ethnically diverse crowd that goes to see Rhodessa Jones's autobiographical pieces—and then both spill over to the Medea Project. Although she respects the social work Jones does and praises her artistic power, the bottom line for Schulman's organization is that Jones attracts an audience and press attention that add to San Francisco's reputation as a creative, unique destination. It is good publicity for the city and good business, part of the "cultural mecca" that attracts people to the city: "Perhaps the unique thing about us is that wonderful as this [the Medea Project] might be from a sort of social service [angle], empowerment, or whatever you want to say, that's not why the city funds [Cultural Odyssey]. The city funds it because it adds to the panoply of unique arts activity that San Francisco produces for the public. When [Rhodessa] gets the kind of press that she gets, she's fulfilling her mission for us. She's helping us to fulfill our mission."[26] The mission is to advertise the diversity, the edgy mix of cultural choice, for the tourist and for the native alike.

Other foundations have other missions, and each of those missions affects the kind of art work that gets produced. In San Francisco, the loss of NEA money over the last five years has pressured private foundations into finding ways to fund the artists and smaller organizations, like Cultural Odyssey, who stand to lose the most from the reduction in federal government money.[27] The Haas family, which funds many local cultural and educational organizations in San Francisco, decided to pool their resources from four family foundations into what they called the Creative Work Fund (CWF).[28] In 1994–95, the director of the CWF, Frances Phillips, oversaw a grant made to the Medea Project. The mission that the CWF carved out for itself was to find individual artists who were already working with different community organizations either in the arts community or outside of it. Phillips says what the CWF board members were looking for were projects in which artists could "make new work within these complex contexts with organizations." She describes the Medea Project's connection to CWF:

Rhodessa was already somebody who was collaborating with other organizations in a masterful way. She was collaborating with the jails, with other social service providers. She's a wonderful artist herself, and the result is excellent art work that's presented to the public. We didn't want to fund artists to do social work or to teach, although that could be part of their process of making the work.

In the case of this particular fund, one of the ideas is that artists are really good at problem solving—beyond the value of the creative work. This fund is arguing [that] both the art work and the making process have meaning and reasons for being and a value in a lot of different contexts. The thought is that artists . . . have ways of solving problems that people in organizations (and many organizations are under stress in these days) could learn from them. At present we are trying to help organizations do what they do better by serving more people. We might look at an organization and think, "The quality of this artistic work is really great. More people should see it," hence an audience development grant. Or sometimes we look at an organization and think the way they're proposing that they're going to develop audiences could not only serve them, but it might also pay off for a whole artistic field. . . . We've been looking at what my boss refers to as developing more demand, as opposed to developing more supply in the arts. And that's where the CWF comes in; it's about the supply side of the equation.

So in Rhodessa's case, she had already established relationships. She had done some of that visionary problem solving in difficult settings with people. The question was, is she going to reach new people? Was this particular way of working and thinking that she had as a particularly gifted artist, was it going to resonate with new constituencies?[29]

Since foundations recognize that they cannot replace every lost federal dollar, they have to decide how to spend their money most effectively. The CWF made a decision to target research and development funding rather than ongoing support. Hence the pressure to find groups on the verge of something "new" and "different." Jones had to convince the committee that awarded the grants that her fourth production, *Buried Fire,* was significantly different from her previous work with the Medea Project. She argued that for the first time she was concentrating on working with formerly incarcerated women and that this presented a different challenge. With these women, Jones wouldn't necessarily be able to count on their showing up, as she might if they were in jail. At this point, she was attempting to create a sort of academy of graduates. That seemed to the CWF a new idea and a substantial step forward. A case of good timing, the Medea Project was ready after so many years to try to expand into an academy, and this fit a particular foundation's granting criteria. Indeed, the Medea Academy was a step forward, attempting to move the project beyond the public performance. But the funding was limited and ended with the production of *Buried Fire.* Jones would have to look for other sources of funding if she wanted to try to institutionalize an academy.

Individual productions of the Medea Project may be fitted to differing missions. For instance, *Slouching Towards Armageddon* was funded partly by a Rockefeller grant that was looking to support interracial conversations, and Jones proposed to carry on conversations among guards and staff as well as prisoners of different races. However, it is much harder to find funding sources willing to support the long-term institutional development of the Medea Project. In the case of both *Buried Fire* and *Slouch-*

ing Towards Armageddon, the foundations were intrigued by the social ambitions of the Medea Project, but the money covered only the cost of producing a show. To sustain an academy and an ongoing conversation about race requires more time, long-term commitment, and money. The question is how to find ongoing means of support for these new ideas that depend on long-term commitment. These experiments are costly precisely because they go beyond the short-term theatrical run, aiming to change the parameters of the community in which we live and do business. If an individual (or organization) is not fortunate enough to have already broken into stardom, then, like the Medea Project, they are at the mercy of the granting market, having to find a way to attract the attention of national and local private foundations with "missions" that change every few years.

The Medea Academy was perhaps the most far-reaching of the Medea Project's ideas, as it hoped to hire teachers other than Rhodessa Jones and would have been a place for formerly incarcerated women to teach and learn together. It would have been serving as a sort of halfway house, a haven or safe house, a public meeting place for the women to retreat to from the neighborhoods they live in. The halfway houses that exist now for women who are released from jail are under enormous pressure to perform the work of rehabilitation that may not have happened in jail. Some of the women who are released from jail do elect (or are required to) attend a halfway house. Milestones, a licensed residential and out-patient drug treatment program for men and women offenders, has been in operation since 1992. Licensed for 100 clients, they have contracts with the State Department of Corrections, with the San Francisco Sheriff's Department, and with other public and private organizations. Parolees are usually on a six-month program, with a year being the maximum time spent at Milestones.

The program director of Milestones, Martha Stein, funnels some of her clients into the Medea Project. Like Sheriff Hennessey, she believes that creative arts can help her clients find different ways to express themselves: "Many of our clients are effective communicators, but it's somewhat superficial oftentimes, and they've really closed down a lot of their emotional, personal, sensitive sides because it's been very painful. So sometimes through drawing, through theater, they really do have the opportunity to express some stuff that has been shut away for a long time." The program at Milestones is a twelve-step program; there is a lot of therapy, but people are also expected to find work. There are very few women at Milestones; the women who are there are surrounded by men, and Stein is convinced that it would be far better if there could be entirely separate programs for women:

This is a coed program, and we have always had a far lower number of women here than men, proportionally. Even more so than would be reflected by the prison population. And there are a number of reasons for that, I believe. One of them is that women tend to have more reasons not to come voluntarily into a program when they're released from prison. They have kids already; they have people ready to get rid of their children. Not get rid of them, but to want to get them back doing their mothering stuff. And working on the other side: even mothers who have not been necessarily responsible mothers, because of addiction and other kinds of things, when they're removed from the streets, they tend to do a lot of idealization and a lot of guilt stuff about being a good mother again; and unfortunately, oftentimes they again have a difficult time accomplishing that.

I think women, even within this setting, are distrustful of each other, that a lot of their self-worth, so to speak, has been due to attention they've gotten from men. And . . . it's very difficult in a coed program to help people focus on themselves. It's difficult to get people to focus primarily on themselves in any kind of group drug treatment, but especially difficult when they're in a coed program. There's advantages in a coed program—because they're going to need to learn to interact with . . . people of both sexes, and they need to learn to interact with the opposite sex in a mutually supportive relationship. But it's been difficult here, and we have done our best to separate the women. We have separate groups; we have a separate hallway; there's a separate dayroom; but there's still plenty of interaction, and it's been a challenge. And we're looking—we have been for a long time—for a different location for this program, where we will have even more separation of women from men. When we got this contract, it was for men and women, and after a year, we could have easily said we'll just take men.

What Stein touches on here is at the problematic center of the Medea Project: women's needs are different from men's, and being treated with men is counterproductive for women, since so often the relations between men and women are the problem. Women can't live with men and change, but they can't live without them either (for the most part). The biological segregation that exists within the Medea Project is sustained only in the artificial community of jail. Most halfway houses cannot afford to be segregated, because there are far fewer women willing to live in them, as they are powerfully drawn back to their families, friends, and children.[30]

Stein knows that mostly what she has to do is adjust her clients to the probable, to keep them from expecting miraculous changes:

> It's not like we're going to have everybody climb a corporate ladder or anything. There are limited job opportunities; jobs don't pay well enough; there is limited housing. How are we going to help them survive and have some semblance of pleasure in life? One needs to help them sort of reconcile all those kinds of things and somehow develop some type of a realistic plan so that that can happen. It's sad when people leave here with the limited places that they can literally afford. Is it going to be collectives and cooperative housing agreements? San Francisco has a very high cost of living; it's probably not as difficult in Los Angeles to find housing. But it's a superhuge challenge right now. And people need to be willing to look at it.
>
> Communities at large need to realize that this is our problem collectively. It isn't just something we can put away in some cow field or some distant remote place like Pelican Bay and think that's going to keep us safe. I really advocate for the kinds of community-level work that's happening, not only with our treatment program, but through developing more community centers around schools, so that families can have some kind of support. Where there's day care, health and education, nutrition, and community policemen. We need to recreate that sort of sense of community.

There is no question that the right alchemy of place, individual, and ideals is necessary to make a multicommunity project work. If Sheriff Hennessey, Michael Marcum, Rhodessa Jones, and Ruth Morgan weren't all in the same place at the same time with some of the same sympathies (and an ability to ignore differences), then this particular project wouldn't exist. There is a T-shirt the Medea Project was selling at shows for awhile, with a red circle and a black line through it, and inside the circle the words, "No Divas." In a way, the joke is that everyone on the project acts like a diva, entitled to center stage, but the sentiment is ultrademocratic: no one is more important than any one else. Of course, each woman must contend against institutional constraints, and none of them believe that her own willpower and desire will make all the social changes necessary for personal changes to happen. A critical mass of people (a majority of voters, for instance, or a group of obstructionist guards) or a drastic change in a foundation's mission statement can block an individual gatekeeper from opening the gate. People try to manage with the limited resources they have, a certain number of beds, funding, time. They chafe at the limitations, and they argue among themselves (in private and off the record) about the proper way to manage the community they've got.

Imagined Transformations

OSUN *(Goddess of Civilization, dressed in orange gown):* In a perfect world everything would be just as I planned. I worked everything out so perfectly. How to have community, how to make love, make babies, how to be good to each other. Simple, just simple, simple rules to follow.

ASWANG *(Taker of the Unborn, dressed in green, face made up in black):* Before the sixteenth century everything was so straightforward. I would crawl into the hut where the mother was ready to give birth. I would take the soul of the infant straight out of the mother's womb before it was born and deposit the soul in the Well of Souls to have it wait to be born in better times. But in 20th-century America the babies are dying in the great land. The babies now do not want to be born. I am getting calls by the hundreds and the thousands. My volume has increased. I cannot handle my workload! I am stressing out!

DIANA *(Goddess of the Hunt):* We are here. Like a thousand flapping locusts. Like a mirror cracked into a hundred shards upon the sidewalk. Get ready. Ready for the battle. Vivid loins, shiny buttons, snapping gum, ancient prayers, guns and salt water. We have them. We have them.
—*Buried Fire*

Buried Fire, the fourth Medea production, refers to a historical event that occurred in 1995 at Point Reyes, just north of San Francisco. A couple of campers had made an illegal campfire. Though they thought they had put it out, the fire smoldered underground and then burst out with terrifically destructive fury. The ground was dry, expensive homes were destroyed, a great part of the forest burned, and it took days to put out. Buried fire provides the key metaphor in this production. As the play begins, the goddesses speak the lines quoted above, and a voice chants, "Buried Fire burns. Smolders in silence. Invisible flames lick the surface not as a flame—as fury, as hatred, as madness. Smoldering self in silence. Visible flames engulf the mind, the body, the spirit. It's time. Sear the secret. Explode the shame." A trapdoor opens, and from underneath the stage, a red glow shines out. One by one, the troupe climbs up onto the stage, as if from the dead, or some hellish space. They keep coming until they fill the stage, form two lines, and explode into a line dance. Initially menacing, they become, by the time the dance is over, a group of exuberant, proud, defiant, joyous women.

The transformation from individual violence to group exuberance is never simple in real life, though it may look so on stage. Community is not simple, though it may always seem to have been simple long ago. It is never without fractures, without furious, smoldering disagreements. Within the Medea Project there are tensions that a group line up on stage covers up. There is competition between individual women—who gets paid what; there are disagreements among professionals about the best way to rehabilitate criminals—a GED or performing in a show. What may be more binding for this community is, again to refer to Benedict Anderson, the way this community imagines itself to be. Everyone believes a different, more expansive community must be created (or perhaps re-created) if everyone is going to get half a chance at a decent life. They each envision a future, sometimes based partly on some mythical idea of the past or on some mythical idea of the powerful goddess within or on their own particular vision of justice.

Much of the time, the idea of the perfect community—at least for these incarcerated women or young girls who have lived much of their lives in abusive homes, foster homes, and juvenile detention—is rooted in the domestic ideal nurturing home. When Jones worked with a group of girls in detention in Harris County Juvenile Probation Department in Houston, Texas, Reynolds visited the first week to set the process in motion, and came away with this almost Louisa May Alcott–Harriet Beecher Stowe utopian vision of a working home:

> Those girls in Houston we were working with, the day we walked in there, the day we finally got in there, jumping through the hoops, I thought, "Oh yeah, [sarcastically] *this* is a progressive institution." Ain't no library, number one. You can't even carry pencils and papers around because the pencils can be used as a weapon. This was a brand new facility, right up the road from NASA. Why didn't they build a facility for kids that is more conducive to education and to community? They put the girls in a little townhouse, a couple rooms downstairs, but no one can use the kitchen because a couple of girls set it on fire. You can't cook your own meals.
>
> If I ran this place, the kitchens would be totally operational. The girls

would be coming from the bedrooms down to the kitchen every morning, washed and pressed, and they'd sit down at the table and they'd ask,

"Would you pass me the grits?"

"Thank you."

"Could you pass me the eggs?"

We'd say a blessing before our food. That's very important. Too many people in the world are hungry, how the *fuck* are you taking this for granted, *that you have food on your table?* That is too arrogant even to be believed. We would have some kind of decorum and manners. People's rooms would be cleaned. We'd have a cool-out session. And every single day we'd have a check-in. Sit down. Take our showers, because I'm a firm believer in comfort. Take our showers, put on our sweatsuits or our pajamas or nightgowns, and we could sit there and check in, do our hair, do our nails, and talk about the day. Every single day you'd have time out to go read by yourself, quiet time. That's your book time. I would encourage reading the Bible, and every other work of fiction. There would be pictures on the walls that they painted and framed. Every two years we would paint the walls. People smoke—it's not good for you, but people do it. We'd have a session where people could smoke and have a cigarette. There would be a garden, and everyone would be encouraged—everybody ain't no gardener, but everybody would be encouraged to participate in this because I can't imagine anything better than growing seeds, knowing that you did this, and tending to something. We would help each other with our homework, because somebody's better at reading, somebody's better at spelling than at reading or math. The older girls would be required to take an interest in the younger girls.

"No, you can't be sitting cussing in front of her. No you cuss in front of me, I'm grown."

I think that what's needed are different therapeutic communities.

The ideal home Reynolds describes has rules, speaks to people's strengths, understands people's weaknesses. With slightly different vices than Alcott's little women, these girls need to smoke. They are not unlike Topsy; with a little loving attention and some structure, they too can be civilized. People need to be taught to take care of each other, to help each other, and so to help themselves. The implicit observation Reynolds makes is that all communities perform some form of therapy. Some are designed as places of discipline and punishment rather than as places for nurturing and growth. An ideal community should provide room for an individual to establish some more creative relationship to the often dehumanizing (or deindividuating) larger communities we belong to—the nation, or one's race, or one's gender. Jones dreams:

> On the other end when the women get out, what they need is protection, the privacy of something of their own. A place where they can be, a room of their own, if you will. A place where they are with their children or they have a connection with their children. Hopefully in a situation where they're surrounded by more women who are helping them. They need therapeutic, psychological counseling.
>
> I have wild ideas. If I had the resources, I'd love to see the Medea Project have its own theater and theater training component, to have a strong Medea Academy. I'd love to see the Medea Project have a solid arm of youth co-ordination, where we could take our Brave Little Girls Institute, with the daughters of the incarcerated women and daughters of the community—come together, interact, and out of that group of people, pluck people out for the performance. See what they might grow into: teachers, counselors, therapists, a part of the future.
>
> I think the dream for ex-offenders would be a complex with clinics, with schools. And for a while a woman should always be escorted, and should go out in a group with other women. It may sound a bit like house arrest. She should also be encouraged to speak out loud about longings. If she wants to see a man, OK. He can maybe spend the night, but then he has to check out in the morning. This is the dream plan. Now when is that going to happen? Because women are not at the top of anybody's list of social redemption.

At the beginning of the twentieth century, a room of one's own seemed a novel idea, but once pointed out, it came to be seen as every woman's right, at least for every woman of a certain class. At the end of the twentieth century, for most women it was still only a "dream plan."

As for the Medea Project, it is unclear whether it can become a different therapeutic community. It now exists, provisionally, from year to year, as an extraordinary public event. The public side of the Medea Project, the performance that produces newspaper reviews and generates grants, is designed to leave members of the audience feeling good, hopeful, with a lump in their throats, participating, cheering not only these women but also themselves, individually and collectively, for coming together as a community. When it functions as boosterism—for both the women's self-esteem and the community's self-image as a place that tolerates, even invites, difference—it may provide the catalyst for individual transformation. It certainly serves as a warning of what could happen to the city if attention isn't paid. But this congratulatory response may, if it is the end rather than the beginning of audience participation, curb the Medea Project's transformative and critical aspirations.

The Medea Project does not, as yet, fulfill its collective potential. Without any way to track ex-offenders, without the ability to offer them incentives and an organization through which they can remain involved, it is a project that ends before it can begin to transform the community. To succeed in that goal, it would have to move beyond the particular locale and timeframe and production schedule, beyond the institutions that now surround it—the jails, the theater, the city—and find others that would support its transformation into a long-term institution, with funding for a longer haul, defined by collaborations with yet more communities. There are many utopian futures that can be imagined for the Medea Project: a Medea Academy, with outreach programs in public schools and inner city projects; a halfway house for women, with private rooms, where policing, counseling, and the expression and acting out of desires can take place safely. Or, like Medea, the Medea Project could become diasporic, leaving home, taking the troupe to workshop and perform in other communities. Jones would like to take the women on the road: "to have a traveling show and have these women out on the road with me, have them talking at universities about their experience, speaking to drug addiction/rehabilitation, to violence against women. Have *them* speak to it. I know people that are ready. They might be better off if I could set something up like that. But I'm just an artist, I'm not a social worker. I'm not a therapeutic community in the technical sense. I don't have the kind of budget Milestones has or Walden House has." The Medea Project could take off from the jailhouse performance and from San Francisco, and even, perhaps, from the directorial control of Rhodessa Jones, to bring the ex-offenders' information to other places. The ex-offenders themselves would be transformed from students to teachers, through something like the Medea Academy, graduating into a traveling, pedagogical, theatrical community.

Jones knows that to change the course of history, one must do more than simply talk, although that's where the workshops begin. The women have to become teachers—and those of us in the audience have to become more than spectators. New pathways must not only be imagined, they must be made navigable. The dream is that the mixture of professions may make the professionals pay attention to their subject in different ways. Health professionals glimpsing the theater professional at work, a lawyer hearing from a woman who is memorizing her lines, actresses becoming more informed about the law and its resources—all may become more effective counselors because they not only will have more information, they may have more resources, and thus be able to dispense some power to people who have very little. Community outreach of the sort the Medea Project practices may make alternative routes possible; resources may flow in different directions. Information might get passed around, instead of imparted top-down, enlightenment circulating to everyone, rather than uplifting just a few.

Jones's cultural project for the twenty-first century means to reconfigure what we recognize as our public sphere. She presents us with new voices, drawing in a new audience—from people who have never set foot in a traditional theater, let alone an experimental one, to an uptown man who found himself surprised by the connection he felt with a woman's burden, so different and yet so similar to his own. The Medea Project provides us now with an example of a voluntary organization that may be a venue for participation and exchanges among publics. It has certainly always been an organization that depends on people who will volunteer to organize themselves and others, to bring their individual skills and knowledge and listen to others. But Jones also wants to transform the way an audience traditionally performs. She wants her audience, not just her actresses, to *act,* to take responsibility, instead of Prozac or crack, one's drug of choice. The Medea Project as it exists now cannot be a solution to the overwhelming problems of life in the early twenty-first century; it is just one response. But it does make us wonder how we might intervene or volunteer here and elsewhere. Jones opens up the public intersection. She shows us different routes we have taken, slouching towards Armageddon or flying off like Medea, leaving the wreckage behind, and inspires us to imagine how we might launch a counter epic on the road and fan the flames.

APPENDIX

Selected Performing and Directing Biography of Rhodessa Jones

1982 to present: Codirector of Cultural Odyssey, an African American nonprofit performing arts organization, located at 762 Fulton Street, San Francisco, CA 94102

1990 to present: Founder and artistic director of The Medea Project: Theater for Incarcerated Women

PERFORMANCES

1989: *I Think It's Gonna Work Out Fine: A Rock and Roll Fable.* Written in collaboration with Ed Bullins, Idris Ackamoor, and Brian Freeman. Directed by Brian Freeman.

1989: *Perfect Courage.* Written and performed in collaboration with Bill T. Jones and Idris Ackamoor. Directed by Brian Freeman.

1989: *Big Butt Girls, Hard-Headed Women.* Conceived and written by Rhodessa Jones. Directed by Idris Ackamoor.

1990: *The Mother of Three Sons: A Dance Opera.* Libretto by Ann T. Green. Music by Leroy Jenkins. Staging and choreography by Bill T. Jones.

1992: *The Blue Stories: Black Erotica about Letting Go.* Conceived, written, and performed by Rhodessa Jones. Directed by Idris Ackamoor.

1992: First Medea Production: *Reality Is Just Outside the Window.* Conceived and directed by Rhodessa Jones. Theater Artaud, San Francisco, January 8.

1992: *Raining Down Stars: Musical Exploration of Miscegenation.* Written in collaboration with Ed Bullins, Don Moye, and Idris Ackamoor.

1993: Second Medea Production: *Food Taboos in the Land of the Dead.* Conceived and directed by Rhodessa Jones. Lorraine Hansberry Theater, San Francisco, April 1.

1994: Third Medea Production: *A Taste of Something Else: A Place at the Table.* Conceived and directed by Rhodessa Jones. Center for the Arts at Yerba Buena Gardens, San Francisco, February 10.

1995: *Street Corner Symphony.* Written in collaboration and performed with Idris Ackamoor. Directed by Harriet Schiffer.

1996: Fourth Medea Production: *Buried Fire.* Conceived and directed by Rhodessa Jones. Lorraine Hansberry Theater, San Francisco, January 10.

1997: *Deep in the Night: Meditation on Aging with AIDS.* Conceived, written, and performed by Rhodessa Jones. Codirected by Adele Prandini and Idris Ackamoor.

1998: *Requiem for a Dead Love.* Conceived and directed by Rhodessa Jones.

Medea Project production with survivors of domestic violence. Glide
Memorial Church, San Francisco.

1999: Fifth Medea Production: *Slouching Towards Armageddon: A Captive's
Conversation/Observation on Race*. Conceived and directed by Rhodessa
Jones. Lorraine Hansberry Theater, San Francisco, January 21.

2000: *Hot Flashes, Power Surges, Private Summer*. Conceived, written, and
performed by Rhodessa Jones. Additional writings by Adele Prandini and
Harriet Schiffer. Directed by Harriet Schiffer.

2000: *Don't Go There: TV without the Tube*. Written by Al Cunningham.
Directed and performed in part by Rhodessa Jones.

2001: The National Tour of *The Vagina Monologues*. Written by Eve Ensler.
Directed by Joe Mantello. Theatre on the Square, San Francisco, March 6.

WORKSHOPS

1. "Creating New Performance."
   Instructors: Idris Ackamoor and Rhodessa Jones.
2. "Jazz, the Origins of America's Indigenous Art Form."
   Instructors: Idris Ackamoor and Rhodessa Jones.
3. "Creative Survival, Creative Performance: An Acting Seminar."
   Instructor: Rhodessa Jones.
4. "The Dismembered Heart: A Theater Workshop for Women."
   Instructor: Rhodessa Jones.

NOTES

PREFACE
1. Mercer quoted in Ugwu, "Keep on Running," 81 (emphasis added).
2. Rose, "Performing Inoperative Community," 195.
3. Collins, *Fighting Words*, xxii.

INTRODUCTION
1. Rhodessa Jones, curtain speech, *Buried Fire*, January 20, 1996, Lorraine Hansberry Theater, San Francisco.
2. Along with the San Francisco Sheriff's Department, which authorized access to the city jails, provided space and correctional staff to supervise inmates, and processed teachers and outside participants, Jones enlisted Milestones, a local residential and outpatient drug and alcohol treatment program, which funneled ex-inmates in their program to work as ushers, stagehands, and actresses for the Medea Project. The Center for African and African American Art and Culture, which houses Jones's and Idris Ackamoor's performing arts organization, Cultural Odyssey, provided rehearsal space for the Medea Project's arts classes and workshops for the ex-prisoners. In addition, two new partners were tapped for this production. The Division of Substance Abuse and Addiction Medicine at San Francisco General Hospital participated through their Stimulant Outpatient Program (STOP), with STOP health professionals recruiting five to ten women to work in the Medea Project. The district attorney's Family Violence Prevention Program offered one-on-one advocacy as well as support services to women in the project who needed counseling or emergency housing.
3. R. Jones, program notes, *Slouching Towards Armageddon*.
4. *Slouching Towards Armageddon*.
5. Jones says she had all the women perform all of the evils and then assigned particular evils to the women who gave the strongest performances. This still begs the question of personal connection: did the women give the strongest performance to the evil they personally knew best, or feared most?
6. Bernard interview.
7. Quoted in Snider, "Just Say Rho!" 8, 11.
8. Quoted in Harvey, "Theater in a Cage," 13.
9. Phelan, *Unmarked*, 146.
10. Mercer, *Welcome to the Jungle*, 30. Mercer is writing specifically about homosexuals of color who do this work of "translation." He goes on to quote Gloria Anzaldua's *Borderlands: La Frontera*, in which she writes: "Our role is to link people with each other—the Blacks with Jews and Indians with

Asians with whites with extraterrestrials. It is to transfer ideas and information from one culture to another." I think Rhodessa Jones, although not gay, performs similar translations.

11. In *But Is It Art?* Nina Felshin writes that the proper response to that question is another: "Does it matter?" (13). Shifting from a purely aesthetic scale to include political and moral concerns provides a more congenial matrix for the Medea Project. But other critics, like Arlene Croce, believe in the critical importance of maintaining strict boundaries between aesthetic and political categories. In her controversial review of Bill T. Jones's performance *Still/Here,* Croce claimed that since it was about terminally ill people, it was beyond aesthetic evaluation. She calls the genre "victim art" and sees it as part of an arts bureaucracy that favors such socially useful works because they in turn justify the bureaucracy that funds them. See Croce, "Discussing the Undiscussable"; and responses in Croce, "Responses to Discussing the Undiscussable."

12. Rose, "Performing Inoperative Community," 195.

13. Scott, "Evidence of Experience," 797. See also essays in two collections edited by Smith and Watson: Smith and Watson, *Getting a Life: Everyday Uses of Autobiography* (especially Smith and Watson, "Introduction"; Peck, "Mediated Talking Cure"; and Alcoff and Gray-Rosendale, "Survivor Discourse"); and Smith and Watson, *Women, Autobiography, Theory: A Reader* (especially Smith and Watson, "Introduction"; and Felski, "On Confession").

14. Alcoff and Gray-Rosendale, "Survivor Discourse," 213.

15. I am thinking of the way Augusto Boal involves the audience in the performative dialogue, either in his "Invisible Theater," in which performers stage actions in public spaces in order to provoke responses from passersby, or where audiences are asked to direct and redirect the actions of a skit. The public performances of the Medea Project have not addressed the audience in this way. See Boal, *Rainbow of Desire* and *Legislative Theatre.*

16. Freire, *Pedagogy of the Oppressed,* 80–81. See also McLaren and Leonard, *Paulo Freire: A Critical Encounter.* For essays on liberation theater and theater for development, see Fido, "Finding a Way to Tell It: Methodology and Commitment in Theatre about Women in Barbados and Jamaica"; Ford-Smith, "Ring Ding in a Tight Corner: Sistren, Collective Democracy, and the Organization of Cultural Production"; Ford-Smith, "Notes Toward a New Aesthetic"; Jeyifo, *The Truthful Lie: Essays in a Sociology of African Drama;* Kidd, "Folk Media, Popular Theatre, and Conflicting Strategies for Social Change in the Third World"; Crow and Etherton, "Popular Drama and Popular Analysis in Africa"; Byam, *Community in Motion: Theatre for Development in Africa.*

17. Ford-Smith, "Ring Ding," 238.

18. Quoted in Byam, *Community in Motion,* 187.

19. See Bhabha, *Location of Culture,* 36–39, for his discussion of a "Third Space"; for other discussions of rethinking community and rethinking cultural geog-

raphy, see Anderson, *Imagined Communities;* Duncan and Ley, *Place/Culture/Representation;* Moore, "Remapping Resistance: 'Ground for Struggle' and the Politics of Place"; Massey, *Space, Place, and Gender;* Massey, *Spatial Divisions of Labor;* Massey, Allen, and Sarre, *Human Geography Today;* Soja, *Thirdspace: Journeys to Los Angeles and Other Real-and-Imagined Places.*

20. Massey, *Space, Place, and Gender,* 152–55.

21. Rhodessa Jones interview. All further quotations from Rhodessa Jones, if not otherwise documented, are from personal interviews with author.

22. Ford-Smith, "Notes Toward a New Aesthetic," 28–29.

CHAPTER ONE

1. Bill T. Jones has gone on to have a flourishing career as a dancer/choreographer. His autobiography, *Last Night on Earth,* gives a wonderful portrait of growing up in this family and the development of his dance company, the Bill T. Jones/Arnie Zane Dance Company.

2. Arnie Zane took photographs of the Jones family production, *Port Royal Sound,* a musical theater work about the Civil War. See Zane, *Continuous Replay: The Photographs of Arnie Zane,* with an introduction by Bill T. Jones.

3. Jones first performed *Lily Overstreet* in 1979 at the Eureka Theater in San Francisco and again at Cultural Odyssey's fifteenth-year retrospective for the Sixth Annual Solo Theatre Festival in San Francisco, September 9– October 15, 1995, a project of Climate Theatre. Original staging by Bill T. Jones and Arnie Zane.

4. Quoted in Snider, "Just Say Rho!", 10.

5. Cultural Odyssey's mission is to "stretch the aesthetic boundaries of American art by creating, producing and presenting original experimental performance works that are firmly rooted in African American music, dance and theatrical traditions and that reflect the experiences of contemporary African Americans." According to its mission statement, "Cultural Odyssey annually premieres at least two original works by the Co-Artistic Directors [Idris Ackamoor and Rhodessa Jones], tours the company's repertoire to venues throughout the world, and conducts community-based residency programs that utilize theater to enhance the self-esteem and self-awareness of incarcerated women and at-risk African American youth. Cultural Odyssey also produces the African American Performance Festival. Founded in 1979, the company's annual artistic programs have historically investigated the socio-economic conditions experienced by the African American community." Ackamoor, "Cultural Odyssey Mission Statement," 2–3.

6. Quoted in Snider, "Just Say Rho!", 10.

7. A selected performing and directing biography of Rhodessa Jones can be found in the Appendix.

8. Fusco, "Performance and the Power of the Popular," 160. The following is a selected list of books about performance art that emphasize its hybridity: Carr, *On Edge: Performance at the End of the Twentieth Century;* Dolan, *Presence and Desire: Essays on Gender, Sexuality, Performance;* Felshin, *But Is It*

Art?: The Spirit of Art as Activism; Fusco, *English Is Broken Here;* Guerrilla Girls, *Confessions of the Guerrilla Girls;* Huxley and Witts, *Twentieth-Century Performance Reader;* Martin, *Sourcebook of Feminist Theatre and Performance;* Parker and Sedgwick, *Performativity and Performance;* Phelan, *Unmarked: The Politics of Performance;* Raven, *Art in the Public Interest;* Schechner, *Performance Theory;* Schutzman and Cohen-Cruz, *Playing Boal: Theatre, Therapy, Activism;* Ugwu, *Let's Get It On: The Politics of Black Performance;* Vanden Heuvel, *Performing Drama/Dramatizing Performance: Alternative Theater and the Dramatic Text;* Joseph, "Introduction: Diaspora, New Hybrid Identities, and the Performance of Citizenship."

Women and artists of color have especially been attracted to the autobiographical form, including Anna Deavere Smith, John Leguizamo, and Jessica Hagedorn, to name just a few. The Chicano balladeer with his *corrido,* the trickster character from Native American cultures, and the African griot are all available models for performance artists who mix myth and personal storytelling.

9. Fusco, *English Is Broken Here,* 33. Kapchan, "Hybrid Genres, Performed Subjectivities," locates this hybridity as a feature of contemporary history, the reaction of postmodernism to modernism's Enlightenment project to establish pure categories in science, morality, and art. In her book *Black Women, Writing and Identity: Migrations of the Subject,* Carole Boyce Davies argues, "[Black women's writing] cannot be located and framed in terms of one specific place, but exists in myriad places and times, constantly eluding the terms of discussion. . . . In the same way as diaspora assumes expansiveness and elsewhereness, migrations of the Black female subject pursue the path of movement outside the terms of dominant discourses" (36–37). Jones can be seen too as living an ongoing cultural migration.

10. Schneider, *The Explicit Body in Performance,* 41.

11. Jill Dolan, like Rebecca Schneider, sharply distinguishes among these practices:

> Radical feminists propose that female identity is coherent and whole, and defined in opposition to male identity. The politics that stem from this position carve out a place in gender, race, and class that is solipsistically unified and that elides the differences within and between women. Radical feminist performance texts, as Elin Diamond has written, tend to romanticize female identity by assuming that a transcendent female self can be mirrored in "woman-identified" theatre.
>
> Asserting a ground of experience from which to theorize feminism is not romanticized or totalized under materialist feminist analysis. . . . Materialist feminist performance criticism uses poststructuralism to deconstruct both traditional, male-identified realism and alternative, women-identified ritual drama and performance art for their belief in coherent, unified identities. (Dolan, "In Defense of the Discourse," 96–97)

12. hooks, *Yearning: Race, Gender, and Cultural Politics,* 29.

13. Bondi, "Locating Identity Politics," 96.
14. Burnham, "Monuments in the Heart: Performance and Video Experiments in Community Art since 1980," 197. Nina Felshin writes about the shift in arts funding to social programs:

> Along with the explosion of activist art in the 1990s, we are also beginning to see cultural and arts funding diverted to social programs. "In L.A., Political Activism Beats Out Political Art," reads the headline of an article that appeared in the *New York Times* in March 1994. The article reports a major change in funding priorities of the Lannan Foundation, formerly a generous supporter of contemporary art exhibitions and acquisitions, including some of a political nature. The article also comments on the general trend among foundations and corporations in recent years of shifting their contributions from the arts to social programs. Earlier in 1994, the *Village Voice* reported a shift in NEA and state arts funding away from individual artists to community-based projects that are essentially educational (and apolitical) in nature. This trend was viewed both as a means of avoiding controversy and as part of a general change in public funding patterns. It parallels a growing tendency among museums in the 1990s to invite artists to engage in community-based projects that can be broadly characterized as empowering. (Felshin, *But Is It Art?*, 28)

15. Peniston interview. All further quotations from Peniston are from the same interview.
16. See Hart and Waren, *The Arts in Prisons,* 12–13, for a similar list of goals that participants in prison arts programs may have. The mixture of politics, therapy, and personal advancement is symptomatic of these kinds of community projects. Hart and Waren attribute some of the difficulties in evaluating art in prison programs to the different objectives that participants may have.
17. Zeitlin, "Playing the Other," 65–71.
18. Rabinowitz, *Anxiety Veiled: Euripides and the Traffic in Women,* 2. Rabinowitz quotes Sue-Ellen Case: "As a result of the suppression of real women, the [Greek] culture invented its own representation of the gender, and it was this fictional 'Woman' who appeared on stage, in the myths and in the plastic arts, representing the patriarchal values attached to the gender while suppressing the experiences, stories, feelings and fantasies of actual women. . . . 'Woman' was played by male actors in drag, while real women were banned from the stage. . . . Classical plays and theatrical conventions can now be regarded as allies in the project of suppressing real women and replacing them with masks of patriarchal production" (1–2).
19. Zeitlin, "Playing the Other," 69.
20. Ibid., 70–71.
21. All quotations from Euripides' *Medea* are from the Vellacott translation.
22. Johnston, "Introduction," 3–5. Besides the well-known play by Euripides, other treatments of Medea include Pindar's ode *Pythian 4,* writings by Apol-

lonius of Rhodes and Ovid, and a play by Seneca. The collection of essays on *Medea* edited by Clauss and Johnston is a useful orientation to various classical interpretations.

23. Rabinowitz writes: "Herodotus mentions that Kolchis was first an Egyptian settlement; according to this evidence, then Medea was not only a foreigner but also a woman of color and, more important, a member of a well-established civilization, not at all 'barbaric.' In Kolchis, Medea would not be an exotic; her wisdom would be a strength, to be sure, but not a weird knowledge." Rabinowitz, *Anxiety Veiled*, 137.

24. O'Higgins, "Medea as Muse: *Pythian 4*," 121.

25. See Graves, *Greek Myths*, 2:215–59.

26. Johnston, "Introduction," 8.

27. Sally Humphreys explains the Greek culture in this way: "The contrast between public and private life in classical Athens was sharp. Public life was egalitarian, competitive, impersonal. Its typical locus was the open arena—market-place, law-court, theatre, gymnasium, battle-field. . . . The *oikos*, by contrast, was in closed space, architecturally functional rather than ornamental. Its relationships were hierarchic: husband-wife, parent-child, owner-slave . . . women, children and slaves had no formal place in public life." Quoted in Rabinowitz, *Anxiety Veiled*, 7–8.

28. For a discussion of the play and other sources of the myth, see McDermott, *Euripides' Medea: The Incarnation of Disorder*, especially chap. 1.

29. Edris Cooper, E-mail correspondence with author, 28 January 1996.

30. Or in Dale Byam's words, alluding to the examples of Brecht and Boal, the goal was "not purging the spectator . . . but transforming the society." Byam, *Community in Motion*, 10.

31. Lipsitz, *Time Passages*, 213.

32. In the twentieth century, Medea can be played still as wholly tragic or as a revolutionary freedom fighter. Like Sethe, in Toni Morrison's novel *Beloved*, Medea can be a tragic figure—someone who kills but who kills a most beloved part of herself. Or, as Marianne McDonald explains, she can be seen as a woman who, by killing her children, rejects the colonization that has taken place, refuses to be the "incubator or soil for the man who sows the seed." McDonald points out, "The children thus can be seen as the product of one who violated her: her body was not her own just as the colonized land does not belong to the colonized but to the colonizer. Medea's heroism then is a protest against her self-alienation." She can also be viewed as an example of the type of revolutionaries who, when coming to power, inflict on others "the abuses they have suffered." McDonald, "Medea as Politician and Diva," 301, 302.

There are so many twentieth-century adaptations of the Medea story, it is clear this myth fits a feminist century. Some of the adaptations are listed in Johnston's introduction to *Medea: Essays on Medea* and in McDonald's "Medea as Politician and Diva: Riding the Dragon into the Future." They include Samuel Barber's ballet score *Cave of the Heart*, created for

Martha Graham and retitled *Medea's Meditation and Dance of Vengeance;* Pasolini's film version of Jean Anouilh's *Médée,* starring Maria Callas; Jules Dassin's film *A Dream of Passion,* with Melina Mercouri as an actress playing Euripides' *Medea* who meets a woman (Ellen Burstyn) serving time for having murdered her children; Maxwell Anderson's *The Wingless Victory;* Güngör Dilmen's *Kurban;* Willy Kyrklund's *Medea från Mbongo;* Brendan Kennelly's *Medea;* Heiner Müller's *Medeaspiel* and *Medeamaterial;* Tony Harrison's libretto for *Medea: A Sex War Opera;* and Valerie Salonas's *SCUM (Society for Cutting Up Men) Manifesto.* I have in my possession an unpublished play written by an Indian academic, poet, and playwright, Nabaneeta Deb Sen, which tells the Medea story of a madwoman, who cannot recognize the lover who left her and who cannot remember her own children. These represent only a selective sampling of a much longer list.

33. For an extremely interesting account of a similar sort of experiment, see Emunah, *Acting for Real: Drama Therapy, Process, Technique, and Performance,* 251–98. Emunah is a drama therapist who founded Beyond Analysis, a drama program for former psychiatric patients. She describes some of the pitfalls that are common to these projects—the depression that the actors may fall into once the performance is over, for instance—but because she is a therapist, she builds into her process/performance schedule one-on-one meetings with her group, which seem to prevent at least some of the retreats into destructive patterns of behavior. She also articulates the benefits of what she calls "self-revelatory" theater performed in public: the affirmation the actor receives from an audience when the actor has performed credibly, communicated effectively; and the understanding the audience gains from hearing a mostly silenced population.

CHAPTER TWO

1. In *Gender Trouble,* Judith Butler sets out to show how gender may be viewed as "*a corporeal style,* an 'act,' as it were, which is both intentional and performative, where '*performative*' suggests a dramatic and contingent construction of meaning" (*Gender,* 139). Attacked for this stance, as a suggestion that gender can be put on and off like clothes, dismissing, so to speak, the power of the normative, Butler went on to write *Bodies That Matter: On the Discursive Limits of "Sex,"* in which she clarifies the limits of performativity. In her discussion of the documentary film *Paris Is Burning,* she carefully asserts that the parodic element of drag performances does not *necessarily* replace or subvert normative cultural habits: "At best, it seems, drag is a site of a certain ambivalence, one which reflects the more general situation of being implicated in the regimes of power by which one is constituted and, hence, of being implicated in the very regimes of power that one opposes" (*Bodies,* 125). Butler argues that "'being a man' and this 'being a woman' are internally unstable affairs" (*Bodies,* 126), while she also understands the ways in which they are utterly imprisoning in their normative utterances. Rhodessa Jones, I want to argue, understands this state of affairs also. That is, perform-

ing difference doesn't necessarily lead to subversion of the norm. On the other hand, as Butler argues, "the increasing politicization *of* theatricality" (*Bodies,* 233) may disrupt complacency, may make people pay attention, may make the performer imagine the boundaries of their self differently.

2. Persephone, the daughter of Demeter (goddess of agriculture), is abducted by Hades and forced to go underground. Demeter, grieving, causes the earth to become dark. Hades is persuaded to let Persephone join her mother for six months out of the year, during which period the earth enjoys spring and summer. Condemned to return to Hell every six months (one for each pomegranate seed consumed), Persephone stands for the women also trapped in hell. The land of the dead here is prison, prostitution, drugs, abuse, abandonment. In the program notes of *Food Taboos in the Land of the Dead,* Jones writes: "*Food Taboos* is a mixture of movement, music and text which journeys into contemporary hell to explore the victimization and criminalization of women. The questions are: Where did Persephone go? What happened to her there? Where is this place? Who did she meet? What is the face of love? And when the soul was found, did it resemble the soul of the mother?"

3. Sean Reynolds from *Food Taboos:*
   "Once Upon a Time Called Now"
   (written and performed by Sean Reynolds)
      Gather round, gather round. I've got a story to tell you. Once upon a time there was a family—a husband, a wife and a baby and they were very poor. And they were very hungry. And because they were very poor and very hungry, they were very pissed off. Poverty and hunger have a way of grinding every emotion with the exception of rage. One day the husband was leaving the house and he told his wife, "When I come home there had better be some food in this goddamned house." *Everyone punches their fist into their hand.*
      But there was no food. There was no food in the refrigerator, there was no food in the cabinets. What was she supposed to do? She was pissed off too. So she looked around, she filled a large pot with water and put it on the stove. She turned the jets on and let it come to a full boil. She didn't have a pinch of salt to put in the water. She wrung her hands for a little while, then suddenly she grabbed the baby and threw it into the pot. Well, the husband came home. Got his wish. The table was spread. And he sat down, ate his food, felt satisfied, belched, picked his teeth, and said "Bring me my baby."
      ALL sing: Mommy killed me.
      Daddy ate me.
      Who's gonna hang me on the Christmas tree? (*Lights out*)

4. Scaggs interview; all further quotations by Felicia Scaggs are from this interview.

5. There is now voluminous literature on drama therapy, arts therapy more generally, and some literature on prison and art therapy specifically. See

Gladstone and McLewin, "Treading on Tales: Telling all Stories," for a dialogue between the education coordinator of Clean Break (a company started by two women in HMP Askham Grange prison in England, which has since become a touring company and education and training program for female ex-offenders) and a dramatherapist at 4ARTS (an organization that explores the boundaries between drama and dramatherapy). The two discuss the difficulties of mixing therapeutic and artistic goals, how individuals sometimes do not feel safe in revealing their personal stories, how or on what basis a director can or should make decisions about how to intervene or even block someone's drama. See also Stamp, "Holding On: Dramatherapy with Offenders"; Cogan, "Educational Drama Programming in Prison"; and Byrne, "Psychodramatic Treatment Techniques with Prisoners in a State of Role Transition," for a discussion of the potential for using J. L. Moreno's psychodramatic techniques with prisoners being prepped for job interviews.

Psychodrama, drama therapy, and drama education are three terms that are sometimes used interchangeably since many of the techniques (role playing, improvisation) are used for therapeutic purposes as well as for dramatic productions. Although it was J. L. Moreno who began and codified the principles of psychodrama (and sociodrama) in Vienna in the twenties, many others have contributed to the now more overarching practice of drama therapy. In the United States, the National Association for Drama Therapy was founded in 1979 and has provided a professional apparatus for practitioners. Compared to drama therapy, psychodrama is more individually oriented, with the leader acting as director and the content mostly culled from real-life experiences. In contrast, drama therapy may be more group oriented, the facilitator may be more integrated into the group, and some of the content may not necessarily be related directly to the individuals' own experiences. Both psychodramatists and drama therapists are explicitly concerned with meeting a therapeutic goal, while drama educators may speak first of theatrical skills. But the language of skills, knowledge, acting, acting out, and healing can be found in each of these disciplines. On one side of the spectrum, the therapeutic, drama is used as one tool in the relationship between patient and therapist, with the goal being easily measurable — successfully competing for a job, for instance. On the other end of the spectrum, drama education, drama is used as recreation with, perhaps, a production as the goal to be performed. Even when the goal is therapeutic enlightenment, the actor might discover the peculiar discipline and joy of memorizing and moving; and when the goal is producing a dramatic scene, the actor may discover something about the particular benefits and limitations of masking the self.

6. Bongolan interview; all further quotations by Fé Bongolan are from this interview.

7. Reynolds interviews; all further quotations by Sean Reynolds are from these interviews.

8. Resistance to therapy, or to therapists, is common among prison inmates.

Some therapists (see Cleveland, *Art in Other Places*) argue that drama and other art forms can help overcome the resistance of people who find it easier to "act out" than to participate in talk therapy or who at least find it more engaging to act than to bullshit (i.e., talk). However, Jenny Hughes, in "Resistance and Expression: Working with Women Prisoners and Drama," argues from her experience in England that women prisoners are more resistant than men to drama workshops. Perhaps, she suggests, because most are working-class women, they "lack confidence in expressing themselves in formal, group or public settings" (49), or perhaps their social conditioning, which tells them to be quiet, to feel guilty, and to hide, makes it initially hard for them to dramatize themselves.

9. Katz, *Open the Gate*.

10. Mayo interview; all further quotations by Tanya Mayo are from this interview.

11. Johnson interview.

12. Kantor, *Journey through Other Spaces*, 113.

13. Spolin, *Improvisation for the Theater*, 17.

14. Iannoli interview.

15. In "Fierce with Reality: Theatre-Making with Women in Prison," Sheryl Stoodley describes another matrilineage exercise called "The Daughter's Cycle," first used by the Women's Experimental Theatre. Stoodley had each woman in prison list her lineage and then respond; for example,

> I am the grandmother of Jessica.
>
> I don't feel like a grandmother
> because I am in prison.
>
> But, I still don't know who I am. (34)

Jones always places her matrilineage at the end of the production, where it comes to seem wholly affirmative. See Coss, Segal, and Sklar, "Notes on The Women's Experimental Theatre."

16. In *From Ritual to Theatre: The Human Seriousness of Play,* Victor Turner gives a helpful etymology of the word "experience": from the hypothetical Indo-European base or root *per-,* meaning "to attempt, venture, risk," whence the Greek *peira,* meaning "experience." It is also the verbal root of the modern English word "fear." More directly, "experience" derives, via Middle English and Old French, from the Latin *experientia,* denoting "trial, proof, experiment," itself generated from *experiens,* the present participle of *experiri,* "to try, test"—from *ex* ("out") plus the base *per,* as in *peritus* ("experienced, having learned by trying." The suffixed, extended form of *per* is *peri-tlo,* whence the Latin *periclum* or *periculum,* meaning "trial, danger, peril." As Turner writes, "Once more, we find experience linked with risk, straining towards 'drama,' crisis, rather than bland cognitive learning!" Finally, "experiment," like "experience," is derived from the Latin *experiri* "to try or test." "If we put these various senses together," writes Turner, "we have ... a journey, a test (of self, of suppositions about others), a ritual passage, an ex-

posure to peril or risk, a source of fear" (17–18). All of these meanings may underlie Jones's admonition to claim the past, to name experience. It is a risky business, fearful, but a necessary moving journey through life. Naming is a testing and creating of the self.

17. Schneider, "After Us the Savage Goddess," 161.

18. Schneider, *The Explicit Body in Performance*, 35.

19. West, "Introduction," xiii.

CHAPTER THREE

1. Marcum's remarks are all drawn from the Marcum interview, as are all further quotations by Marcum. Marcum, now assistant sheriff of San Francisco, is himself an ex-offender, convicted of second-degree murder. After serving time, he worked as a community organizer, when he heard about a grant to do prison advocacy. It was he who hired Michael Hennessey, now the sheriff of San Francisco, onto the project, and so began their association in the San Francisco County Jail system.

2. There are various kinds of information about prisons: the literature written by prisoners, the sociology of prisons, the history of prisons, contemporary policy issues, and prison advocacy. Mary Helen Washington, president of the American Studies Association (ASA), published a call for more prison studies by academics in the March 1999 newsletter of the ASA and gave notice of a prison website sponsored by the ASA: http://www.georgetown.edu/crossroads/asa/prison.html. There are multiple routes on the information highway for prisons. The following is a small selection of sources I've found useful: *Bibliography on Issues Concerning Women in Prison*, published by the National Prison Project, 1616 P Street, NW, Washington, D.C., 20036; Chesney-Lind, *The Female Offender: Girls, Women, and Crime*; Cole, *No Equal Justice: Race and Class in the American Criminal Justice System*; Cummins, *The Rise and Fall of California's Radical Prison Movement*; A. Y. Davis, "Race and Criminalization: Black Americans and the Punishment Industry," and "Racialized Punishment and Prison Abolition"; M. Davis, "A Prison-Industrial Complex: Hell Factories in the Field"; Donziger, *The Real War on Crime: The Report of the National Criminal Justice Commission*; Ferrell and Sanders, *Cultural Criminology*; Flowers, *Female Crime, Criminals and Cellmates: An Exploration of Female Criminality and Delinquency*; Franklin, *The Victim as Criminal and Artist*; Harlow, *Barred: Women, Writing, and Political Detention*; Kennedy, *Race, Crime, and the Law*; McConnel, *Sing Soft, Sing Loud*; Miller, *Search and Destroy: African-American Males in the Criminal Justice System*; Rafter, *Partial Justice: Women, Prisons, and Social Control*; Rosenblatt, *Criminal Injustice: Confronting the Prison Crisis*; Russell, *The Color of Crime: Racial Hoaxes, White Fear, Black Protectionism, Police Harassment, and Other Macroaggressions*; Schlosser, "The Prison-Industrial Complex"; Simon and Landis, *The Crimes Women Commit, The Punishments They Receive*; Sulton, *African-American Perspectives: On Crime Causation, Crimi-*

nal Justice Administration, and Crime Prevention; Wilbanks, *The Myth of a Racist Criminal Justice System;* Zedner, "Wayward Sisters: The Prison for Women."

3. Foucault, *Discipline and Punish,* 216–17.

4. Steven Donziger explains how the two main sources for tabulating the number of crimes, the Uniform Crime Reports (UCR) and the National Crime Victimization Survey (NCVS), come up with different numbers. The UCR numbers, drawn up by the FBI, are based on arrest information submitted by police departments; often, if two persons are arrested for a single assault, police will count the incident as two arrests rather than one assault. The NCVS, considered more accurate by academics, employs staff at the Census Bureau to conduct by telephone representative samplings of households to determine how many people have been victimized. See Donziger, *Real War on Crime,* 3–4.

5. Schlosser, "Prison-Industrial Complex," 52.

6. Ibid.

7. A. Y. Davis, "Race and Criminalization," 63.

8. Schlosser, "Prison-Industrial Complex," 54.

9. Cole, *No Equal Justice,* 141, 201.

10. Schlosser, "Prison-Industrial Complex," 54.

11. Gage, "The Kids Get Pain," 237.

12. Donziger, *Real War on Crime,* 150.

13. Hutchinson, "Overcoming the Odds Getting Tougher for Jailed Black Women," 6.

14. Kurshan, "Behind the Walls," 150.

15. Barry, "Women Prisoners and Health Care," 250.

16. Legal Services for Prisoners with Children, "Statistics on Women and Girls."

17. Zedner, "Wayward Sisters," 336, 342, 352–55. See also Freedman, *Their Sister's Keepers: Women's Prison Reform in America, 1830–1930.* Freedman describes the efforts of prison reformers to create separate institutions for female criminals because women were believed to have different needs and to present a different sort of threat to society than men.

18. There may be many reasons behind the turn away from rehabilitation and treatment programs, all intertwined with the conservative swing of the 1970s, responses to the radicalization of prisoners that occurred in the 1960s, the riots, strikes, and rebellions at Attica and Santa Fe. The most influential study on rehabilitation—*The Effectiveness of Correctional Treatment* (1975) by Douglas Lipton, Robert Martinson, and Judith Wilks—stated that rehabilitative efforts generally have no effect on recidivism, the authors' conclusion being that "nothing works" and that crime is not a disease but a social phenomenon. That still leaves unresolved the problems of what to do with the social phenomenon of crime and how prisoners should be treated. If prisoners no longer are considered sick or deviant, in need of medical intervention, then the criminal can revert to being simply a criminal, serving his or her time in jail for a specific amount of time. This has been the trend through

the last part of the twentieth century, though clearly there are large numbers of reformers still working in and out of prisons.

Larry Sullivan's book *The Prison Reform Movement: Forlorn Hope* includes a good survey of the history of American prison reform from the eighteenth century to the present. Sullivan argues that there is a built-in incompatibility of goals within the modern prison. While earlier manifestations of social punishment reflected some form of theology, redeeming a sinner and a society through punishment, the modern prison has attempted to rationalize crime. The prison is supposed to deter crime, rehabilitate the criminal, and punish him or her at the same time. But whether in the silent confinement attempted in the Philadelphia prison, the congregate labor model of the Auburn, New York, prison in the nineteenth century, or in various types of therapeutic treatment in the twentieth century (including psychotherapy, art therapy, and group interaction), Sullivan's overarching argument is that custody prevents the criminal from learning how to live in society. The prison punishes, but, he claims, it cannot rehabilitate.

19. A. Y. Davis, "Racialized Punishment and Prison Abolition," 97.

20. Ibid., 100–101. As Randall Kennedy asserts, "criminal law—not simply the biased administration of law but the law itself—was the enemy of African-Americans" (*Race, Crime, and the Law,* 26).

21. Kurshan, "Behind the Walls," 152.

22. Schlosser, "Prison-Industrial Complex," 76.

23. Donziger, *Real War on Crime,* 9–11, 196. Donziger reports that the percentage of women in state prisons for violent offenses declined from 48.9 percent in 1979 to 32.2 percent in 1991 (149). Jerome Miller also argues that violent crime has dropped; the number of homicides in Manhattan fell significantly between 1975 and 1994, from 648 to 330 (see Miller, *Search and Destroy,* 32).

24. Donziger, *Real War on Crime,* 146.

25. For a discussion of black male ghetto culture, see Robin Kelley's chapter, "Kickin' Reality, Kickin' Ballistics: 'Gangsta Rap' and Postindustrial Los Angeles," in *Race Rebels* and his *Yo' Mama's Disfunktional: Fighting the Culture Wars in Urban America.* For a very interesting discussion of the young black woman rebel/criminal, see Austin, "The Black Community, Its Lawbreakers, and a Politics of Identification."

26. Miller, *Search and Destroy,* 143.

27. See Schlosser, "Prison-Industrial Complex," for this argument.

28. A. Y. Davis, "Racialized Punishment and Prison Abolition," 97.

29. Sean Reynolds is also convinced that the judicial system is racist:

I am not crazy enough to talk about crime without talking about responsibility. However, I do think, and I think any rational person has to know, that if all these black folks are sitting up here in jail, something is wrong with the system of incarceration. It is not directly related to crime that is being committed in this city. It has to be related to something else. I know people in San Francisco, my white friends, gays and lesbians, who couldn't tell me how to get to Third and Bayview [a largely African

American neighborhood]. The questions kept being raised in my mind. Sure, I saw white people come to jail, but then they bail out.

I would talk to women in jail [who would say,] "I was selling so much dope when I was out there, I had a gold chain."

And I'd say, "Well then, did you save your bail money? That's the issue isn't it? Did you have a public defender or a public pretender? Well, did you have a private lawyer? Why are you in here telling me this story?" These are the questions. It's not about crime in my mind. It's about access. You know? Because people who had access weren't sitting in there. Those who did not, were.

I remember the time they brought in the man who was accused of having sex with child prostitutes. A big real estate magnate here in the city. I remember the day they brought him in. I couldn't figure out what the hoopla was about. He was flanked by about thirty lawyers. I see this little white man. I'm saying, "What the hell is this? Who is this guy? Must be a dignitary to visit the jail." Then I saw they did a private booking with him. I said, "That's the man who's been going to bed with child prostitutes. He'd have to pay a child, looking at him." I went up to him, I said, "You look like Moses. You ought to be ashamed of yourself. You got all this money and you're going to bed with children." And they clean up the jail. They took everyone and threw them in cells, so he could be in the booking room by himself. If it were me, they'd give me the gas chamber.

Others concede the charge of historical racism, but do not believe it infects the criminal justice system at present. Instead they argue (along with those who attack the system as racist) that certain *policies* may seem to target minorities, but rather than argue against these policies as racist, they argue they are not effective modes of discipline. For instance, putting offenders who commit nonviolent crimes to support their drug habit into jail and prison, without enrolling them at the same time, or instead of, in drug programs is a waste of money, ineffective either as punishment or rehabilitation. Without treatment that might help overcome addiction, upon release from prison, people are more than likely to take up the same habits and the same ways of supporting those habits.

30. Foucault, *Discipline and Punish*, 264–68.
31. Ibid., 272.
32. Ibid., 304.
33. Ibid., 251–52 (emphasis added).
34. For discussions of the difficulty of but necessity for providing evaluations that prove that art makes a personal impact and thus can cause at least small-scale social change, thereby ensuring funding for such projects, see Cogan, "Educational Drama Programming in Prison"; and Balfour and Poole, "Evaluating Theatre in Prisons and Probation."
35. See Ferraro, "You Can't Look Away Anymore: The Anguished Politics of Breast Cancer."

36. Hennessey interview; all further quotations by Michael Hennessey are from this interview. Sheriff Hennessey comes from Iowa. He graduated from St. John's University in Minnesota with a degree in history and went to law school at the University of San Francisco School of Law. In 1975 he founded the San Francisco Jail Project, a legal assistance program for indigent prisoners. The project helped prisoners with civil legal problems and provided training for law students and new lawyers while offering technical assistance to the Sheriff's Department. As Assistant Sheriff Michael Marcum says, "We never thought Michael Hennessey ever had a chance to be elected. But that Irish face carried him." Elected first in 1979, he was reelected in 1983, 1987, 1991, 1995, and 1999. Both Hennessey and Marcum are progressives; they want to try different ways of running jails, experimenting with different programs. The San Francisco County jails employ about 800 workers. There are 2,600 prisoners.

37. Levine interview.

38. P. Jones interview.

39. Wilson interview.

40. Bailey interview.

41. Butler argues that gender identity is a "regulatory fiction" (*Gender Trouble*, 141).

42. Andrea Justin's testimony from *Buried Fire:*
    Women form cluster with Andrea at front.
    ANDREA: I was fifteen years old when I met Aaron. I got married at twenty-one. We had three kids. It was a happy family. His friends started coming over and these guys always looked like they were asleep. I said, "Damn, they look like they missing everything." Then this crash came from the bathroom. Aaron came running out. He was getting a cold towel to put on somebody's head. There's a guy on the floor. I thought he was dead. That was the first time I ever seen anything like this. That passed. Then one day Aaron called me to the bathroom. I went in. He was holding his heart. There was this black syringe on the floor. He asked me to get a cold towel to put on his head. From that day on every time he went to the bathroom I was there with the cold towel. I didn't know anything about drugs. Aaron introduced me to heroin, cocaine. He was the first person to put a needle in my arm. He started calling me bitch and ho. Telling me I wasn't worth shit, I couldn't do nothing right. I went into a bad state of depression. I took pills, I cried. One day I woke up in intensive care with tubes in me. And the first person I heard was Aaron's voice saying, "You stupid bitch, you can't do nothing right." And that reminded me that he was right, I couldn't even kill myself.
    He had someone teach me to steal. Pick up purses. Boost. He fucked my cousin, my auntie. But the last straw, the last straw was when he said he wanted to knock the shit out of my mama. I had to pack my bags and I left.

43. Justin interview.

44. Amnesty International, "Not Part of My Sentence: Violations of the Human Rights of Women in Custody." See http://www.amnesty.org for a copy of the full report.

45. Colhour interview. In *Offending Women: Female Lawbreakers and the Criminal Justice System,* Anne Worrall describes how and theorizes why women offenders are seen in particular ways by magistrates and solicitors; she also explores the ways in which women may resist these authorities' attempts at character construction. Worrall's work relies on a small selection of case studies, and she recognizes that her methodology is insufficient to support generalizations. However, she regards the statements made by the women offenders "as opportunities for the critical analysis of the social, political, and economic context which makes such statements both possible and ineluctable" (13). I have followed the same approach to methodology in this chapter. It should be noted that characterizations and generalizations like those that Worrall and I present (as, for instance, the claim that women are more complicated) are just the sort of rhetorical gesture a critic could analyze and a subject might wish to resist, endorse, and/or elaborate upon.

46. Stein interview; all further quotations by Martha Stein are from this interview. For statistics on incidences of abuse among incarcerated women, see Pasternak, "Half of Women in Prison Systems Were Victims of Abuse."

47. Quoted in Thrift, "Steps to an Ecology of Place," 296.

CHAPTER FOUR

1. Benhabib, "Models of Public Space," 86.

2. Habermas, *Structural Transformation of the Public Sphere,* 247.

3. Berlant, *The Queen of America Goes to Washington City,* 3. Berlant's argument is that the intimate domestic sphere of eighteenth-century modernity described by Habermas produced a sense of citizenship that was separate from the domestic sphere, "abstracted and alienated in the nondomestic public sphere of liberal capitalist culture." "In contrast," argues Berlant, "the intimate public sphere of the U.S. present tense renders citizenship as a condition of social membership produced by personal acts and values, especially acts originating in or directed toward family life. No longer valuing personhood as something directed toward public life, contemporary nationalist ideology recognizes a public good only in a particularly constricted nation of simultaneously lived private worlds" (5). The Medea Project depends upon activating an expanded sense of what constitutes a shared public sphere and shared public good.

4. McCarthy, "Practical Discourse: On the Relation of Morality to Politics," 63. He elaborates: "Having abandoned the hope that he [Habermas] earlier placed in the democratization of all governmentally relevant and publicly influential organizations, he now pursues the rather different line that locates rational collective will formation *outside* of formal organizations of every sort. In this view, it is the variegated multiplicity of spontaneously formed

publics engaged in informal discussions of issues of public interest that is the core of the democratic public sphere. The 'nodal points' of this 'web of informal communication' are voluntary associations that organize themselves and secure their own continued existence" (63).

5. Soja, "Thirdspace: Expanding the Scope of the Geographical Imagination," 276.

6. Ibid., 268.

7. Ibid., 269.

8. Massey, "Spaces of Politics," 286.

9. Bhabha, *Location of Culture*, 39.

10. Anderson, *Imagined Communities*, 6 (emphasis added).

11. Schulman interview; all further quotations by Kary Schulman are from this interview.

12. Wirt, *Power in the City: Decision Making in San Francisco*, 21.

13. The history of San Francisco's politics, especially in the last thirty years, is intimately tied up with the pro- and anti-growth movements. See McGovern, *Politics of Downtown Development;* Issel, "Liberalism and Urban Policy in San Francisco"; and DeLeon, *Left Coast City.*

14. DeLeon, *Left Coast City*, 20.

15. Ibid., 3. An example of this attitude arose on 14 January 1991, when the Board of Supervisors and Mayor Art Agnos declared San Francisco to be a sanctuary for conscientious objectors to the Persian Gulf War. DeLeon recounts the tale:

> After hostilities began, the board unanimously passed another resolution supporting American troops. What was reported around the country, however, was the sanctuary resolution, and this against the backdrop of thousands of antiwar protestors closing down the Bay Bridge, setting bonfires, and rampaging through the downtown area. Chamber of Commerce leaders were so distressed by the image cast of San Francisco as an antiwar, unpatriotic city that they launched a bicoastal advertising campaign in the *Wall Street Journal* and *USA Today* apologizing for the demonstrations and assuring readers that most San Franciscans supported national policy in the Persian Gulf. One indicator of just how stereotyped San Francisco has become as the nation's premier "Left Coast" city was Republican Congressman's Newt Gingrich's dismissal of the antiwar protests as a "cheap date"—so predictable that they need not be taken seriously as expressions of outrage against the war. (3–4)

16. Claiborne, "San Francisco Race Turns Out to Be a Contest."

17. DeLeon, *Left Coast City*, 14.

18. Cleveland, *Art in Other Places*, 77. By 1981, arts funding had been incorporated into the budget of the Department of Corrections. Rhodessa Jones, however, was paid for her work from CAC Artists-in-Residency grants, as well as from private grants. While the CAC funds Arts in Corrections to some degree, Arts in Corrections also has a massive budget separate from

the CAC. Ruth Morgan, the director of Multi-Residencies for Artists in the San Francisco jails, also gets money from the San Francisco Art Commission and some money from within the local sheriff's department.

M. C. Richards's *Centering in Pottery, Poetry, and the Person* is a mystical how-to book about liberation through art. She writes:

> Ordinary education and social training seem to impoverish the capacity for free initiative and artistic imagination. We talk independence, but we enact conformity. The hunger in many people for what is called self-expression is related to this unrealized intuitive resource. Brains are washed (when they are not clogged), wills are standardized, that is to say immobilized. Someone within cries for help. There must be more to life than all these learned acts, all this highly conditioned consumption. A person wants to do something of his own, to feel his own being alive and unique. He wants out of bondage. He wants in to the promised land. (43)

Like Viola Spolin's belief that anyone can act, Richards believes anyone can produce imaginative work—and that this artistic expression will free a person from bondage. Such a belief meshed perfectly with the Arts in Prison movement.

19. Morris, "The Contemporary Prison," 243, 237.
20. California Task Force, quoted in Cruikshank, "Revolutions Within: Self-government and Self-esteem," 232.
21. Ibid., 234. Cruikshank goes on to quote the California Task Force report of 1990: "Government and experts cannot fix these problems for us. It is only when each of us recognizes our individual personal and social responsibility to be part of the solution that we also realize higher 'self-esteem.'" And then she argues: "This is a social movement premised upon the limits of politics and the Welfare State, the failures of American democracy and upon the inability of government to control conflict; it is a 'revolutionary' movement seeking to forge a new terrain of politics and a new mode of governing the self, not a new government. In short, the question of governance becomes a question of self-governance in the discourse of self-esteem" ("Revolutions Within," 232). She argues further that much of the statistical "evidence" for this social science is largely imaginary:

> The California Task Force to Promote Self-Esteem and Personal and Social Responsibility was charged by the State legislature with compiling existing research on the relationship between "self-esteem" and six social problems: "chronic welfare dependence," alcoholism and drug abuse, crime and violence, academic failure, teenage pregnancy and child abuse. Neil Smelser, a sociologist and member of the task force, admits the failure of social scientists to identify the lack of self-esteem as the cause of social problems. "The news most consistently reported, however, is that the associations between self-esteem and its expected consequences are mixed, insignificant, or absent."
>
> Despite the fact that a "disappointing" correlation was found between the lack of self-esteem and the social problems listed, the task force forged

ahead, calling for increased funding for further research. Task force members and the social scientists involved did not diagnose, empirically discover or even describe an already existing malaise and its cure. Instead, the social scientists devised methods to measure what was not there: the focus of research was on the *lack* of self-esteem and its (non-)relation to social problems.

The task force included in its final report the following quotation from Professor Covington who claims that self-esteem "challenges us to be more fully human. In addition to being an object of scientific investigation and also an explanation for behavior, self-esteem is above all a metaphor, a symbol filled with excess meaning that can ignite visions of what we as a people might become."

From the "discovery" of an absence of the thing, social scientists have created a tangible vision of a "state of esteem." Here the social sciences can be seen as productive sciences; the knowledges, measurements and data they produce are constitutive of relations of governance as well as of the subjectivity of citizens. In devising the methods for measuring, evaluating and esteeming the self, social science actually devises the self and links it up to a vision of the social good and a programme of reform. In short, social scientists have helped to produce a set of social relationships and causal relations where there were none before. (236–37)

22. The arts also compete with other sorts of rehabilitative programs in the jails. Marcum describes the conditions:

There are people who are fanatics about education and believe it's the key to everything. When I say "fanatics," I don't say that in a derogatory sense. But to me, if we would go around bragging that 180 people got their GEDs last year, it's hypocrisy to pretend that that made a huge difference in those folks' lives unless we're also addressing a slew of other things. If they're beating up on their spouse, if they're not supporting their kids, if they're not dealing with their anger, if they're not dealing with their shame, those GEDs don't mean a thing. Now that's hard for some of our teachers, not all of them, but some—who have a hard time embracing everything—because there's a scarcity of resources in this business. There isn't in the custodial end. No scarcity at all. But there is in the treatment end. So there's a lot of infighting. And also something like theater gets an enormous amount of attention compared to a teacher who's plugging away trying to teach people math and English, or a domestic violence counselor who's doing small, ten-person groups in private, or a parenting teacher who thinks that he or she is really doing something to affect this person and their kids and maybe break the cycle of institutionalization. So it's just part of the uneven morale in this business.

23. Morgan interview; all further quotations by Morgan are from this interview. Morgan began as a volunteer in the San Francisco County jails. She had read an article in the *Village Voice* about a photographer who had been teaching

photography in jail in New York, and she decided to try to do the same in San Francisco. She worked for six months as a volunteer, teaching photography and also taking photographs of prisoners, then applied for an Artist-in-Residency grant in the jails, which she held for three years. She then was appointed director of Multi-Residencies for Artists, expanding the program and bringing other artists into the jail.

24. A range of programs designed to reduce recidivism have been instituted at the San Francisco County jails. The Sisters Project and the Horticultural Project are two others. In addition, there are a host of other people and groups who work in the jails: artists, church groups, AA groups, and teachers. Perhaps because Sheriff Hennessey came from the legal side of prisoners's lives rather than the law enforcement side, he has a different take on arts programming in his jails:

> Before I was elected Sheriff of San Francisco, I was a lawyer and I represented prisoners for a living. I did that for five or six years. So I come to the Sheriff's Department from a different philosophy or perspective, I think, than most cops, or most elected sheriffs. Most of them come up from within the ranks of peace officers. And I come from the perspective of knowing prisoners as persons first and as criminals and as defendants second. And I also know that prisoners as a group have a wide variety of influences and backgrounds and goals for themselves. Some of them have no goals, but a lot of them have different goals and I know that different things reach them. Different things affect them. And so for that reason I think it's very good and healthy and important to allow experimentation in prisons and jails to find out what things work, and what things work on a broad base, and what things work on a small scale, and what things don't work at all. The problem with doing that for most jail and prison administrators is when you experiment and take risks you are courting problems and you may be bringing in people who cause administrative problems. You may be causing security breaches. You may occasionally have an injury or disaster of some sort. But ultimately the institution survives. It has survived prison riots, and smugglings in, and smugglings out. The institution survives.

> So I guess I kind of look at it from a perspective of, "What kind of things can we do in our jails that might help people be better citizens when they get out?" For some people, their time in jail or prison and getting reacquainted with their religion or with a new religion is what changes their life. I was brought up Catholic, though I'm not an overly religious person. But I recognize the truth in that. Other people who are nonreligious may scoff at religion, but for some people, what I truly, personally believe, religion has changed their life. Now they're active in their church, they're more god-fearing, or they're more conscious of the Ten Commandments, or something like that. For some people, I believe, exposure to arts, their ability to communicate through the arts, has helped them change their lives.

It needs to be pointed out that not everyone in the jail feels the same way. Michael Marcum speaks of schisms in the jails between old-timers who do not approve of these experiments and some of the newer employees:

[It's been slow,] much slower, which is frustrating for me, but . . . we have turned around about half the department, and this is a long, long process. This is sixteen years. Half of the department . . . is supportive of this jail, the new jail at Bruno, programs like Rhodessa's—those kinds of things. Half the jail is dug in and doesn't want anything to do with it—usually old-timers who are still real bitter and angry and kind of take it out on whatever they can. And that's the case pretty much in jails all over the country. I mean that kind of schism. We've brought in a lot of women, a lot of people of color, a lot of gays and lesbians, and that also helped open up the hearts and minds of people in uniform.

25. Steinberg, "The San Francisco Hotel Tax Fund: Twenty-Five Years of Innovative Arts Funding, 1961–1986." The Ford Foundation, founded in 1936 and reconstituted in 1950 as a national philanthropic institution, did not create an arts and humanities program until 1957, and that program did not begin to fund arts organizations until 1962. In 1973, the arts still accounted for only 8.7 percent of all corporate philanthropic contributions in the United States.

26. The committee that passes on the recommendations of Schulman and her staff is made up not of peers from the art world but of representatives from the hotel industry, developers, and people who work with neighborhood activities and other nonprofits. Schulman says: "They know the arts, but they have no conflict of interest, which in this city is really hard to do because it's such a small city that everybody is connected in some way or another. So to identify people with no conflict is one of our biggest challenges."

27. Phillips estimated in 1996 that the Bay Area would lose $5 million with the downsizing of the NEA. The San Francisco Bay Area had been receiving more money per capita from the NEA than any other city in the United States.

28. The four foundations supporting CWF are the Walter and Elise Haas Fund, the Columbia Foundation, the Miriam and Peter Haas Fund, and the Evelyn and Walter Haas Jr. Fund. The Creative Work Fund began as a pilot program in July 1994; in July 1996 it was renewed for three additional years. Between July 1996 and July 1999, the fund awarded six rounds of grants to organizations and collaborating artists in San Francisco and Alameda Counties. Grants ranged from $10,000 to $35,000. The grant guidelines stress the role of artists as problem solvers and "the making of art as a profound contribution to intellectual inquiry and to the strengthening of communities." To that end, the CWF looked for projects that brought together artists and arts organizations or artists and non-arts community organizations in human services, education, or the environment. For a listing of CWF grant recipients and guidelines, see www.creativeworkfund.org.

29. Phillips interview.

30. The Sisters Project runs a program inside the San Francisco jail and Walden House, a halfway house outside of jail in San Francisco, both of which are for women only. Sean Reynolds does not believe that women have a chance in a coed program like Milestones. She also believes that even in women-only programs like Walden House therapeutic decisions are still being made on the basis of male expectations. She asks:

> How can you have a woman at Milestones? It's so simple to me. How can you have a woman at Milestones who's been in jail for selling crack, prostitution? I would be willing to bet she's been sexually abused by a man in her family—father, stepfather, uncle, grandfather—raped in the streets because the streets are not safe, selling crack and at best being ripped off by men, at the worst being beaten up and raped. Killed? How many women who have left San Bruno [prison] are dead? And then you put her in an environment with all these men and expect change to occur? At what point in the continuum do you expect change to occur? That's a question that must be asked.
>
> At Walden House, if you're a woman and you're overweight, the first thing they do is put you on a diet. You know why? It's not because they think that being overweight affects your health, which is a legitimate concern. We know about high blood pressure, hypertension, diabetes. That's not the concern. Because they say you lack self-esteem if you're overweight. And this is the party line. And so women eat lettuce for six fucking weeks. It's so fucking cruel. And this woman really wants to talk about prostitution. And then you have men who are in charge of your life. Men who tell you, "No. You have to sit on that bench for twelve hours because you were being disrespectful." You're bound to fail. That's why women don't make it in those places.

BIBLIOGRAPHY

INTERVIEWS

All interviews were conducted by the author.
Bailey, Barbara. 26 June 1996
Bernard, Darcell. 31 January 1999
Bongolan, Fé. 25 May 1996
Colhour, Marcia. 26 June 1996
Hennessey, Michael. 20 August 1996
Iannoli, Hallie. 25 June 1996
Johnson, Nancy. 24 May 1996
Jones, Paulette. 23 January 1999
Jones, Rhodessa. March 1996–August 2000
Justin, Andrea. 25 May 1996
Levine, Karen. 26 June 1996
Marcum, Michael. 26 June 1996
Mayo, Tanya. 25 May 1996
Morgan, Ruth. 19 August 1996
Peniston, Pam. 19 August 1996
Phillips, Frances. 25 June 1996
Reynolds, Sean. 15–16 July 1996, August 2000
Scaggs, Felicia. 26 June 1996
Schulman, Kary. 24 June 1996
Stein, Martha. 24 May 1996
Wilson, Angela. 20 June 2000

MEDEA PROJECT PRODUCTIONS

Reality Is Just Outside the Window (first production). Conceived and directed by
   Rhodessa Jones at Theater Artaud, San Francisco, January 8, 1992.
Food Taboos in the Land of the Dead (second production). Conceived and
   directed by Rhodessa Jones at Lorraine Hansberry Theater, San Francisco,
   April 1, 1993.
A Taste of Something Else: A Place at the Table (third production). Conceived
   and directed by Rhodessa Jones at Center for the Arts, Yerba Buena
   Gardens, San Francisco, February 10, 1994.
Buried Fire (fourth production). Conceived and directed by Rhodessa Jones at
   Lorraine Hansberry Theater, San Francisco, January 10, 1996.
Slouching Towards Armageddon: A Captive's Conversation/Observation on Race
   (fifth production). Conceived and directed by Rhodessa Jones at Lorraine
   Hansberry Theater, San Francisco, January 21, 1999.

OTHER SOURCES

Ackamoor, Idris. "Cultural Odyssey Mission Statement." Cultural Odyssey, San Francisco, 1997–1998.

Alcoff, Linda Martin, and Laura Gray-Rosendale. "Survivor Discourse: Transgression or Recuperation?" In *Getting a Life: Everyday Uses of Autobiography*, edited by Sidonie Smith and Julia Watson, 198–225. Minneapolis: University of Minnesota Press, 1996.

Amnesty International. "Not Part of My Sentence: Violations of the Human Rights of Women in Custody." *Amnesty International—International Womens Day 1999*, 19 March 1999. <*http://www.amnesty.org/ailib/intcam/women/reporto.html*>.

Anderson, Benedict. *Imagined Communities: Reflections on the Origin and Spread of Nationalism*. London: Verso, 1983; reprint, 1991.

Austin, Regina. "The Black Community, Its Lawbreakers, and a Politics of Identification." *Southern California Law Review* 65 (1992): 1769–1816.

Balfour, Michael, and Lindsey Poole. "Evaluating Theatre in Prisons and Probation." In *Prison Theatre: Perspectives and Practices,* Forensic Focus series no. 4, edited by James Thompson, 217–30. London: Jessica Kingsley Publishers, 1998.

Barry, Ellen M. "Women Prisoners and Health Care: Locked Up and Locked Out." In *Man-made Medicine: Women's Health, Public Policy, and Reform,* edited by Kary L. Moss, 249–72. Durham, N.C.: Duke University Press, 1996.

Benhabib, Seyla. "Models of Public Space: Hannah Arendt, the Liberal Tradition, and Jürgen Habermas." In *Habermas and the Public Sphere,* edited by Craig Calhoun, 73–98. Cambridge: MIT Press, 1992.

Berlant, Lauren. *The Queen of America Goes to Washington City: Essays on Sex and Citizenship*. Durham, N.C.: Duke University Press, 1997.

Bhabha, Homi K. *The Location of Culture*. New York: Routledge, 1994.

Bibliography on Issues Concerning Women in Prison. Washington, D.C.: National Prison Project, n.d.

Boal, Augusto. *Legislative Theatre: Using Performance to Make Politics*. Translated by Adrian Jackson. New York: Routledge, 1998.

———. *The Rainbow of Desire: The Boal Method of Theatre and Therapy*. Translated by Adrian Jackson. New York: Routledge, 1995.

Bondi, Liz. "Locating Identity Politics." In *Places and the Politics of Identity,* edited by Michael Keith and Steve Pile, 84–101. New York: Routledge, 1993.

Borris, Chris. "Curtain Calls." *San Francisco Weekly,* 7 April 1993.

Burnham, Linda Frye. "Monuments in the Heart: Performance and Video Experiments in Community Art since 1980." In *Art in the Public Interest,* edited by Arlene Raven, 193–208. New York: Da Capo, 1993.

Butler, Judith. *Bodies That Matter: On the Discursive Limits of "Sex."* New York: Routledge, 1993.

—————. *Gender Trouble: Feminism and the Subversion of Identity.* New York: Routledge, 1990.

Byam, L. Dale. *Community in Motion: Theatre for Development in Africa.* Westport, Conn.: Bergin & Garvey, 1999.

Byrne, Kenneth. "Psychodramatic Treatment Techniques with Prisoners in a State of Role Transition." *Journal of Sociology and Social Welfare* 3, no. 6 (July 1976): 731–41.

Carlen, Pat, and Anne Worrall, eds. *Gender, Crime and Justice.* Philadelphia: Open University Press, 1987.

Carr, C. *On Edge: Performance at the End of the Twentieth Century.* Hanover, N.H.: Wesleyan University Press, 1993.

Chesney-Lind, Meda. *The Female Offender: Girls, Women, and Crime.* Thousand Oaks, Calif.: Sage, 1997.

Claiborne, William. "San Francisco Race Turns Out to Be a Contest, Not a Coronation." *Washington Post,* 4 November 1995, A3.

Clauss, James J., and Sarah Iles Johnston, eds. *Medea: Essays on Medea in Myth, Literature, Philosophy, and Art.* Princeton: Princeton University Press, 1997.

Cleveland, William. *Art in Other Places: Artists at Work in America's Community and Social Institutions.* Westport, Conn.: Praeger, 1992.

Cogan, Karen B. "Educational Drama Programming in Prison." Master's thesis in Education, University of Alberta, 1995.

Cole, David. *No Equal Justice: Race and Class in the American Criminal Justice System.* New York: New Press, 1999.

Collins, Patricia Hill. *Fighting Words: Black Women and the Search for Justice.* Minneapolis: University of Minnesota Press, 1998.

Come into the Sun Coalition. "Come into the Sun: Findings and Recommendations on the Needs of Women and Girls in the Justice System." San Francisco: Delinquency Prevention Commission, Commission on the Status of Women, City and County of San Francisco, March 1992.

Coss, Clare, Sondra Segal, and Roberta Sklar. "Notes on the Women's Experimental Theatre." In *Women in Theatre: Compassion and Hope,* edited by Karen Malpede, 235–44. New York: Drama Book Publishers, 1983.

Croce, Arlene. "Discussing the Undiscussable." *New Yorker,* 26 December 1994–2 January 1995, 54–60.

—————. "Responses to Discussing the Undiscussable." *New Yorker* 30 January 1995, 10–13.

Crow, Brian, and Michael Etherton. "Popular Drama and Popular Analysis in Africa." In *Tradition for Development: Indigenous Structures and Folk Media in Non-Formal Education,* edited by Ross Kidd and Nat Colletta, 570–94. Berlin: German Foundation for International Development and International Council for Adult Education, 1980.

Cruikshank, Barbara. "Revolutions Within: Self-government and Self-esteem." In *Foucault and Political Reason: Liberalism, Neo-liberalism and Rationalities of Government,* edited by Andrew Barry, Thomas Osborne, and Nikolas Rose, 231–51. Chicago: University of Chicago Press, 1996.

Cummins, Eric. *The Rise and Fall of California's Radical Prison Movement.* Stanford: Stanford University Press, 1994.

Davies, Carole Boyce. *Black Women, Writing and Identity: Migrations of the Subject.* London: Routledge, 1994.

Davis, Angela Y. "Race and Criminalization: Black Americans and the Punishment Industry." In *Angela Y. Davis Reader,* edited by Joy James, 61–73. Malden, Mass.: Blackwell, 1998.

———. "Racialized Punishment and Prison Abolition." In *Angela Y. Davis Reader,* edited by Joy James, 96–107. Malden, Mass.: Blackwell, 1998.

Davis, Mike. "A Prison-Industrial Complex: Hell Factories in the Field." *Nation,* 20 February 1995, 229–34.

DeLeon, Richard Edward. *Left Coast City: Progressive Politics in San Francisco, 1975–1991.* Lawrence: University Press of Kansas, 1992.

Dolan, Jill. "In Defense of the Discourse: Materialist Feminism, Postmodernism, Poststructuralism . . . and Theory." In *A Sourcebook of Feminist Theatre and Performance: On and Beyond the Stage,* edited by Carol Martin, 94–107. New York: Routledge, 1996.

———. *Presence and Desire: Essays on Gender, Sexuality, Performance.* Ann Arbor: University of Michigan Press, 1993.

Donziger, Steven R., ed. *The Real War on Crime: The Report of the National Criminal Justice Commission.* New York: HarperPerennial, 1996.

Duncan, James, and David Ley, eds. *Place/Culture/Representation.* New York: Routledge, 1993.

Emunah, Renée. *Acting for Real: Drama Therapy Process, Technique, and Performance.* New York: Brunner/Mazel, 1994.

Euripides. *Medea and Other Plays.* Translated by Philip Vellacott. Baltimore: Penguin, 1963.

Felshin, Nina, ed. *But Is It Art?: The Spirit of Art as Activism.* Seattle: Bay, 1995.

Felski, Rita. "On Confession." In *Women, Autobiography, Theory: A Reader,* edited by Sidonie Smith and Julia Watson, 83–95. Madison: University of Wisconsin Press, 1998.

Ferraro, Susan. "You Can't Look Away Anymore: The Anguished Politics of Breast Cancer." *New York Times Magazine,* 15 August 1993, 24–27.

Ferrell, Jeff, and Clinton R. Sanders. *Cultural Criminology.* Boston: Northeastern University Press, 1995.

Fido, Elaine Savory. "Finding a Way to Tell It: Methodology and Commitment in Theatre about Women in Barbados and Jamaica." In *Out of the Kumbla: Caribbean Women and Literature,* edited by Carole Boyce Davies and Elaine Savory Fido, 331–42. Trenton, N.J.: Africa World Press, 1990.

Flowers, R. Barri. *Female Crime, Criminals and Cellmates: An Exploration of Female Criminality and Delinquency.* Jefferson, N.C.: McFarland, 1995.

Ford-Smith, Honor. "Notes Toward a New Aesthetic." *Melus* 16, no. 3 (Fall 1989–90): 27–34.

————. "Ring Ding in a Tight Corner: Sistren, Collective Democracy, and the Organization of Cultural Production." In *Feminist Genealogies, Colonial Legacies, Democratic Futures*, edited by M. Jacqui Alexander and Chandra Talpede Mohanty, 213–58. New York: Routledge, 1997.

Foucault, Michel. *Discipline and Punish: The Birth of the Prison*. Translated by Alan Sheridan. New York: Vintage, 1995.

Franklin, H. Bruce. *The Victim as Criminal and Artist: Literature from the American Prison*. New York: Oxford University Press, 1978.

Freedman, Estelle B. *Their Sisters' Keepers: Women's Prison Reform in America, 1830–1930*. Ann Arbor: University of Michigan Press, 1981.

Freire, Paulo. *Pedagogy of the Oppressed*. Translated by Myra Bergman Ramos. New York: Seabury, 1970.

Fusco, Coco. *English Is Broken Here: Notes on Cultural Fusion in the Americas*. New York: New Press, 1995.

————. "Performance and the Power of the Popular." In *Let's Get It On: The Politics of Black Performance*, edited by Catherine Ugwu, 158–75. Seattle: Bay, 1975.

Gage, Beverly. "The Kids Get Pain." *Nation* 250, no. 7 (1995): 237.

Gladstone, Pauline, and Angus McLewin. "Treading on Tales: Telling All Stories." In *Prison Theatre: Perspectives and Practices*, Forensic Focus series no. 4, edited by James Thompson, 67–88. London: Jessica Kingsley Publishers, 1998.

Graves, Robert. *The Greek Myths*. Vol. 2. Baltimore: Penguin, 1960.

Guerrilla Girls. *Confessions of the Guerrilla Girls*. New York: HarperCollins, 1995.

Gussak, David, and Evelyn Virshup, eds. *Drawing Time: Art Therapy in Prisons and Other Correctional Settings*. Chicago: Magnolia Street Publishers, 1997.

Habermas, Jürgen. *The Structural Transformation of the Public Sphere: An Inquiry into a Category of Bourgeois Society*. Translated by Thomas Burger. Cambridge: MIT Press, 1991.

Harlow, Barbara. *Barred: Women, Writing, and Political Detention*. Hanover, N.H.: University of New England Press, 1992.

Hart, Steven. "The Family: A Theatre Company Working with Prison Inmates and Ex-Inmates." Ph.D. diss., City University of New York, 1981.

Hart, Steven, and Mark Waren, eds. *The Arts in Prisons*. New York: The Graduate School and University Center of the City University of New York. Center for Advanced Study in Theatre Arts (CASTA), 1983.

Harvey, Dennis. "Theater in a Cage." *San Francisco Weekly*, 30 December 1992, 13, 19.

hooks, bell. *Yearning: Race, Gender, and Cultural Politics*. Boston: South End, 1990.

Hughes, Jenny. "Resistance and Expression: Working with Women Prisoners and Drama." In *Prison Theatre: Perspectives and Practices*, Forensic Focus series no. 4, edited by James Thompson, 43–62. London: Jessica Kingsley Publishers, 1998.

Hutchinson, Earl Ofari. "Overcoming the Odds Getting Tougher for Jailed Black Women." *Chicago Tribune,* 25 February 1996, sec. 13, p. 6.

Huxley, Michael, and Noel Witts. *The Twentieth-Century Performance Reader.* New York: Routledge, 1996.

Issel, William. "Liberalism and Urban Policy in San Francisco from the 1930s to the 1960s." *Western Historical Quarterly* 22, no. 4 (1991): 431–50.

Jeyifo, Biodun. *The Truthful Lie: Essays in a Sociology of African Drama.* London: New Beacon, 1985.

Johnston, Sarah Iles. "Introduction." In *Medea: Essays on Medea in Myth, Literature, Philosophy, and Art,* edited by James J. Clauss and Sarah Iles Johnston, 3–17. Princeton: Princeton University Press, 1997.

Jones, Bill T., with Peggy Gillespie. *Last Night on Earth.* New York: Pantheon, 1995.

Joseph, May. "Introduction: Diaspora, New Hybrid Identities, and the Performance of Citizenship." *Women and Performance: A Journal of Feminist Theory* 7.2–8.1, nos. 14–15 (1995): 3–14.

Kantor, Tadeusz. *A Journey through Other Spaces: Essays and Manifestos, 1944– 1990.* Edited and translated with a critical study of Tadeusz Kantor's Theatre by Michal Kobialka. Berkeley: University of California Press, 1993.

Kapchan, Deborah A. "Hybrid Genres, Performed Subjectivities: The Revoicing of Public Oratory in the Moroccan Marketplace." *Women and Performance: A Journal of Feminist Theory* 7.2–8.1, nos. 14–15 (1995): 53–85.

Katz, Kathy. *Open the Gate: The Making of Cultural Odyssey's The Medea Project: Reality Is Just Outside the Window* (video). 1991–1992.

Kelley, Robin D. G. *Race Rebels: Culture, Politics, and the Black Working Class.* New York: Free Press, 1994.

———. *Yo' Mama's Disfunktional: Fighting the Culture Wars in Urban America.* Boston: Beacon, 1997.

Kennedy, Randall. *Race, Crime, and the Law.* New York: Pantheon, 1997.

Kidd, Ross. "Folk Media, Popular Theatre, and Conflicting Strategies for Social Change in the Third World." In *Tradition for Development: Indigenous Structures and Folk Media in Non-Formal Education,* edited by Ross Kidd and Nat Colletta, 280–301. Berlin: German Foundation for International Development and International Council for Adult Education, 1980.

Kornfeld, Phyllis. *Cellblock Visions: Prison Art in America.* Princeton: Princeton University Press, 1997.

Kurshan, Nancy. "Behind the Walls: The History and Current Reality of Women's Imprisonment." In *Criminal Injustice: Confronting the Prison Crisis,* edited by Elihu Rosenblatt, 136–64. Boston: South End, 1996.

Legal Services for Prisoners with Children. "Statistics on Women and Girls in State Prison and Juvenile Facilities" (internal report). San Francisco, February 1996.

Liebmann, Marian, ed. *Arts Approaches to Conflict*. London: Jessica Kingsley Publishers, 1996.

Lipsitz, George. *Time Passages: Collective Memory and American Popular Culture*. Minneapolis: University of Minnesota Press, 1990.

Lipton, Douglas, Robert Martinson, and Judith Wilks. *The Effectiveness of Correctional Treatment: A Survey of Treatment Evaluation Studies*. New York: Praeger, 1975.

McCarthy, Thomas. "Practical Discourse: On the Relation of Morality to Politics." In *Habermas and the Public Sphere*, edited by Craig Calhoun, 51–72. Cambridge: MIT Press, 1992.

McConnel, Patricia. *Sing Soft, Sing Loud*. New York: Atheneum, 1989.

McDermott, Emily A. *Euripides' Medea: The Incarnation of Disorder*. University Park: Pennsylvania State University Press, 1989.

McDonald, Marianne. "Medea as Politician and Diva: Riding the Dragon into the Future." In *Medea: Essays on Medea in Myth, Literature, Philosophy, and Art*, edited by James J. Clauss and Sarah Iles Johnston, 297–323. Princeton: Princeton University Press, 1997.

McGovern, Stephen J. *The Politics of Downtown Development: Dynamic Political Cultures in San Francisco and Washington, D.C.* Louisville: University Press of Kentucky, 1998.

McLaren, Peter, and Peter Leonard, eds. *Paulo Freire: A Critical Encounter*. London: Routledge, 1993.

McLaren, Peter, and Tomaz Tadeu da Silva. "Decentering Pedagogy: Critical Literacy, Resistance and the Politics of Memory." In *Paulo Freire: A Critical Encounter*, edited by Peter McLaren and Peter Leonard, 47–89. London: Routledge, 1993.

Martin, Carol, ed. *A Sourcebook of Feminist Theatre and Performance: On and Beyond the Stage*. New York: Routledge, 1996.

Massey, Doreen. *Space, Place, and Gender*. Minneapolis: University of Minnesota Press, 1994.

———. "Spaces of Politics." In *Human Geography Today*, edited by Doreen Massey, John Allen, and Philip Sarre, 279–94. Cambridge: Polity, 1999.

———. *Spatial Divisions of Labor: Social Structures and the Geography of Production*. New York: Routledge, 1984; reprint, 1995.

Massey, Doreen, John Allen, and Philip Sarre, eds. *Human Geography Today*. Cambridge: Polity, 1999.

Mercer, Kobena. *Welcome to the Jungle: New Positions in Black Cultural Studies*. New York: Routledge, 1994.

Miller, Jerome G. *Search and Destroy: African-American Males in the Criminal Justice System*. New York: Cambridge University Press, 1996.

Moore, Donald S. "Remapping Resistance: 'Ground for Struggle' and the Politics of Place." In *Geographies of Resistance*, edited by Steve Pile and Michael Keith, 87–106. London: Routledge, 1997.

Moreno, J. L. *Psychodrama*. New York: Beacon House, 1946.

Morris, Norval. "The Contemporary Prison: 1965–Present." In *The Oxford History of the Prison: The Practice of Punishment in Western Society,* edited by Norval Morris and David J. Rothman, 227–59. New York: Oxford University Press, 1995.

Nardone, Diane Christine. "The History of the San Quentin Drama Workshop." Ph.D. diss., New York University, 1978.

National Prison Project. *Bibliography on Issues Concerning Women in Prison.* Washington, D.C.: n.p., n.d.

Neal, Leslie. "Miles from Nowhere: Teaching Dance in Prison." *High Performance* 19.1 (1996): 6–9.

O'Higgins, Dolores M. "Medea as Muse: *Pythian 4.*" In *Medea: Essays on Medea in Myth, Literature, Philosophy, and Art,* edited by James J. Clauss and Sarah Iles Johnston, 103–26. Princeton: Princeton University Press, 1997.

Parker, Andrew, and Eve Kosofsky Sedgwick, eds. *Performativity and Performance.* New York: Routledge, 1995.

Pasternak, Judy. "Half of Women in Prison Systems Were Victims of Abuse, Report Says." *Los Angeles Times,* 12 April 1999, A4.

Peck, Janice. "The Mediated Talking Cure: Therapeutic Framing of Autobiography in TV Talk Shows." In *Getting a Life: Everyday Uses of Autobiography,* edited by Sidonie Smith and Julia Watson, 134–55. Minneapolis: University of Minnesota Press, 1996.

Phelan, Peggy. *Unmarked: The Politics of Performance.* London: Routledge, 1993.

Rabinowitz, Nancy Sorkin. *Anxiety Veiled: Euripides and the Traffic in Women.* Ithaca: Cornell University Press, 1993.

Rafter, Nicole Hahn. *Partial Justice: Women, Prisons, and Social Control.* 2d ed. New Brunswick, N.J.: Transaction, 1990.

Raven, Arlene, ed. *Art in the Public Interest.* New York: Da Capo, 1993.

Richards, Mary Caroline. *Centering in Pottery, Poetry, and the Person.* Middletown, Conn.: Wesleyan University Press, 1962; reprint, 1989.

Rose, Gillian. "Performing Inoperative Community: The Space and the Resistance of Some Community Arts Projects." In *Geographies of Resistance,* edited by Steve Pile and Michael Keith, 184–202. London: Routledge, 1997.

Rosenblatt, Elihu, ed. *Criminal Injustice: Confronting the Prison Crisis.* Boston: South End, 1996.

Russell, Katheryn K. *The Color of Crime: Racial Hoaxes, White Fear, Black Protectionism, Police Harassment, and Other Macroaggressions.* New York: New York University Press, 1998.

Ryan, Paul Ryder. "Theatre as Prison Therapy." *Drama Review* 20.1 (1976): 31–42.

Schechner, Richard. *Performance Theory.* London: Routledge, 1988.

Schlosser, Eric. "The Prison-Industrial Complex." *Atlantic Monthly,* December 1998, 51–77.

Schneider, Rebecca. "After Us the Savage Goddess: Feminist Performance Art of the Explicit Body Staged, Uneasily, Across Modernist Dreamscapes." In *Performance and Cultural Politics*, edited by Elin Diamond, 157–78. New York: Routledge, 1996.

————. *The Explicit Body in Performance*. New York: Routledge, 1997.

Schutzman, Mady, and Jan Cohen-Cruz, eds. *Playing Boal: Theatre, Therapy, Activism*. New York: Routledge, 1994.

Scott, Joan W. "The Evidence of Experience." *Critical Inquiry* 17 (Summer 1991): 773–97.

Simon, Rita J., and Jean Landis. *The Crimes Women Commit, The Punishments They Receive*. Lexington, Mass.: Lexington Books, 1991.

Singer, Mark I., Janet Bussey, Li-Yu Song, and Lisa Lunghofer. "The Psychosocial Issues of Women Serving Time in Jail." *Social Work* 40.1 (1995): 103–13.

Smith, Sidonie, and Julia Watson, eds. *Getting a Life: Everyday Uses of Autobiography*. Minneapolis: University of Minnesota Press, 1996.

————. *Women, Autobiography, Theory: A Reader*. Madison: University of Wisconsin Press, 1998.

Snider, Burr. "Just Say Rho!" *San Francisco Examiner*, 3 October 1993, 7–11.

Soja, Edward W. "Thirdspace: Expanding the Scope of the Geographical Imagination." In *Human Geography Today*, edited by Doreen Massey, John Allen, and Philip Sarre, 260–78. Cambridge: Polity, 1999.

————. *Thirdspace: Journeys to Los Angeles and Other Real-and-Imagined Places*. Cambridge, Mass.: Blackwell, 1996.

Spolin, Viola. *Improvisation for the Theater: A Handbook of Teaching and Directing Techniques*. Evanston, Ill.: Northwestern University Press, 1963.

Stamp, Sally. "Holding On: Dramatherapy with Offenders." In *Prison Theatre: Perspectives and Practices*, Forensic Focus series no. 4, edited by James Thompson, 89–108. London: Jessica Kingsley Publishers, 1998.

Steinberg, Corbett. "The San Francisco Hotel Tax Fund: Twenty-Five Years of Innovative Arts Funding, 1961–1986." *Encore: Studies in West Coast Arts Philanthropy* (Archives for the Performing Arts Quarterly), Spring 1986.

Stoodley, Sheryl. "Fierce with Reality: Theatre-Making with Women in Prison." Master's thesis, Smith College, 1989.

Sullivan, Larry E. *The Prison Reform Movement: Forlorn Hope*. Boston: Twayne, 1990.

Sulton, Anne T. ed. *African-American Perspectives: On Crime Causation, Criminal Justice Administration, and Crime Prevention*. Boston: Butterworth-Heinemann, 1996.

Thrift, Nigel. "Steps to an Ecology of Place." In *Human Geography Today*, edited by Doreen Massey, John Allen, and Philip Sarre, 295–322. Cambridge: Polity, 1999.

Turner, Victor. *From Ritual to Theatre: The Human Seriousness of Play*. New York: PAJ Publications, 1982.

Ugwu, Catherine. "Keep on Running: The Politics of Black British

Performance." In *Let's Get It On: The Politics of Black Performance*, edited by Catherine Ugwu, 54–83. Seattle: Bay, 1995.

Vanden Heuvel, Michael. *Performing Drama/Dramatizing Performance: Alternative Theater and the Dramatic Text.* Ann Arbor: University of Michigan Press, 1991.

Washington, Mary Helen. "Presidential Address: Prison Studies as Part of American Studies." *American Studies Association Newsletter* 22.1 (1999): 1–5.

West, Cornel. "Introduction." In *Paulo Freire: A Critical Encounter*, edited by Peter McLaren and Peter Leonard, xiii–xiv. London: Routledge, 1993.

Wilbanks, William. *The Myth of a Racist Criminal Justice System.* Monterey, Calif.: Brooks/Cole, 1987.

Wirt, Frederick M. *Power in the City: Decision Making in San Francisco.* Berkeley: University of California, 1974.

Worrall, Anne. *Offending Women: Female Lawbreakers and the Criminal Justice System.* New York: Routledge, 1990.

Zane, Arnie. *Continuous Replay: The Photographs of Arnie Zane.* Edited by Jonathan Green. Cambridge: MIT Press, 1999.

Zedner, Lucia. "Wayward Sisters: The Prison for Women." In *The Oxford History of the Prison: The Practice of Punishment in Western Society*, edited by Norval Morris and David J. Rothman, 329–61. New York: Oxford University Press, 1995.

Zeitlin, Froma I. "Playing the Other: Theater, Theatricality, and the Feminine in Greek Drama." In *Nothing to Do with Dionysos? Athenian Drama in its Social Context*, edited by John J. Winkler and Froma I. Zeitlin, 63–96. Princeton: Princeton University Press, 1990.

Emunah, Renée, 215 (n. 33)
Essentialism, 8, 35

Feminist theater, 35, 212 (n. 11). *See
also* Jones, Rhodessa: as feminist
First Memory, 104–5, 111. *See also*
Theater techniques
Food Taboos in the Land of the Dead,
72–74, 105, 113; "Ho Stroll," 113–
19; photograph, 116; Abiku myth,
216 (n. 3)
Ford-Smith, Honor, 22, 24
Foucault, Michel, 121, 129–32
Freeman, Brian, 45, 46
Freire, Paulo, 21–22, 70, 87, 119, 191
Funding for the arts, 193–97; 213 (n.
14), 229 (nn. 25, 26, 27). *See also*
Creative Work Fund; Grants for
the Arts; Medea Project: funding
of; Phillips, Frances; Schulman,
Kary
Fusco, Coco, 33–34

Garret, Chenique, 11, 12, 13, 16
Gavin, Ellen, 45
Gender, 113, 215–16 (n. 1)
Grants for the Arts, 182, 193, 194
Greek classical theater, 2, 48–49, 213
(n. 18), 214 (n. 27)

Haas family, 182, 195
Habermas, Jürgen, 179, 224 (n. 3),
224–25 (n. 4)
Halfway houses, 136, 146, 198–99,
201–4, 230 (n. 30). *See also* Milestones Human Services, Inc.;
Walden House
Hall, Stuart, 34
Hand Dancing, 98–101. *See also* Theater techniques
Hennessey, Michael, 5, 19, 46, 193;
on arts in prison, 133, 187, 188–89,
190, 192, 228 (n. 24); as gatekeeper,
183, 199; biography of, 219 (n. 1),
223 (n. 36)

hooks, bell, 37, 180
*Hot Flashes, Power Surges, and Private
Summers,* 34
Hybridity, xvii, 19, 20, 34, 180, 212
(n. 9). *See also* Jones, Rhodessa: as
connector

Iannoli, Hallie, 46–47, 106
Identity, 12–13, 16, 110–11, 164
Incarcerated women in the Medea
Project: interviews with, xiv, xvi,
xvii, xviii, 135, 224 (n. 45); general
profile of, 3, 7, 81–82, 84; and violence, 10–11, 16, 127, 230 (n. 30);
crimes of, 15, 136, 172; and language, 40, 78; fragmented lives of,
133; recidivism of, 133; and men,
170; and treatment programs, 173;
as mothers, 173–74; complicated
lives of, 172–75. *See also* Bailey,
Barbara; Jones, Paulette; Justin,
Andrea; Scaggs, Felicia; Wilson,
Angela

Jealousy, 114–15
Johnson, Nancy, 46, 97–98, 145
Johnson, Stephanie A., 46
Johnston, Sarah, 51
Jones, Bill T., 27, 31, 99, 113, 145, 210
(n. 11)
Jones, Paulette, 7–8, 47, 149–51;
interview, 136–147; photograph,
137
Jones, Rhodessa: as director, xvi, 1,
6–7, 9, 16, 46, 69, 88–89, 192–93,
218–19 (n. 10); as connector, 18–
19, 24, 36, 119, 199, 209–10 (n. 10);
on politics, 23–24, 100; on theater,
27, 39, 65, 66; as feminist, 31–32,
34–37; as performer, 31–37; as
community worker, 38, 203–5; in
the jails, 38–45, 77; on *Medea,* 43–
44, 54, 65–66; as teacher, 77, 106,
109–10
Jones Company, 31

74; rants, 88–94; Hand Dancing, 98–101; Women Are Waiting, 101–2; First Memory, 104–5, 111; composition, 105–7; Matrilineage, 107–9, 218 (n. 15)

"There Are Women Waiting: The Tragedy of Medea Jackson," 53, 55–56; text of, 56–64

I Think It's Gonna Work Out Fine, 41

Third Space, 23, 180

Tims, Jeannette, 56, 107–9

Tocqueville, Alexis de, 122, 125

Trounstine, Jean, 43

Tumbleweed, 31–32, 35–36

Turner, Tina, 34

Voluntary organizations, 179, 205

Walden House, 136, 149

Walker, Rene, 46

Welk, Lois, 99

West, Cornel, 119, 180

West Side Story, 114–15

Williams, Angellette, 56

Wilson, Angela, 12–13, 47, 136; interview, 147–51

Wittgenstein, Ludwig, 177–78

Women Are Waiting, 101–2. *See also* Theater techniques

Women's Theater Festival (San Francisco), 41–42

Zeitlin, Froma, 48–49

GENDER AND AMERICAN CULTURE

Imagining Medea: Rhodessa Jones and Theater for Incarcerated Women, by Rena Fraden (2001)

Painting Professionals: Women Artists and the Development of Modern American Art, 1870–1920, by Kirsten Swinth (2001)

Remaking Respectability: African American Women in Interwar Detroit, by Victoria W. Wolcott (2001)

Ida B. Wells-Barnett and American Reform, 1880–1930, by Patricia A. Schechter (2001)

Taking Haiti: Military Occupation and the Culture of U.S. Imperialism, 1915–1940, by Mary A. Renda (2001)

Before Jim Crow: The Politics of Race in Postemancipation Virginia, by Jane Dailey (2000)

Captain Ahab Had a Wife: New England Women and the Whalefishery, 1720–1870, by Lisa Norling (2000)

Civilizing Capitalism: The National Consumers' League, Women's Activism, and Labor Standards in the New Deal Era, by Landon R. Y. Storrs (2000)

Rank Ladies: Gender and Cultural Hierarchy in American Vaudeville, by M. Alison Kibler (1999)

Strangers and Pilgrims: Female Preaching in America, 1740–1845, by Catherine A. Brekus (1998)

Sex and Citizenship in Antebellum America, by Nancy Isenberg (1998)

Yours in Sisterhood: Ms. Magazine and the Promise of Popular Feminism, by Amy Erdman Farrell (1998)

We Mean to Be Counted: White Women and Politics in Antebellum Virginia, by Elizabeth R. Varon (1998)

Women Against the Good War: Conscientious Objection and Gender on the American Home Front, 1941–1947, by Rachel Waltner Goossen (1997)

Toward an Intellectual History of Women: Essays by Linda K. Kerber (1997)

Gender and Jim Crow: Women and the Politics of White Supremacy in North Carolina, 1896–1920, by Glenda Elizabeth Gilmore (1996)

Delinquent Daughters: Protecting and Policing Adolescent Female Sexuality in the United States, 1885–1920, by Mary E. Odem (1995)

U.S. History as Women's History: New Feminist Essays, edited by Linda K. Kerber, Alice Kessler-Harris, and Kathryn Kish Sklar (1995)

Common Sense and a Little Fire: Women and Working-Class Politics in the United States, 1900–1965, by Annelise Orleck (1995)

How Am I to Be Heard?: Letters of Lillian Smith, edited by Margaret Rose Gladney (1993)

Entitled to Power: Farm Women and Technology, 1913–1963, by Katherine Jellison (1993)

Revising Life: Sylvia Plath's Ariel Poems, by Susan R. Van Dyne (1993)

Made From This Earth: American Women and Nature, by Vera Norwood (1993)

Unruly Women: The Politics of Social and Sexual Control in the Old South, by Victoria E. Bynum (1992)

The Work of Self-Representation: Lyric Poetry in Colonial New England, by Ivy Schweitzer (1991)

Labor and Desire: Women's Revolutionary Fiction in Depression America, by Paula Rabinowitz (1991)

Community of Suffering and Struggle: Women, Men, and the Labor Movement in Minneapolis, 1915–1945, by Elizabeth Faue (1991)

All That Hollywood Allows: Re-reading Gender in 1950s Melodrama, by Jackie Byars (1991)

Doing Literary Business: American Women Writers in the Nineteenth Century, by Susan Coultrap-McQuin (1990)

Ladies, Women, and Wenches: Choice and Constraint in Antebellum Charleston and Boston, by Jane H. Pease and William H. Pease (1990)

The Secret Eye: The Journal of Ella Gertrude Clanton Thomas, 1848–1889, edited by Virginia Ingraham Burr, with an introduction by Nell Irvin Painter (1990)

Second Stories: The Politics of Language, Form, and Gender in Early American Fictions, by Cynthia S. Jordan (1989)

Within the Plantation Household: Black and White Women of the Old South, by Elizabeth Fox-Genovese (1988)

The Limits of Sisterhood: The Beecher Sisters on Women's Rights and Woman's Sphere, by Jeanne Boydston, Mary Kelley, and Anne Margolis (1988)